12 × 12

12 × 12

Conversations in 21st-Century Poetry and Poetics

Edited by Christina Mengert and Joshua Marie Wilkinson

University of Iowa Press | Iowa City

University of Iowa Press, Iowa City 52242
Copyright © 2009 by the University of Iowa Press
www.uiowapress.org
Printed in the United States of America

Design by April Leidig-Higgins

The University of Iowa Press is a member of Green Press
Initiative and is committed to preserving natural resources.

Printed on acid-free paper

Library of Congress Cataloging-in-Publication Data
12 × 12: Conversations in 21st-century poetry and poetics /
edited by Christina Mengert and Joshua Marie Wilkinson.
     p.   cm.
Includes bibliographical references and index.
ISBN-13: 978-1-58729-791-5 (pbk.)
ISBN-10: 1-58729-791-4 (pbk.)
1. American poetry — 21st century.   2. Poets, American —
20th century — Interviews.   3. Poets, American — 21st
century — Interviews.   4. Influence (Literary, artistic, etc.)
5. Poetry — Authorship.   6. Poetics.   7. Poetry — Social
aspects.   8. Poetry — Political aspects.   I. Mengert, Christina.
II. Wilkinson, Joshua Marie, 1977– .   III. Title: Conversations
in 21st-century poetry and poetics.
PS617.C67   2009
811'.608 — dc22   2008048819

for Bin Ramke and Eleni Sikelianos,
and for our students

Influence

"Influenza," [o]ur formal name for the disease . . . is actually the Italian word for "influence," which derives from the same medieval Latin word *influentia*, "to flow into," as our English equivalent. At first, *influence* was a term specific to astrology, an ethereal fluid given off by the stars that was supposed to affect humans. It was only in the sixteenth century that the modern meaning, a "power to produce effects," began to gain the dominance it now possesses.

— Michael Quinion, World Wide Words Web site

xiii   Introduction

JENNIFER K. DICK | LAURA MULLEN

2   Poems by Jennifer K. Dick
Anatomy 2
In the Garden 3
Claudia 3

4   Jennifer K. Dick and Laura Mullen in Conversation

14   Poem by Laura Mullen
Wake 14

JON WOODWARD | RAE ARMANTROUT

20   Poems by Jon Woodward
from *Rain*: "newer sore spots blossomed open" 20
from *Rain*: "looking over the bomb inventory" 20
from *Rain*: "it's not that he died" 21

22   Jon Woodward and Rae Armantrout in Conversation

35   Poems by Rae Armantrout
Sake 35
The Subject 36
Worth While 37

SABRINA ORAH MARK | CLAUDIA RANKINE

40   Poems by Sabrina Orah Mark
The Dumb Show 40
The Song 41
In the Origami Fields 42

43   Sabrina Orah Mark and Claudia Rankine in Conversation

51 Poems by Claudia Rankine
from *Don't Let Me Be Lonely*: "Or Paul Celan said that . . ." 51
from *Don't Let Me Be Lonely*: "Or one meaning of here is . . ." 51
from *Plot*: of course. of course. 52

CHRISTIAN HAWKEY | TOMAŽ ŠALAMUN

54 Poems by Christian Hawkey
Fräulein, can you 54
There is a Queen inside 55
Unhoused casements 56

57 Christian Hawkey and Tomaž Šalamun in Conversation

67 Poems by Tomaž Šalamun
19.IX.1982 67
Spring Street 69

CHRISTINE HUME | ROSMARIE WALDROP

72 Poems by Christine Hume
Comprehension Questions 72
What Became of the Company You've Kept,
    According to One Who Left 74

76 Christine Hume and Rosmarie Waldrop in Conversation

89 Poem by Rosmarie Waldrop
Music Is an Oversimplification of the Situation We're In 89

SRIKANTH REDDY | MARK LEVINE

96 Poems by Srikanth Reddy
Evening with Stars 96
Hotel Lullaby 97
Corruption (II) 98

99 Srikanth Reddy and Mark Levine in Conversation

114 Poems by Mark Levine
Work Song 114
Counting the Forests 115
Triangle 116

KAREN VOLKMAN | ALLEN GROSSMAN

120 Poems by Karen Volkman
Sonnet ("I asked every flower") 120
"Although the paths lead into the forest . . ." 121
"And when the nights . . ." 122

123 Karen Volkman and Allen Grossman in Conversation

131 Poems by Allen Grossman
Rain on a Still Pond 131
"Warble," Says the Bird 132
I Am That I AM 133

SAWAKO NAKAYASU | CARLA HARRYMAN

136 Poems by Sawako Nakayasu
9.19.2004 136
3.21.2004 137
6.21.2003 138

139 Sawako Nakayasu and Carla Harryman in Conversation

170 Poems by Carla Harryman
from *Baby*: "Now. Word. Technology." 170
Fish Speech 170
Membership 171
Matter 173

PAUL FATTARUSO | DARA WIER

176 Poem by Paul Fattaruso
from *The Submariner's Waltz*:
"I opened the brushed steel box" 176

180 Paul Fattaruso and Dara Wier in Conversation

189 Poems by Dara Wier
Hypnagogic 189
Corrosion 191

MARK YAKICH | MARY LEADER

196   Poems by Mark Yakich
Pretzels Come to America 196
An Untenable Nostalgia for Chernobyl 197

199   Mark Yakich and Mary Leader in Conversation

217   Poem by Mary Leader
When the Wind Ever Shall Be Like a Black Thread 217

MICHELLE ROBINSON | PAUL AUSTER

222   Poems by Michelle Robinson
From This Miserable Mutineer a Stutter . . . 222
Keith 223
When Smithson Looked into the Salt Lake What He Saw 224

226   Michelle Robinson and Paul Auster in Conversation

234   Poems by Paul Auster
Narrative 234
from "White Spaces": "Something happens,
   and from the moment" 235

BEN LERNER | AARON KUNIN

238   Poems by Ben Lerner
from *The Lichtenberg Figures*: "We must retract our . . ." 238
from *The Lichtenberg Figures*: "I'm going to kill . . ." 238
from *The Lichtenberg Figures*: "The sky is a big . . ." 239

240   Ben Lerner and Aaron Kunin in Conversation

251   Poems by Aaron Kunin
Enclosed Please Find 251
Enclosed Please Find 252
The Sore Throat 253

255   Contributors
259   Acknowledgments and Permissions
263   Index

JMW: In one of the early conversations in this anthology, Claudia Rankine explains that privacy is a kind of architecture. Sabrina Orah Mark — one of the twelve younger poets we selected for this project — responds by saying that privacy could also be "a box you can rest inside." I have to confess: I have no idea where exactly to begin by way of introduction. This is because what has been gathered here by these twenty-four poets (their poems and their conversations) exceeds my initial expectation so much that I am no longer sure of what I expected. It's sort of like how you imagine a new city only to arrive for the first time and have the landscape, the scents — everything — overwhelm your initial notion of what it was supposed to be like. It was Claudia Rankine and Juliana Spahr's anthology *American Women Poets in the 21st Century* that first inspired the idea for this assemblage of poets. But as I read through these conversations — in which twelve younger poets were invited to select a more established poet to have a conversation with — I'm struck by the hugeness, the sprawl, and the myriad connections of the architecture over what was otherwise private — that is, these twenty-four poets writing alone, in privacy.

CM: I'm reminded of what Allen Grossman once said — that poetry "is the least solitary of enterprises." Poetry is, I think, in its nature, equal parts private and public. I'm reminded of the troubadours who stood at court and recited aloud their compositions and then the sonneteers of the Renaissance who composed privately, self-consciously. It seems poets are always negotiating this boundary. Language itself is this boundary, and poets as the acute sculptors of it seem particularly bound to that threshold.

I think what we have in these conversations, in this manuscript, is triangular in a way. And by that I mean that we have the poets writing alone, as you point out (point A), and then the dialogue generated between each pair of poets (point B), and then the conversation that arises between conversations (point C). For example, a number of the conversations speak to the relationship between poetry and politics, and/ or poetry and nuclear holocaust, but from different angles. These three forces (the poet's solitary production, the deliberate exchange, and the resonances between conversations) are constantly playing off each other. Or maybe another way of thinking about it is that the gesture of bringing one's thoughts into written language has a kind of ripple effect of public-ness. There's an exponential expansion of the conversation.

JMW: I like your thought that "language itself is this boundary." And influence — how one writer's work comes into a new poet's sense of writing — marks this boundary too, as when Laura Mullen writes, "The idea of influence as that which flows across — permeates — the boun-daries of self-hood: suddenly 'I' and 'you' are a little less safely separate." And the anthology presents a concatenation of "less safe" modes of influ-ence. I think of Ben Lerner's long line, "If it is any consolation, we admire the early work of John Ashbery" and it's here where even influence is reduced to cliché, yes, but also marked with humor, homage, playfulness, anxiety (in Bloom's sense too), and of course recognition. In these conver-sations, I'm continually struck by the vast differences and the overwhelm-ing number of other poets, writers, texts, films, artists, and places that are cited. Many of the conversations seem to take up that node of the par-ticular, the private, or the singular — and yet they all seem to radiate out, as when Christian Hawkey describes, for Tomaž Šalamun, how he woke up and found himself saying "good morning" to a deer in the yard as this disarming interior/exterior moment.

CM: Oh, I'm glad that you cite Laura Mullen here. I really appreciate her attempt, in her conversation with Jennifer Dick, to distinguish between "influence" and "symptoms of influence" (stylistic or textual appropria-tions). I wonder if influence is understood here as a shaping of thought, or a generation of impulses, both, neither? It does seem clear that influence is somehow generative. I like what Jon Woodward says: "Being influenced has always felt more than anything like being given permission, or being shown possibilities." I like that influence is liberating for him, a force upon his writing, yes, but a liberating force.

JMW: And on political or ethical levels, I'm impressed by the degree to which the poets included in this book want to talk through the ethical tasks (or obligations or uncertainties) of being a poet. Here is Mark Levine responding to Srikanth Reddy: "It troubles me a bit that, as poets, we seem to feel put on the spot to pretend that everything we put in poems emerges from a very supportable rationale." And then Karen Volkman: "There is also an increasing concern on the part of many poets over the last decades that this [ancient] modeling [of lyric poetry] has an ethical imperative to assert freedoms rather than affirming what can be viewed as a falsely consoling cohesiveness — instability, indeterminateness, lack of closure representing a consciousness in action, a model of the self as open, exploring, and dynamically engaged." It's this attention to the ethics of writing the self, the interrogation of the lyric "I," which I find particularly moving. Yet, Mary Leader and Mark Yakich approach it with humor, volleying spryly through Grossman and Dickinson to Eliot, Ginsberg, and back to Blake's *Four Zoas*, whereas Ben Lerner and Aaron Kunin shift coordinates between the preservation of the self in Shakespeare's sonnets to the ubiquity of apocalypse narratives in California, where they both live, and in the Midwest, where they're both from. There is a strong propulsion in so many of the conversations to step cleanly around issues of craft and the culture of workshops, and move right into their working theories of writing, subjectivity, futurity, the role of the ethico-political all under the constellations of their influences — of whom there are hundreds named throughout the twelve conversations.

CM: What I find particularly fascinating is the overlap — how many times Emily Dickinson is cited, for example, and by very different poets. It speaks to a sharing of poetic DNA — it's as if the top of Dickinson's head came off and released a poetic charge upon the poetry landscape that finds its way into almost every cranny of American poetic discourse and production. That Laura Mullen refers to Rosmarie Waldrop and that Mary Leader references Allen Grossman is another kind of overlap, and one of the wonderful surprises of this anthology as I read it. I think we both envisioned, from the outset of this project, a way of thinking about "the power to produce effects" in poetry that sidesteps the canonical patrilineal notion of influence. Here, influence looks something like a spiderweb with no truly discernible middle (the Eve of influence?! Sappho perhaps, though she had her own influences), spinning out and out. One disruption of this old-guard notion of influence is the way in which other mediums are considered swaying to a poet — visual art, music — for instance, Rae Armantrout and Jon Woodward talking about counting the syllables of hymns, "absorb[ing] their rhythms." Again, I want to draw a line to Dickinson — her influences finding new poets — the traversal of time.

JMW: Your response makes me think about what's gone into this through our role as editors. Perhaps the metaphor of curating is an apt one. Intimately involved in the worlds of art and poetry, John Yau observed: "Curating is like doing an anthology, or editing a book. It enables you to shape something — a way of looking or a way of seeing." And, yet, while this is similar to curating a show, it's more like inviting artists to select other artists that have been important to them and having *all* of them paint the gallery. The way these conversations diverge — and as you said, overlap — is incredible. Dickinson and Ashbery keep reappearing, but so do Stein, Barbara Guest, and so many other art forms . . .

CM: The book as gallery — that's lovely. I don't think we've really sculpted a "way of seeing" so much as we've offered space to twenty-four poets to show their ways of seeing, whatever those ways might be. It does feel a bit like watching poets paint the gallery, as you say.

I've noticed we have a number of student/mentor pairs among our poets (Sabrina Orah Mark and Claudia Rankine, Paul Fattaruso and Dara Wier, to name a couple). I think this is something rather unique to our moment (and by that I mean the last few decades), that poets "study" poetry with other poets in a formal academic setting; and yet, perhaps it's only novel insofar as it's been formalized. We've always learned to write from other writers. I wonder what you think about this. And I wonder if you think this might have something to do with the sustained interrogation of the lyric I, its ethics or even existence, that we find pervasive amongst our poets.

JMW: It is unique when the teaching poet has a significant, even irreparable, influence on the student poet — a bond, perhaps, that lasts beyond the walls of the acadame. What I admire about the two pairings you mention is how these pairs seem like collaborators with one another, especially in the ways that they differ. These marked differences as a form of collaboration also surface with Karen Volkman and Allen Grossman, where their difference with respect to what happens to the lyric I when you add all the dross of the contemporary (e.g., the ubiquitousness of television, advertising, visuality, etc.) forces them to reinvent the terms of engagement. Christina, I know that some of your own favorite poets are here, especially Rosmarie Waldrop and Rae Armantrout. I wonder what in their responses to Christine Hume and Jon Woodward have surprised you, moved you, or offered you pause?

CM: There is a moment I do keep coming back to (I've underlined it in three different pens in my manuscript!) wherein Rae Armantrout is thinking about silent screen comedians, and she says, "I think jokes and dreams have a similar structure in that they both show us what we don't know we know. . . . I like poems that embody that dynamic." I thought this was remarkable. I remember Alice Notley remarking, at one point, "The reader likes you to tell her/him what she/he already knows in a familiar form whether in mainstreamese or avant-gardese," and at the time this struck me as unsettlingly true. What Rae does is let this still be true, but takes the comfortable consciousness out of the reader. Reading a poem is not just being told what we know, but being shown what we "don't know we know." It seems that it would take quite a bit of humility on both the part of the poet and the reader to be part of such a poem. It also reminds me of Augustine's theories of memory, that there are those things which we do not learn but which live in us, and which we are simply given a more formal way of knowing (which he calls an act of memory). A dream or joke or poem gives us a more formal way of knowing what already lives in us. The other thing that strikes me about this is that, I suspect for a poem like this to work, foresight would have to be abandoned. (Rae notes, just prior to this observation, that the joke of silent screen comedians is "the apparent failure of foresight.") The poet would have to have to be shown what he/she doesn't know he/she knows for the reader to read that in the poem. It foregrounds the discovery element of writing without ever explicitly naming it.

I think in Rosmarie's conversation, I found myself struck (in addition, of course, to Christine Hume's incredibly attentive and thoughtful readings) by this tiny little moment wherein she plays out this axiom of rhythm, a poetic "proof," if you will, that concludes, "the meaning of the words changes the rhythm. And so we're back with rhythm as cultural." First, I simply found this proof astonishing on a visceral level. It was a belated eureka moment for me —"Of course!" I thought, and then felt badly for having not thought this exact thing before. She showed me what I didn't know I knew. I also wondered what this kind of understanding does for her translation work. If the meaning of the words is being approximated across languages, but the cadences of the two different languages diverge, then where does a translated poem find its rhythm? I do remember reading a review by Marjorie Perloff of her translation of Jacques Roubaud's *Some Thing Black* (which I am deeply, deeply grateful to Rosmarie for translating) in which Perloff notes how deftly Rosmarie carries rhythm from the French into the English. She claims that Roubaud is eminently translatable, a comment that just confirmed in my mind how truly remarkable Rosmarie's translations are.

Now, can I throw this question somewhat back to you? I know you to be a very committed reader of new poetry. Is there a poet, or poets, perhaps on the younger order, who you found yourself particularly surprised by here?

JMW: There is a generosity in Tomaž Šalamun's responses that is staggering; you cite Christine Hume's careful, brilliant readings of Rosmarie Waldrop's poems; the connection that Jennifer Dick and Laura Mullen have — and the way they further each other's responses — is remarkable; Ben Lerner and Aaron Kunin's humorous approach to the history of literature and imminent destruction is also renewing and fascinating, you know, to see those minds at work together — playfully talking about Lyn Hejinian, the beautiful boy in Shakespeare's poems, and nuclear holocaust and the chain stores of the Midwest. I love, and continue to return to, Claudia Rankine's responses to Sabrina Orah Mark which are so deft, and I'm heartened by the way that Sabrina keeps pushing on the answers she garners. In all, I think it is seeing these minds at work, shifting between modes of attentiveness: the ethical, the humorous, the teacherly, and the poet as engaged theorist. And also, it's the utter lack of reliance on old, easily assimilable narratives of what poetry is, what a poet does, etc.

When we started this project, it was in part to disrupt notions of canonicity: to let a disparate, uncategorizable pack of new poets self-select their influences. What strikes me now that the project is complete is the strange simultaneity of how far-reaching the conversations are, how unique the poems are, on the one hand; and on the other hand, how much overlap, continuity, and shared ground of influence there is among these twenty-four writers.

CM: I feel that there's something very honest, almost to-the-point, about the fact that such different writers have, in this way, so much commonality. Shelley and Coleridge could hardly be more different on the page, and yet they share much by way of aesthetic and cultural influence. Or Stein and Pound. We may, it seems, be wearing very different clothes, but the thread stitching the pockets is spun from the coat of the same silkworm. And if not the pockets, the sleeves; and if not the sleeves, the buttons. But this is too surface; poetry is *in* the body, not adorning it. That silk is stitching our lungs.

12 × 12

JENNIFER K. DICK | LAURA MULLEN

Anatomy

Some words I know: scapula, ventricle, organ, liver, femur.
The body pieced back. The body pieced. The body in

Let's begin simply. Locate the_____

A reference point, as when we stretch our heads back to see
clearly the pole wobbling in the grasp — and the feet? Somewhere,
at first beyond vision, the cornea taking in light, adjusting
until the line between tightrope and toe, heel, ankle, thigh, hip,
waist, chest — in, out — neck then head wobbling
eyes eyeing out of sight the white pole

where. we meet. An interstice — two perpendicular lines.
Completely still that instant all eyes fix

together.

As here, his voice behind my own larynx vibrating
behind me eyeing the rail, no, between the rails, the wooden
crossties. Eyeing between. My voice eyeing, eyes eyeing me and it
was there, slowing, our train so that

In the Garden

She comes into vanishing words. Scintillating, rounding the hollow vowels she whispers against to re-evoke peaceful views. Forgetting eaves, she scavenges in her throat. Turns her back in sleep, closes the vast plains like musk. Herself mixing with his. Forgets the body. Language before in that other breast, bending, flower blooming against his breath. Her distaste, body sweat, wants the first apple rounding smooth as a poison icicle. She mouths the rotund, opening mouth over him, eyes trying her childhood. Great barriers against salt. Her ejaculation returning to Eve. Before the woman's palm, to taste of it.

Claudia

The small girl, the night "Claudia" her name becomes. Mosaics echo a song, perhaps another place. She imagines the pile of perfume, scarves, table, the bare leather clogs, inhales orange burnt-out. Unlatched. "Shhhh" she calls in the holding. The "u" nebulous, cumulous with her plaintive something. Here the springs of incense, beaded, draped over the middle of "owd" i.a.: so that rainmaking, the voice is, perhaps, needed. In next-door creek, jewelry, bottles, small seagreen bureau or perhaps slim burning. She, nose of the, and with a sign. Dark hallway. The small girl with her feet pat-patters.

JD: I was thinking, this being a collection of younger poets and their "influences," we might start on the topic of influence.

LM: I keep hearing the words under the word — don't you? "Influence" is itself influenced, coming from an Italian word for the outbreak of a disease (*influenza*, outbreak, meaning here a breaking into the body). The idea of influence as that which flows across — permeates — the boundaries of self-hood: suddenly "I" and "you" are a little less safely separate. Whether it's a successful use of your will upon another (*How to Win Friends and Influence People . . .*) or whether it's a virus, it's still going where it's not supposed to go, you know? By which I mean to say it is a very interesting topic to have chosen. In art we have a certain acceptance of the fact of influence (it happens, you can trace it, talk about it), but in the world, the fact that the well-guarded borders of the intact individual fail has a darker glow.

JD: Yes, it is traceable, and so we backtrack like epidemiologists trying to locate a poet's source infections! Thus I would start here by asking you to do that epidemiological work for me. In other words, who are some writers that you feel influence you now, and who were some that influenced you when you started writing, and at the stages when you first published a book?

LM: I'm very responsive, reactive, permeable (and willful); I'm sure I'm always being influenced. The question is indeed the one you ask: by whom and when (along with the question of how). So any list I make here is going to leave way too many writers, artists, lovers and landscapes out! But *influencing me since I first saw the work* would be a list of *mostly* women in order of appearance: Sylvia Plath, John Ashbery, Jorie Graham, Carol Snow, D. A. Miller, Joseph Lease, Carole Maso, Brenda Hillman, Rikki Ducornet, Erin Mouré, Gertrude Stein. That's a timeline, by the by; you can see it in the work. But "influence," as the word implies, flows! I've been influenced by my students — the people I'm supposed to be influencing, right? I have a very strong, brilliant slam poet student here at Louisiana State University and I just wrote (after an independent study on slam poetry with her last spring, and having gone to local slams because of her) a slam poem. My joke is "Yeah, I wrote this, but it's your poem!" (She goes by Dr. Madelyn Hatter on myspace.com.) But maybe it's because I'm a huge Anne Waldman fan and have been reading *In the Room of Never Grieve*? Influence is like paternity: without DNA testing it's hard to be sure exactly who, what, when, and how. And the truth is that I hope not to influence my students in any direct way; it makes me so sad when you can tell that X student studied with Y teacher because X writes watered-down Y-ish poetry. So it almost seems as if successful teaching teaches students to resist influence? (I always tell students that part of what they will learn in workshop is when to say, *No way! I'm not changing this at all!*)

JD: So do you think that influences are (too) important? Or that in fact they aren't given enough importance nowadays? For myself, I have always tended to think of influence as, first, an awareness that writing and attention to words exist. For me, that started with Dickinson and a high school teacher who turned me on to her and to poetry in general. Then, as one begins to actually write, I began to see influence like a painter might — looking to writers and classics and traditions to learn technique, gestures, ways to use syntax, grammar, and vocabulary, and also as lessons in knowing what has already been done and therefore has lost its interest or would be seen as simple imitation or déjà vu — what I'd also call writing like one's teachers in the context of MFA or literary studies, as you've mentioned. Now, however, influence comes to me more in other art forms than in writing, yet reading continues to constantly impact how and what I write in littler ways than it at first did, milder ways than when I was younger, placing me more in a space of dialogue with and expansion off of what has been or is now being written.

LM: I think that the pressure on modern art to "make it new" has made the suspect side of "influence" (in its roots) more present for us. We are afraid of "catching" something from what we read, see, get involved with somehow. I vividly recall Robert Pinsky telling his students not to worry about writing like the people they were reading, it was the people they weren't reading . . . *that* was who they might be imitating, *and they wouldn't know.* It's a wonderful image, don't you think? Ghostly! Spooky! I haven't read Kafka for a decade: maybe he's running me (or I'm running him, the Kafka bug) right now. I do have outbreaks of others, we might say. Nathaniel Hawthorne is chronic; I've got a touch of Henry James I just can't shake — not even a heavy dose of French feminism could cure that "flu." But I love that you bring in other mediums (even the word "medium" — it's the place where the boundary between self and other, self and world, must be permeable); this is why my books always end (now) with long lists of names. I have so many "influences" I am grateful to — as diverse as Eve Aschheim, Jean-Luc Godard, and Hole.

JD: Film, music, pop culture — these are "influences" some would certainly tend to see as infections, necessary to eradicate, as if terminal — risky (or unpoetic). Despite all that's happened over the past century, they still seek a poetry that they perceive will speak across timelines, into a future where the reader won't know or "get" Hole. What would you say to a reader who discourages such pop music and film culture references, or to a writer who shies away from them in fear of ostracizing a reader?

LM: Ah, but we don't have a crystal ball, do we? I mean, I was going to say, how do you know what will last "across timelines" and what won't? Take that crystal ball, for instance (please): Eliot was taking quite a risk to introduce his tacky faddish "famous clairvoyant" into a poem, the same kind of risk Dante took, deciding to write in the vernacular, but it turns out that Latin's the dead language, right? And Frank O'Hara, whose work might be characterized — arguably — as a list of ephemera, turns out to be one of the most important, influential poets of his generation. We don't know what will last ("what thou lovest well remains," those words from Pound come back to me), and we write, as Cecilia Vicuña says, to find out what poetry can be.

JD: In your most recent work, it seems to me that you are constantly also in dialogue with writings and reflections of others, yet they've become wholly your own and are your voice in your poems. Do you yourself see/ feel that, and do you see it as different from the relationship you had with influence when writing your first book (*The Surface*)?

LM: I think you are really putting your finger on an important distinction when you change "influence" to "dialogue." With *Subject* I am in conversation with Stein in many ways and responsive to Charles Olson's pressure to use the whole page, and I'm teasing Eliot and citing O'Hara and George Oppen straight-faced . . . but an increasing (if increasingly desperate) reliance on my own vision allows me to do that. As for *The Surface*, I like that book, but I can't think of it without thinking of Kaspar Hauser (in the Peter Handke play) reeling around repeating "I want a sentence like somebody else had once." I'm probably murdering that — from memory — quote. It's solid, that collection, it makes some useful discoveries, but I wanted a poem not too different from poems other somebodies had once. In *Fluorescence* you leaped over that step — I'd love to hear you talk about how you managed that.

JD: Wow, I guess I take that as a compliment, since in ways I do relate still to that "I want a sentence like somebody else had once" — fearing being too far from the fold. But as with most poets, the problem is we often fail to blend (are "left of center" to take up that Suzanne Vega lyric that has haunted me since high school!). Maybe we're just too dissatisfied — wanting something more, needing what we still can't express and thus strive towards. So even when we are trying desperately to match, our spots show (as Ani DiFranco put it). Concretely, I think that aiming for the sentence I knew, the ones I felt for, I still wanted it to take a little detour on the way, to explore itself. In *Fluorescence*, influence, striving toward dialogue, does still show some of its imprints — Steinian and Christophe Tarkos-like syntax or repetitions and reflections, stretching between a concrete abstract that I sense in Michael Palmer, or stealing outright the images I spent so much time examining in the Breugel works that I reference for certain poems. But I think my mind mixes and melds too easily. Influenza is usually a traceable strain, but I remember being a teenager with mono and learning that it was sometimes hard to diagnose since so many other viruses got into the mix. In *Fluorescence*, Palmer meets Stein meets Breugel meets Rauschenberg meets Laynie Brown, Carol Snow, Carole Maso, John Ashbery, Cole Swensen, Laura Mullen, Keith Donovan, Julie Brown and, less evidently, the rhythmic influences ingrained in my head by years as a Joseph Brodsky student reading lyric and Russian poetry by Robert Frost, W. H. Auden, Dylan Thomas, A. E. Housman, Anna Akhmatova, Osip Mandelstam, Boris Pasternak, Marina Tsvetaeva, etc. We are a sum of what we have read, seen, and thought, and I think the poems in *Fluorescence* reflect a *sum* of influence rather than, I hope, being distinct imitations of someone else.

LM: Hmmm — sounds like a "some" rather than a "sum," or that's what I think(s). What is it Rimbaud said — "If brass wakes a trumpet that's not its fault"? Do we, making our trumpet out of the brass that is language, just pour out "brass" (music) for others to melt down, meld with, melody off of? Whose trumpet are we holding, heated to liquid and flowing, to our lips? I do have a strong sense that it would be wrong not to know, and, not (where you can) to credit. But *Murmur*, the book coming out in the spring, is a murder mystery, and it's full, on the level of the language itself, of murder, dismemberment, and theft.

JD: This also makes me think of the question of "appropriation of language" of which you and I have spoken before. Is it possible to be appropriating the language of someone else? Is there a distinguishable line between a poem you write and a text you have used to write it? And how do we locate or define this line, or must we? (This seems to me less appropriately addressed to your work than to other people working in the States that we've talked of or have seen the work of — for example, Susan Howe, Carla Harryman, Carol Snow, Stacy Doris, etc.) I also think of this in relationship to my recent *Circuits* manuscript and its use of the popular science text by George Johnson that they fragment and play off of.

LM: You know, I was just wondering if my work will be more "mine" the more there is of others in it. I'm laughing — but I'm serious. As my work gets more collage-y, it gets more original? Rosmarie Waldrop has that extraordinary essay ("Alarums & Excursions") in *The Politics of Poetic Form*, where she seems to lay out a basis for the inevitability of that paradox.

What's engrossing about this issue right now, nationally, is the question of permissions and intellectual property. All language is "appropriated," obviously — but at what point we violate copyright law remains a question of some urgent complexity. Carol Snow's *The Seventy Prepositions* includes a group of poems (the "Karesansui") in which quoted (recalled or thought) language is arranged (as are stones in a Zen garden) to emerge like solid peaks from the flow of clouds or water around them, the ongoing, always-in-motion thinking. To use, in that context, a few words from *The Sound of Music* costs money. That's the "distinguishable line between a poem you write and a text you have used to write it" — at least legally! To go back to your question about *Circuits*: scientists, in my experience, find their research used in a poem charming — but I haven't been breaking state secrets. What is your experience with this appropriation? And perhaps this is a good point to draw another distinction: neither appropriation nor dialogue seem to me to be "influence" (though they might be symptoms of influence). What do you think?

JD: Tough delineation! And I laugh, as I initially mistyped "touch"— this is the issue really, no, to touch delineation? To be able to see things as separate from when we speak of the question of appropriation? To whom does the language belong? Who is speaking in this "dialogue"? Let's draw lines! Have you ever had a critic (since I think it is via critics, via being explored and read critically, for better and worse, that questions of influence and appropriation most often arise) "accuse" you of being too influenced by a poem or a poet you have never yourself read, or at least don't recall? How did this make you feel? Do you feel that a writer should let a critic know they are off base, misreading your influences? Or does this misreading enter into the realm of enlarging the poetic dialogue, that by seeing strains of connection, quotes, echoes, etc., that you were yourself not conscious of, the critic opens the realm of potentially subconscious influence and also, therefore, dialogue — a dialogue that leads a writer (and reader) back to other authors and books, to other voices?

LM: Don't you distrust lines drawn ("in the sand," for instance, as the first Bush said), and attempts to control readings? I do! Your questions made me recall the fact that Laura Riding Jackson used to write to anyone who read her work to correct their misunderstandings. That seems as awful, to me, as the fact that Bill Knott writes in and on, actually, his books, endlessly revising his poems. The two gestures seem similar to me in ways I'm not sure I can explain. One of the things I'm really dealing with in *Subject* (by enacting it) is the ongoing dialogue between the two mutually exclusive impulses: to contain, and to continue. What isn't a revision? What isn't a misreading? The revised answer to your questions is that I once got a bad review of *The Tales of Horror* in which the critic — another poet — and the magazine's editor missed the fact of collage and they tore into William Carlos Williams, or rather the critic Williams was (in *Paterson*) quoting! So a bad review got a bad review: "It is a fashionable grocery list." Hilarious, in a way. But as Roland Barthes says in *S/Z*, we write our reading. Don't you find that great criticism is as active, as influential, as poetry?

JD: Certainly. In fact, as I mature as a writer and reader, I appreciate a developing relationship with critical writing, and I enjoy reseeing work I love from another perspective. Though I have always felt the influence of criticism as present in the essays of poets like Octavio Paz, Czeslaw Milosz, Wallace Stevens, Gumilyov, and Ezra Pound — great essayists that try to tackle the giant boulders of thought and questions of "being and poetry," to often find themselves, like Sisyphus, again and again back at the drawing board, the starting point, the bottom of the hill, for better and worse, in constant exploration and striving. Their essays are a map of this effort stretching across their lives!

Another question here, relating to influence or use of others' materials, is how do you see your relationship with the other arts — for example visual artwork and music — as portrayed, embodied, intertwined with(in) your poems? Where is the limit between ekphrasis and the creation of a work wholly apart from a work of art which may have instigated it? And are we as writers, who work in a medium which lacks the messy physical nature of paint, canvas, brush, etc., merely borrowing language assigned to that medium because we are stretching toward it, thus using the page in increasingly visual manners? Or, if it is something else entirely to physically manipulate the typography on a page or to borrow the vocabulary of another art, then what is it?

LM: These are excellent questions — so good I would rather duck out here, maybe ask you to ask Joanna Drucker to answer them rather than me — or ask Cole Swensen to come in and take up the thread, because I really feel Cole is pressing language in important ways by using other mediums to force it past its inclinations, don't you? Lisa Samuels's work does this also — brilliantly. The source for me is *Tender Buttons*: the need to capture seeing and the present/presence in the action of seeing (not just the seen) fractures the usual order, brings the sentence to anacoluthon and fragmented ecstasies. And then, as Brenda Hillman puts it, there was a hole in "about," so maybe "inspiration" has turned to "influence"? In my first poetry collection and my third there are Joseph Cornell poems. In the first, the artist and work are named in the title, and I was (this may be important) working off a catalogue; I had never seen an actual Cornell box. But the "Cornell" poems in *Subject* — written when I was teaching at Columbia College and spending a lot of time in the Chicago Art Institute — never reference the actual works (which I stood in front of, writing) in any direct way. (The change comes by way of the dialogue with the Robert Ryman in my second book, possibly?) Now I am no longer telling you "about" the artwork; I am making another work — that's the change. With your work, I can read your poems without having to see the paintings that influenced you. On the other hand, while Auden's poem about Bruegel is tremendous, I don't really want to see the particular Breugel Auden describes without finding "Musée des Beaux Arts" nearby (or vice versa). They've infected each other? It's symbiosis, actually. Auden reads the painting, or he tells us (he is also "never wrong") how to read. It's profound — and deadly.

JD: This makes me think of Rodrigo Toscano. Recently, reading him on places like the bus (since he is such a light read!) I find myself murmuring the words aloud, moving through the poems just as I am moving through the city on the bus. Then I get off. I realize even in the moment of reading that I have "understood" nothing. I cannot summarize, encapsulate, explicate, or explain what is happening in his poems for me. Even their language, his vocabulary, at times depresses me, entangling me in a confounded web. Yet, they tend to haunt the rest of my day, my week. Images, lines, reflections, some sort of question recurs which I recognize is his. Am I wounded? Because I am certainly infected, but not influenced, have no language of my own to speak in return to this potential sense that I have received an invitation into a dialogue, a hand held out saying "speak," since his work has "inspired" reflections on myself, on life, on him, on what poetry is. In the end, what does this mean?

LM: What "end"? Especially in the context of that definite article?! Whew! What end, which meaning? *Means without End* — the (English translation of a) title of a Giorgio Agamben book — has belatedly become a crucial idea for me. I always loved, loved, loved the great endings of poems, the feeling that things were summed up, even if softly: "and everyone and I stopped breathing." That feeling of a meaningful death, we might say. Walter Benjamin first, and then Stein, and Agamben, and other influences including a recent hurricane started my distrust of the longing for a death to warm my shivering life with, as Walter Benjamin in "The Storyteller" scorchingly says. I'm interested, just now, in the films of Matthew Barney, which are all process, either an ending in every frame or no ending, meaningful at every instant or completely without meaning.

JD: These thoughts take me back again to the questions above on being influenced by other mediums, such as contemporary art. I find that the general public/populous is willing to go to a contemporary art show and "take it in" even if they don't "get" it, but with poetry, there is such fear about "not getting it," and there is such a desire in readers to be able to summarize a poem in one or two words, or else to give up on it. I notice this in classes I am teaching and when talking to friends and acquaintances and family members that don't often read poetry. It also comes up, though, with other writers who dismiss authors as potentially "too difficult," "too experimental," or "too out there" for them. This is often said by people who have yet to actually sit down and read through an entire book by any of the writers they are referring to, however. So how can we get over these aesthetic barriers? What would be some advice you might give to readers coming to poetry for the first time? How would you encourage them to "take it in"? And, when it comes to a book like *Subject* which many first-time poetry readers will find mind-boggling or difficult, how might you advise they proceed?

LM: Oh, compared to experimental music or films, we're fine; as poets, we have it easy! At least what we do doesn't cost $1000 per minute, or involve an orchestra. . . . And recently I have been thinking we are too worried, too quick to complain about our lack of audience. I mean, after watching those who were left behind in New Orleans struggle to survive, I never, ever want to hear any poet talk to me about how poetry is "marginalized"! And I think we have to face, squarely, the fact that we have chosen to work with language, which holds out — unlike paint — a promise of communication. That is a social promise! So the public has some right to feel betrayed, you know? But the shift of perspective that opens us to "means without end" is old now. Which is to say that part of what we face is simply the failure of the educational system. It's as if evolution was never taught, or the work of Copernicus were ignored: that's the best analogy for what is happening, in high schools and colleges, vis-à-vis so-called "experimental" art. Stein's *Tender Buttons* is nearly one hundred years old; nobody should be that shocked or angry when they encounter this work. It's one of the great thefts of our century, the fact that this space of freedom and play has been kept from us and labeled "too difficult"! Really, what that means is "I'm not going to teach this book because I don't know the *right* answer and I can't tell you what you are supposed to think about it." About Stein you are always wrong — or always right? Or neither? And you have to pay attention to each word, each moment; you can't look off somewhere else and sum it all up neatly. What's so bad about having your mind boggled? Luckily — this is the good news — "first time poetry readers" are often less invested in the rigid gestures and careful hierarchies imposed by our accustomed and trained desire for "a sentence like somebody else had once," and more willing to explore what Keats called "negative capability."

Wake

Widening line of light
What isn't inked
          ("the area of its competence

A visit to the morgue at night?
(Averse?)
                    Traversed
By the frame
A hand (reaching in? withdrawing
                    (From outside

To lift   (this sheet)

Sheer homesickness — the text

+

Awoke a serial homesickness (the text)
for a place you lived in — off and on — for years
(yes) but never liked. *Why wait?* Sickness:
a visit to the morgue at night. Home:
You never lived there, never left. Lift (now):
And part the white canvas they draped

And waking white the scattered where
they dropped

Or wither — dreamed as grasped — reversed:
"I sang in my chains" ("like"); the corpse

Laughed until the top of "my" head also
Came off and   What   can o' mystery

/ or in among the roots a sickness
suckled or mouthed a gap confess

And woke in the secret blacked out
obscene of what you'd never, ever, ever

And woke ("sheer nonsense") layers of plastic
Or *What is it between us?*

The doors flung open the drawers pulled out
a hectic fever burning in what whithered

Tie me tie me please he was heard to murmur
weakly to the past

I did not think that I would sing to you
he seemed to say

Or something like that

+

Wake: outside the frame beyond his 'fit'
Wake: frothed a blankness in the passage of what
Wake: we waited   (and silence)
Wake: tilted sudden and sick in the chop

We kept our heads
We held our posts
                Our *secrets*, one frothed,
                        hissed
Wake: *j'accuse eau*

Wait: she wet
Her fingers and (reaching in) snuffed
Wake: the flames (reaching over
                    their heads

Wait:

Wake: outside the designated unable to recall
What she had smoked

(What weed we'd) (spooked, spoke
Woke: uneasily beached in the bleached out

+

O, widening   (perfidious
To lift   ("The beloved features

+

Abruptly woken ("and") where we'd left her out of reach
Of the too much Watteau flowers out of focus in the arms

Tied she turned to watch her watch while waiting drenched
On the edge of a grave preoccupied by violent argument
What nostalgia I think this is praying (yes) *precisely*
Your hands at my throat

+

Something of the original some harmony of the original white

+

Of or like?

And woken again later What? Can a mystery
girl get no sleep (a "smoldering glance")

Kept trying to find out what she knew what
she could remember and What

Can a mystery girl get no mystery
back to recall herself to herself as she

Once

(No shut

/ chained in "my" song
                              (distrust

JON WOODWARD | RAE ARMANTROUT

from *Rain*

newer sore spots blossomed open
in the dam overnight full
wheelbarrows were brought we spent
all night and into the
morning trying to lick the

wounds closed my late grandmother
sat on top of the
dam it would've been unsafe
for a person but she'd
come back a sunlight finch

and vocalized for a while
by ten in the morning
the sun wasn't out yet
the dam gave way we
let it go what else

from *Rain*

looking over the bomb inventory
looking at the huge list
I heard the strangest music
my eyes were loudspeakers I
was shivering cold I must've

caught a bad fever the
local witch doctor stood my
ankles in a shallow place

in the river and affixed
good examples of a certain

kind of plant to me
in three places chest neck
and head I shivered I'm
made of molecules he said
over me certain preprogrammed words

from *Rain*

it's not that he died
it's that he won't stop
dying and reemerging fully ordinarily
through ordinary doors saying in
his own voice hey brother

if he were in fact
my brother one says the
air keeps getting warmer being
that it's spring the trees
are all telling the same

story hone it down plunge
it with the piano music
we just listened to into
a bottle it won't help
him untwist from his rope

JW: I thought maybe we could start with your poem "Sake," in which there's a delicate interplay of a number of deeply formal choices. I would like to track a way through this particular poem because the obvious care given to its composition is characteristic of your work, and (paradoxically) because this poem so thoroughly troubles the idea of characteristic authorial choices. I'm thinking especially of the lineation, emphasis (as organized by italicized words), and the paired stanzas (mostly couplets) which are the poem's repeated segments and which enforce a constant reevaluation of each other. The italics in "*as if* / for their own sakes" in the third pair of couplets in a row draws renewed attention to "*always marry*" (because it's also italicized and in the same position in the couplet-pair above it), at the same time it raises the question: for what sake if not their own? The peculiar double emphasis of "*always marry*" creates a figure-ground flux between those two words and also resonates with "repeat / a passage" above and "repeated passages" below it. By the time we get to "(self / as repertoire)" we're wondering if the choice the Princesses make repeatedly might itself be thought of as a formal one, and, if it's habitual, is it a choice at all? And the deteriorating echoes of "at some length" and "from here on" heard after the poem's terminal question "*how* far?" sound like answers, but not all the way.

So I wonder what you think about characteristic choice. Is it a productive dilemma for you? Do you recognize your own writing (or does it recognize you) in the way alluded to in the first couplet? And are there forms or formal strategies that you've studied and admired in other people's work, and in which you've found the potential for careful choices (or, on the other hand, any kind of freedom from their necessity) but which you wouldn't use in your own work?

RA: I like your phrase "deeply formal" because I like the idea of form being deep. Or maybe I like the idea of form being subtle. I like broken symmetries. I wouldn't be likely to ever write a villanelle! All that rhyme is cloying. But I'm a sucker for half-rhymes and assonances. I also like what you might call "subject rhymes." That's what you see in "Sake." I like to somehow extend one concept into and through several really different scenarios or types of "discourse." In "Sake," the issue of the value of repetition comes up in different situations. First it's the repetition of musical passages; then it's the repetition of bad marriages; then the structure of a child's cry is seen in terms of the architecture of a cathedral. These ways of envisioning repetition are both utopic and dystopic. In the first section, the person who repeats is sending a signal, hoping for recognition. Recognition (identity?) depends on repetition. But the results that follow, in the poem, are uncertain. Is there a form I admire but wouldn't use? I probably wouldn't write a novel in verse.

I've been reading your new book, *Rain*, and it's clear that you have an interesting relation to form. *Rain* is a narrative poem, written in five line stanzas, and divided into what might be called chapters. It's written in first person, has characters (Patrick, Oni), and is, sometimes at least, in the past tense. In other words, it could be called a novel in verse. One thing that interests me about the writing is the terrific momentum with which it keeps moving forward, with seeming continuity, yet without ever becoming predictable. In fact, it takes one startling swerve after another. It reminds me just a bit of the tension between continuity and disjunction in John Ashbery's *Three Poems*. I haven't really asked you a question but I wonder if you want to talk about the fictive element in this poem. Do you see a relation between *Rain* and, say, Ashbery's work, or perhaps Lyn Hejinian's novel in verse, *Oxota*? How did you keep the forward momentum going through so many twists?

JW: I think any credit for the momentum you perceive should go to the formal constraints I was working with, since they enabled and propelled the writing and hopefully they create part of the reader's experience. A lack of punctuation certainly moves things forward by making the sentences cling kind of heedlessly to each other, but the real benefit I got from the constraints was that so many decisions (five words per line, five lines per stanza, three stanzas, and done) were made beforehand, so that I could begin any sentence even if I didn't know how it would end, link observations and dream-fragments and overheard remarks without any understanding of their relevance to one another, and negotiate emphasis especially at the endings of the poems. It was only much later, two years after the poems were written, that I noticed the narrative thread running through them, along which I rearranged and revised. (I like your idea of a novel in verse — I wouldn't have thought of it, but it seems correct.) Maybe this is where the fictive element comes in — what emerged was an inaccurate composite picture of my mental life from the spring of 2002, full of inconsistencies and exaggerations and falsifications, a little bit like a set of close-up polaroids taken of individual parts of the body and taped together to resemble the person. In that sense *Rain* might have a lot to do with *Oxota*, though I confess I've only read patches of it. But the urge to relay some portion of one's life, the horizontal creep and smear of observational particulars out into adjacent contexts, and the fixed shortness of the chapters all seem familiar to me.

I've read more of *Three Poems*. Part of what amazes me about that book is how it never seems to stop! There's never a landing place, which creates its own momentum in a way; the short form I used in *Rain* gave me the advantage of so many extra leaving-off places, to shoot the reader out into the white space and on into the next poem, but Ashbery never gives himself that opportunity.

As a writer of many short poems, do you have a sense of the emphasis looming at the end of a poem, or is emphasis the right word from your point of view? You said a few years ago in your interview with Daniel Kane that you like a kind of "false bottom" ending in your poems, one which feels stable at first but gives way under scrutiny. How do you engineer the kind of ending that you want? Does it have anything to do with emphasis, for you, even as an act of resistance against an easy or built-in drama? "The Subject," from the new poems you sent me, has an ending that just astonishes me — somehow, at the end of a poem filled with constantly shimmering and arbitrary(?) metamorphoses, you manage to snatch the rug out from underneath everything — and it happens every time I read it. Does that poem's ending in particular have anything to do with how you think about endings in general?

By the way, this, the ending of *Oxota* chapter 126, was what got me going on this ending business. Maybe the fact that I feel indicted by it says something:

The strictness of the walls of the room had been lost —
      withdrawn or removed
Here, said Arkadii — a letter from Chekhov
One must always suspect the beginning and end, since it's
      there that the writer puts his lies

RA: Of course, I had to finish *Rain* to see if that's "where you put your lies" as Lyn says (Arkadii says that Chekhov says). Well, don't ask, don't tell. Actually, I see some value in lies. They remind us we can be deceived and that we can deceive ourselves.

To answer your question, I suppose I often begin a poem with a sense of puzzlement, with a knot in my thinking. In that case, the poem is a version of the knot. In "The Subject," there are several strands. I don't really want to try to paraphrase it but, certainly, in the first two sections there are transformations that get out of control or have a dark side. I was thinking of the transformations in fairy tales (I like to write faux fairy tales) and also of ads on computer screens or television. In that final section, on the other hand, stasis and continuity don't seem any more satisfying. When one moment resembles, repeats the last, "we" start wanting to "change the subject." "What is a surface?" is the strangest line, I suppose. It's as if the human subject feels that all these changing manifestations are *only* a surface concealing something else.

You ask how I "engineer" the endings in my poems. It's more intuitive than that, I'm afraid. I know when it feels right. I like to produce something that reproduces my own initial puzzlement. Or maybe stopping short is, in fact, aggressive. It's like throwing something to the reader suddenly. "Your turn. Catch."

There are a lot of sudden transformations in *Rain* too, for that matter. I'm thinking of these two stanzas:

newer sore spots blossomed open
in the dam overnight full
wheelbarrows were brought we spent
all night and into the
morning trying to lick the

wounds closed my late grandmother
sat on top of the
dam it would've been unsafe
for a person but she'd
come back a sunlight finch

Those lines certainly ask us to refocus and envision something unexpected. There's something humorous, too, about the way they combine practical considerations with surreal shifts. This makes me want to ask about humor. Do you see humor in those lines? Do you think "The Subject" is funny? What's humorous (to you) in poetry?

You know, what I'd really like is to stop and ask some basic questions. You know a thing or two about me, I think, but I know nothing about you. Well, it says on the back of your book that you're from Wichita. Was it very far from Wichita to poetry? How did you come to poetry? Which poets drew you in?

JW: Yeah, you've been at a kind of weird unspoken disadvantage thus far, in terms of who knows what about whom. Basic questions are minefields, but here goes.

I only lived in Wichita until I was nine, so all my memories of living there are worn out and disconnected. I have tornado dreams fairly frequently, but I'm not sure if I ever saw an actual tornado. My first poetry memory, other than children's books, comes from Denver, after we moved: at church, I discovered a section in the back of the hymnal which indexed all the hymns by the syllable count of their lines. I don't know how many sermons I ignored by studying that section. I had a great English teacher in fifth and sixth grade who taught Shakespeare and Greek myth, which I loved. She also gave us an assignment to write a sonnet. I wrote mine about silence, and was extremely proud of it. I liked e. e. cummings in high school. There's a Blake poem from *Songs of Experience*, "The Garden of Love," which turns intensely about halfway through; I used to read it over and over again to feel my hairs stand on end. I attended Lutheran schools all the way through high school, and had my eyes opened when I got to college (Colorado State University), which I think is why "The Garden of Love" hit me so hard. Laura Mullen led my poetry workshops and introduced me to (among many others) Russell Edson and James Tate, both of whom gave me permission for humor in poems. After college, while working in the Harvard University Accounts Payable department, I took three semesters of workshops with Jorie Graham, which was like swallowing rocket fuel once a week.

I think I can try to answer the humor question too, though I distrust opinions about humor, including (especially) my own. I think there are many different kinds of humor in poetry; most of them are useful and great, and there are a few I could do without. I prefer an understated, ambient sense of humor, and deadpan poets who are either still investigating or wholly unaware of the humorous situation around them, and tripping over themselves as a result, like Buster Keaton (as opposed to the kind of poet who's always smirking and winking). I certainly think that a lot of your work (including "The Subject" and especially your dream poems) has that circumspect kind of humor, perforated with paranoia, like the humor in Kafka. I hope *Rain* does too. After a reading recently, I talked to one of my fellow readers who said she was very confused that I had read what was for her a patently absurd poem ("Wall") in such a serious way. She expected me to smile at the end of it, she said. I wasn't sure how to respond. I think the doggerel in the middle of Ashbery's "Variations, Calypso and Fugue on a Theme of Ella Wheeler Wilcox" is one of the funniest things ever, but it's also kind of sad and poignant. I wouldn't want it packaged as either serious only or absurd only. Borges says Charlie Chaplin is "absent-minded to an almost saintly degree." I can't think of a poet like that, but I would love to read their work. At any rate, I take the degree to be a more important factor than the absent-mindedness. One could be, for example, awkward to an almost saintly degree, I believe. I'm not sure why I keep using silent-film comedians for my comparisons.

I don't know, what do you think about humor in poetry? Do you ever laugh out loud when you're reading a poem? Do you reread poems you find funny? Is there any truly unfunny poetry that means a lot to you?

And, since you asked me some basic questions: I know from your memoir *True* that Denise Levertov, among others, was an important early influence on you, and that you have favorite poets that you often return to. For me, being influenced has always felt more than anything like being given permission, or being shown possibilities — is that how it felt for you when you were younger? These days, do you often have that experience when you read, or not? And how does it feel now to be an influence for other poets?

RA: It sounds like we both spent a lot of time in church as kids, listening to hymns. I absorbed the rhythms but I didn't actually count syllables. You remind me a bit of my friend Ron Silliman. If he had gone to church, he would have spent his time there on hymn syllabics. It seems like a fairly direct route for you, really, from studying the syllable count in hymns to counting words into your poem *Rain*.

I love what you say about humor and I agree completely. I like a kind of split-screen humor that's just as serious as it is funny. Or I like what's funny by accident, what stumbles into humor. That's why I like the way you bring in the silent screen comedians.

They were always sallying forth to trip over some unnoticed aspect of reality. The joke is the apparent failure of foresight. I think jokes and dreams have a similar structure in that they both show us what we don't know we know. It's that split screen again. One part of the mind may foresee the conclusion or punch line, while the other part, the part that takes action and proceeds, seems to have no clue. I like poems that embody that dynamic. I think your poem "Wall" does that. It isn't simply absurd. It's also rather ominous. "Mental gymnastics" give the rock wall "reasons to fall," including "Yeah car-bomb okay." Like Charlie Chaplain, the speaker blithely trips into some heavy weather — or at least one could see it like that.

I don't want you to think, though, that I only appreciate poems I find funny. I love William Carlos Williams, after all, and he seldom makes me laugh.

I'm really not certain how to answer your final question. I'm not sure I am much of an influence. I seldom see poems that remind me of my own. I was quite pleased when Graham Foust said that I had influenced him because I'm very fond of his work. But I have trouble recognizing my influence there. Foust's poems are minimalist, yes, more so than mine, in fact, but his sensibility is very much his own. No one would confuse a poem of his for one of mine. I'm cautious about attributions of influence, I guess.

Are there poets you think are often imitated? Too often? No need to name names, if you don't want to. Are there devices or ticks or shticks you see too much of in contemporary poetry? What trends do you see and are they good or bad?

JW: How great that you like Foust's work! I'm pretty fond of it too. And it makes perfect sense to me that he would cite you as an influence — instead of a model for imitation, maybe what he got from your work was a shove in a good direction. That seems healthier; or at least, influence comes in many flavors.

I'm not sure about trends. I read a good amount of contemporary poetry, but I read deep rather than wide. I usually duck out of a book before I read ten poems, especially if it's just soft-surrealist cotton candy (okay, that's a schtick). But, when I find something I like and/or don't understand right away, I'll just about burn a hole through it with constant rereading. Foust was one of those. I also always enjoy reading the work of my friends, even (or especially) if it's the kind of thing I might ordinarily put aside.

There are just too many books to wade through, and journals, and Web journals, and all the (with rare exceptions) claustrophobic little blogs, and on and on. Maybe that's a trend in itself. I know it wasn't like this when you were my age.

I had a helpful conversation with a friend the other day about contemporary poetry and all its entrenchments and trivialities. My friend had been reading ancient Athenian poets whose work is known today only in fragments, much of it lost forever. The implications of that really restored a sense of perspective for me.

There's something else I wanted to ask you about, with respect to your dream poems, before we get too far from them. I like your split screen idea, the half-presence of foresight (or hindsight). "Visibility," from *Made to Seem*, seems to speak to this idea explicitly: "The invisible barricades won't be in the right places, and I won't be able to maneuver around them, neatly, in the roadster I don't have — which is *supposed* to be funny!" It's like one half of the dreaming mind jabbing the perplexed other half in the ribs, trying to get it to laugh at the terrible predicament it constructed and/or stumbled into — the last clause indicating either that it's funny *because* it's supposed to be, or that it's not funny at all, in spite of what was intended. Another one of the new poems you sent, "Worth While," has a similar dynamic, in that all the examples of counting, and the urge to count, to list, or to add up, are seen as "opportunities for / clarity," and yet they encounter a resistance (from dead parents, angry ghosts, and the unspoken affinity between the small-denomination bills and advancing years — it's Mary's birthday, of course) that stops just short of nightmarish. It's the stopping short I want to ask you about. For all the anxiety and paranoia in your dream poems, there's very little outright terror that I've been able to find. Is it that nightmares have a different dynamic, or a different kind of information transfer, than the split-screen one we've been discussing? Have you had any nightmares which you've used as material for poems? Or any that you haven't?

RA: You're right to suspect that none of my dream poems involve outright nightmares. The tone, in all my poems, is probably too equivocal for that. And, also (I almost feel as if I'm talking to a therapist now), I don't really have nightmares. If a dream starts to get too scary, I seem to be able to wake myself up. I don't know what that means. I read somewhere that men have many more nightmares than women do.

I really like your descriptions of "Visibility" and "Worth While." As you must have guessed, I am the Mary at the end of "Worth While." My full name is Mary Rae Armantrout.

I notice that your poem "Golem" is a nightmare poem. And yet you are able to be inside and outside the dream at the same time, asking the kinds of questions that fascinate me: Who is the self that "encodes" our dreams? Who is the self that attempts to interpret? How are these two beings different? Is the golem whose vision clouds a character in the dream or the dreamer himself?

In a number of your poems the surreal and the mundane seem to merge. We seem to occupy a quasi-dream state. That happens, for instance, in "Outside the Minigame" — which could be a dream or, alternatively, a movie or a video game in which you've inserted yourself as a figure. This makes me want to ask about the role of self in your poems. Most of them are in first person. But the self often seems not so much a participant as a mirror in which a strange world is reflected. Is the self in a poem similar to the self in a dream? Do you write pseudo-dream poems as well as real dream poems?

Do you think of your work as "surreal"? You mentioned earlier being influenced, in various ways, by Laura Mullen, Russell Edson, James Tate, and Jorie Graham. I can see your link to the deadpan surrealism of Edson and Tate. And, even though I said before that I didn't see many poems out there that looked like mine, I can see some kinship between, say, your "Golem" and my poetry. For instance, there's the way "Golem" is divided into three parts, as well as the oblique relation among the sections, and the ambiguous/ambivalent position of the speaker. So perhaps I have been an influence too? But, then, what an eclectic group of influences we make! Did you know that Marjorie Perloff devoted a chapter of her most recent book, *Differentials*, to contrasting my work with Jorie Graham's? We're like the matter and antimatter of poetry. I see her as an essentially descriptive poet. That might sound dismissive but it isn't. I respect her project, actually. She seems to take on the tremendous, doomed task of describing complex phenomena (wave action, a school of minnows, blow-ing leaves) in their entirety. These descriptions border on the mystical be-cause she wants to know and say more than can be known or said. Maybe we do have something in common; we're both obsessed with the limits of knowledge. But our approaches to the problem, our styles, are completely different. Anyway, how do your various mentors and/or influences meet and mingle and reconcile or, perhaps, become transformed in your work?

JW: I think about this a lot and I'm still working it out. As far as I can tell I'm not much of a synthesist. I'll be interested to read what Perloff has to say. One of the valuable lessons of Jorie's work, for me, is its variety. From one book to the next she's always trying different approaches, though some stay the same (the descriptive aspect you mention is certainly one of them; a grappling with the specifics of history is another, which I think also differs from your work). She said something in class once which I was predisposed to find frightening, so I've never forgotten it. We were reading Berryman's *The Dream Songs* (also important for me), and she said that he never let the Dream Song form go, or it never let go of him, and it killed him as a result. However overstated that might be, it certainly found a seat in my brain. Of the list above, I think of Edson in particular as a kind of walking-dead, self-similar automaton. As has been said, that might sound dismissive but it isn't; I find it fascinating. The technologies one creates or adapts for oneself become so eager to please, maybe too much so. As much as I receive from people who influence me (yourself, of course, included) a kind of permission to try new structures or sounds, I have a fear of excessive influence which goes beyond the social prohibition against being derivative, a fear of being taken over by one poetic mode or voice only, no matter whether mine or anyone else's. All the worst nightmares I've had in my life have been about possession, in the demonic sense, about something or someone occupying a body (mine or whomever's) that they're not supposed to. To the same degree, and in exactly the same way, the video games I've enjoyed the most have been the ones which created space and movement my brain recognized as physical, like a bodysuit to climb into and (hours or days later, or never) out of. "Outside the Minigame" deals with this, a self that's both permeable and predatory to the degree that the two are alike.

I do write pseudo-dream poems, probably more often than real dream poems. I get them mixed up and mixed in with one another very easily. Your poem "Later" isn't too far from any of this, particularly the aim taken by the questions of the second section. It quickly becomes difficult to imagine a body and a world sufficiently "otherwise" — how could one's own imagination generate something which wasn't one's own? And yet there's something else going on, besides a perpetual hermit crab-like reoccupation of identity. There's something so haunting and indirectly assertive in all the temporal cues, not only the title, but also for example "Then not" in the third section, which stands out because of its redundancy. The fourth section seems to come after the death which has been hinted at (therefore "They drive me / out to sea") which makes the word "still" resonate so powerfully. The question I've got in mind risks already having been answered by the poem itself, unless I include another poem of yours I've always admired and thought of as a kind of self-diagnostic poem. "Now This," from *Up to Speed*, is superficially unlike "Later," in that it seems to be directed much more outwardly, but they share an investigation of the intersection of writing and time: "Later" seems to switch between past and future, and "Now This" wants to pinpoint the exact present moment. Also, they both have a concern with rarity, and there's a similar concern in both with the need for one's writing, along with one's self, to be capable of redemption (or to be justified, as "Now This" has it). Do these two poems pretty well map out what you think is at stake with your writing, and/or with reading and being read by other people? Has this changed over the course of your life? Not unrelatedly, how do you feel about the thought of your work disappearing partially or entirely, like the ancient Greeks my friend was telling me about?

RA: I wouldn't write faux dream poems myself — and I'm not sure why. I'm phobic, somehow, about "making things up." I feel as if I need to be ambushed by material, the way one is by a dream. Then it has authority. I'm not saying that's good. If I did write from imagination, I'd have written more.

I'm interested in your fear of demonic possession. In a sense, I think, we're all in danger of that, given the way we're deluged more and more by mass media. The words of a Dylan song just popped into my mind: "There's voices in the night, asking to be heard / I'm sitting here listening to every mind-polluting word." How do we coexist with all the talking (and singing) heads in our environment without being possessed? One way is to try to hand it back, somehow, by the often ironic use of "found language." I seldom write entire found language poems, but the things I hear, overhear, or read do often make their way into my poems. Does that happen to you? I don't know whether that's exorcism or just proof of possession. How do you feel about it? I don't see a lot of obvious borrowed language in the poems you sent me — though there is "Typical Wish" where you're at a party and "somebody won't stop putting words in my mouth." These words, alarmingly, morph into "an improvised explosive" "thrown down a gaping wishing well." So, I guess my question is, how do you maneuver in your writing to avoid possession, either by demons or by poets you admire?

The questions you ask me are difficult and a little scary — which is good. How do I feel about the possibility of being forgotten? I think it's more than a possibility. Soon enough the world runs out of fuel — and then the stars. Unless there is a God and a heaven, everything we humans do is gone (already). But then how would our poems (so full of anxiety) look in heaven anyway?

Sigh.

But it's so great that you connect "Later" with "Now This." I had never thought of those connections. "Later" speaks from the future, when I won't exist, and from the past, where a slight difference (how slight?) might have caused me not to exist — and yet it still deals with ego needs and claims. And "Now This" asks how the moment and the self in the moment can be justified. As if it ever could! As if it needed to be! As if writing could do it! But we do write. I could ask you why you write. That's a big one. Do you want to take that on?

JW: The more I've thought about the "possession" stuff, the more I feel like I'm going in circles with it. I think you're right to connect it to mass media — the dispensation of blunt little messages from all sides is alarming and ridiculous. It sometimes feels like the ambient temperature of the language as a whole is slowly rising. How could that be avoided? It's a different kind of possession than the influence of poets I admire, which I'm at least grateful for, if also careful of taking too seriously. With both kinds, though, avoiding them would mean losing access to what makes them fascinating.

In practical terms, when revising, I find it's sometimes necessary (and better for the poem in the long run) to disrupt a pattern or strategy which is clearly someone else's by substituting something unexpected or intentionally wrong. But too much of that can turn into a superstition, too.

I am very interested in found language, and I do make use of it (a little in what I sent; more so in other poems) though it's often hidden, misquoted, slowed down, chopped in half, or faked. I don't know if any of that annuls its found-ness, or what it might mean in terms of resisting unwanted intrusions. "Typical Wish" is about sixty percent found or post-found material. It's something I'm more and more interested in.

On the "why write" question, I'll pass, mostly. My reasons are like anyone's.

Sake

In order to be found —
or *recognized* —

one must repeat
a passage at some length.

*

"Why do Princesses
Caroline and Stephanie

always marry
the wrong men?"

*

Repeated passages
are gathered

as if
for their own sakes.

*

A child's cry breaks
into spires
and alcoves;

glass
is stained.

*

From here on
it's *all* metaphor

(self
as repertoire)

*

Music extends "at once"

how far?

The Subject

It's as if we've just been turned human
in order to learn
that the beetle we've caught
and are now devouring
is our elder brother
and that we
are a young prince.

*

I was just going to click
on "Phoebe is changed
into a mermaid
tomorrow!" when suddenly
it all changed
into the image
of a Citizen watch.

*

If each moment is in love
with its image
in the mirror of
adjacent moments

(as if matter stuttered),

then, of course, we're restless!

"What is a surface?"
we ask,

trying to change the subject.

Worth While

A rod: a list,

a mop-top palm
cut-out
against sunset,

chocolate
pastries in the shape
of pyramids,

an elderly, bent figure
beneath a feathered Stetson.

*

Terri fears
she may be risking her job
as an afterlife consultant.

Melinda is comforted by Jed
when she twists her ankle trying
to evade an angry ghost.

Unanswered questions
change things
between Booth and Bone.

*

A string of raindrops
dangling
from an iron bar reveals
opportunities for
clarity.

At the breakfast table,
Mary's dead parents
become impatient
when she counts the wad

of small denomination bills
they presented her with
on her birthday.

SABRINA ORAH MARK | CLAUDIA RANKINE

The Dumb Show

Because the gods believe they ought, like buried
corsets, to make the best of a bad bargain, they have
begun to show their flesh a little;

their black hair expanding into heaven knows
what . . . the muddy scratch of stick figures in the
dark, the ones who have begun to delicately call
themselves Madeleine rub their sleepy eye from
behind that blue monocle, and the others with a
futurist thirst for tin, crimson curtain lowering on
the last act, I assure you: there was no beginning,

as in: *before he even made his entrance . . .* The
whole place was in an uproar. And after? And before?
I went back behind the curtain and returned in a
woman's blouse, battle-weary . . . The men above me
were shouting. The women above me were shouting.
The electric lights went out as arranged. I felt on the
ground for the black wig, though it was not clear
whose was whose. I caressed the bone-hard surface
of a stranger's chest until he pulled me to his lap and
brought my fingers to his mouth.

The Song

The milk is mildly foxed. The sky, too, is mildly foxed. And it is wonderful to see the dexterity with which the dark beak hangs on, although it too, is mildly foxed. As are the woods. As is the fox. We are all mildly foxed. Even Mama. Even Mama is mildly foxed.

When Mama fell in love with the ornithologist she began to sneak from the house at night and return with her pockets full of water lettuce, feathers, bits of nest. She began to save electricity. She began to like certain people. The ornithologist, according to the papers, spoke in a mischievous language and had a beard. The ornithologist, according to Mama, knew exactly how he made her feel. "Like a mildly foxed apricot!" she would say, swinging me around by the hips. She would hold me up to the light. She would kiss me on the neck. She would put me down. Over and over again. For hours. It is true that jealousy is what brought me to spy on Mama that night. I too wanted to feel like a mildly foxed apricot. I too wanted to like certain people. It was February. I wore a blouse with large red pockets. Although Mama had already lost me as a mother, what happened is still difficult to say. I saw Mama. I saw the ornithologist. I followed them to the green balcony where he cut for her a loaf of bread with a large pair of scissors. I could hear through his mischievous language. He had a plan. To get rid of the birds, he said. All the mildly foxed birds. He called it *end low song*. He sang it softly.

In the Origami Fields

where I fold and unfold my left arm into November, my hair
      into my sister,
where the black-gloved woman plays my heart like a crumpled
      violin,
where I stand creased and lusting for paper, where I have no
      more dead lovers
than you, where beautiful girls are always asked for directions,
where I keep myself real, flirting with the ventriloquists,
where my father holds me like a paper doll, where doors can be
      torn down
swiftly, where neither one of us is a miracle,

I understand only this:

It is lonely in a place that can burn so fast.

SOM: As I prepared for our conversation, I dug out my List of Things to Do: #1 bewilder, #2 harvest, #3 oil, rouge, and curtsy. I like, as you know, secret and impossible worlds. I like a good-soiled spectacle. I like a gleeful disturbance. One of the most important things you taught me was how to autopsy the impossible, and revive its organs into instruments that can confront what we call "the real live world." It was about slowing down, wasn't it? It was about watching the image as closely as possible. You taught me how to make rules for my wonderlands. If the father's feet are birds, for example, then these feet must squawk through the entire poem and for a reason. You taught me the difference between necessity and groundlessness. If the father with birds for feet ends up in the kitchen cooking soup for his children, the soup should be stirred ever so slightly with a winged gravity. His children should have traces of feathers between their toes. I suppose this is another way of saying that the bewildering things we make happen to our creatures should move them as deeply as they hold them in place. You taught me that.

CR: Or you knew that a poem was like the unconscious; it needed a body in which to create its depths. I saw that you knew that. In the first days when the poems broke and shattered porcelain dolls, you brooded in and over your lines with such finesse I knew to be in awe.

SOM: I like that word, "brood," and how it crosshatches the mind and the body. It is a reminder that thinking creates. And it is a creation produced out of a sort of moody incubation. This crosshatch reminds me of Aimé Césaire's caution you use as an epigraph in your most recent book, *Don't Let Me Be Lonely*. You know how it goes, it goes like this: "And most of all beware, even in thought, of assuming the sterile attitude of the spectator, for life is not a spectacle, a sea of grief is not a proscenium, a man who wails is not a dancing bear." I remember when you first showed me *Don't Let Me Be Lonely* in its early stages you said you were working on creating a timeless, placeless voice that could receive news through a kind of stripped sensory apparatus. And I remember when I first read pieces of the book I felt like I was fumbling through someone's secret belongings whose belongings belonged to the everywhere/nowhere of a news broadcast. I thought of Walter Benjamin's flâneur who walks through the streets of Paris and slowly materializes through his seeing. And we talked about how what once were our streets are now our televisions.

CR: This reminds me of an image I saw of three hundred televisions washed up onshore of a beach in Tokyo. They fell from a ship in a storm — media saturated.

SOM: Ah! Three hundred dead televisions! As if they were lost explorers . . . What is so unsettling and so brilliant about your newest work is that it resurrects the poet as a witness through a wildly different kind of scrutiny than what we normally associate with the poet's eye. I imagine the voice of *Lonely* walking around on that shore, turning on those televisions, and hearing what only a shipwrecked television could tell us of our news. You make the poet say it as it is, and this is very strange, and very daring. You throw the whole nature of the poet-as-witness up in the air for a closer look. And while the poet is up in the air, I'd like to return to Césaire's wailing man who is not a dancing bear. I wonder what you think about this bear. Is a man who wails *never* a dancing bear? Is transformation a kind of exploitation? A blindness? I'm thinking of Breton's *Nadja* where photographs, like those in *Don't Let Me Be Lonely*, are fastened to the text — but the photograph of a woman's glove proves Nadja's existence no more than it turns her existence suspect. And then there's W. G. Sebald's *Austerlitz*. He uses images too, but to remind us how evidence refuses to remember us. In Sebald, we are always being led to an invisible reference. To the one thing we cannot see. He begins with an image of the nocturama — a captivity made out of artificial dusk. And isn't this captivity made out of artificial dusk no different than the television set that you use to interrupt *Lonely*? I guess my question is whether or not it's ever possible, as poets, to *only* see the wailing man. I like to think of my poetry as responsible. But as consumed as I am with history, I'm a bad historian. I would always rather see the dancing bear.

CR: We should all see your dancing bears. They are constructed from history in such a way that they dance as if the earth just finished burning. In *The Babies,* I feel as if innocence and levity are free to be because everything has already been destroyed. In your work, the terror is not the threat but the memory. It frightens me a little. The work suggests that human desire and need are the only things that cannot be extinguished. It suggests a raw physicality, a new beginning in the origami garden, A and Evie running around giggling. Or is it snickering?

SOM: I think it's a little of both. And speaking of A and E running around in that garden like that, I wonder what you think about privacy. I've lined the titles of your books up and inserted a few words to make a sentence: "(Even though) *Nothing in Nature is Private* (enough to) *Plot The End of the Alphabet — Don't Let Me Be Lonely.*" Forgive me if it's startling to see them holding hands like this, but I've been thinking about the poetics your titles make in succession. "Privacy" means to be free from the state of disturbance. It means to belong to a singular. On one hand, it is a setting that won't leak a plot that ends at confession. But on the other hand, it is the confession. We all, according to the textbooks, have "a right to privacy." We have the right to a hush. "It is true," writes Lucie Brock-Broido in *The Master Letters*, "that each self keeps a secret self which cannot speak when spoken to." When I think of privacy I think of silence. And when I think of silence I think of how often silence is not silent enough to make a story out of all the things we cannot hear, or bear to hear. It's like that riddle I first heard in Roberto Benigni's *Life is Beautiful*: "If you say my name . . . I'm not there anymore. Who am I?" "Silence."

CR: When I think of privacy I think of space: a form of letting alone. Our bodies, without mouths, without words, talk and talk and talk to the world. And we are so "already" that even if we could not speak everyone already has lived this and this and this for us. If they want to they can see us clearly; so privacy is not about the other. It is architecture. It is a moment of rest in the self, beyond language, that allows you to see how close you are to the others, another. Silence as perception maybe is a road I could take.

SOM: I love that idea of privacy as an architecture. Or a box you can rest inside. Over the years I studied with you, I became obsessed with not only how to write standing at the end of an alphabet, but how to create in that place at the end something other than dissolution. Something other than loneliness. The oxymoronic nature of the prose poem helps. I love that box. Charles Simic calls the prose poem "the result of two contradictory impulses, prose and poetry, and therefore cannot exist, but it does." It's a funny little form, and I believe it holds me firmly enough in two places at once so that I can attempt to make things that cannot exist until they do. The prose poem, I suppose, is my déjà vu. I always have the feeling I've been here (in that box) before. It is my unsettled settlement.

I think you know this already, but the idea behind *The Babies* came from Freud's *non vixit* (or *non vivit*) dreams where Freud tries to *explain* to his deceased friend (in a dream) that the reason his friend cannot understand him is because his friend is dead. The babies off-sprung an entourage of those sorts of nonbeing, characters that become. I used them to plot company for silence. And now I'm thinking again of Césaire asking us to "beware, even in thought, of assuming the sterile attitude of the spectator, for life is not a spectacle." And I wonder about this caution. What do you imagine is the scene that keeps us from participating? When you think of a nonbeing, what do you think of? And I wonder about the last exquisite and chilling lines of *Don't Let Me Be Lonely* (accompanied by a photograph of a billboard in the middle of a grassy field that reads "HERE"): "In order for something to be handed over a hand must extend and a hand must receive. We must both be here in this world in this life in this place indicating the presence of." I wonder, in the grasp of those hands and in the light of Césaire's caution, what you imagine *beside* the spectacle. I'm very much a materialist. I'm all object. I see a spoon, or a horse, or a bucket and I dissect them until they make a seeing out of what goes among them unseen. But I believe your poetics keep much closer to Césaire's caution. If life is not what we see then where do you locate presence? Is it in the reaching hand? Where is privacy? Does it only exist once it is disturbed?

CR: You do like objects. One of the gifts of *The Babies* is that its prose poems hold objects that your reader can vicariously hold too. Even your people with their bones sticking to things are like objects. They are literally grounded. I am always trying to get rid of objects. I must think they are in my way, blocking my ability to see. I think it is because I feel I am searching for something, some connection to peace or community maybe. One day I will find I am the one in my way. But to return to Césaire, I am cautioned by his words. I sometimes must remind myself that I am implicated in the moments that distress me. There is a line in your poem "Amen": "I did not fear them until I wanted to be afraid." It's connected to the Césaire because you are both asking and recognizing that one has to take responsibility for the self. The moment of perception will position the self alongside the other in both good and bad ways.

SOM: Or maybe one day you will find out that it's you who left those objects there. It's like the photograph by John Lucas on the cover of *The End of the Alphabet*. The letters are like shells washed up on a beach. Exhausted and empty. Like those dead-television-explorers, they are there because something else has been worn away. Sometimes I wonder if all we'll ever understand about language dwells in a set of children's alphabet blocks. When you make a word out of those blocks it is such an impermanent architecture. The words are always waiting to be formed, torn down, and made again. Like a Tower of Babel, blocks are used to assemble a word or a name; "Let us make us a name," goes Genesis, "lest we be scattered abroad upon the face of the whole earth." Of course, we learn in that story that this desire to make one name gives us the "punishment" of metaphor. It reminds us of the impossibility of ever calling anything again by its (only) name. Language, as I understand it, is always occupied by strangeness and exile. Its illumination is also a glare. I like that word, "block." What we create (or make out of blocks) always blocks. Maybe we should start calling the icy refreshment we drink after we make a word, or a sentence, or a poem, a blockade. Down, down it goes . . .

To restore, or to return something to its former condition, means that something else has been misplaced. Is a poem a restoration? And if it is a restoration then what was there before it was written? I am reminded of that chilling example of the uncanny in the beginning of Nabokov's *Speak, Memory*. He is looking at home movies taken before the viewer's birth: "He saw a world that was practically unchanged — the same house, the same people — and then realized that he did not exist there at all and that nobody mourned his absence. He caught a glimpse of his mother waving from an upstairs window, and that unfamiliar gesture disturbed him, as if it were some mysterious farewell. But what particularly frightened him was the sight of a brand-new baby carriage standing there on the porch, with the smug, encroaching air of a coffin; even that was empty, as if, in the reverse course of events, his very bones had disintegrated." I love how the goodbye or hello of the mother's wave turns the carriage into a coffin. The Jewish Messianic idea of creation relies on that same kind of paradoxical topography the carriage/coffin sets up: the Kabbalists understood that there were these "vessels" or garbs that once held a divine light that the creator had to exile himself out of in order to effect creation. I am currently buried under the Kabbalistic concept called *Tsim Tsum* (or that creation cannot happen without the creator's departure from the creator's creation). It calls the poetics of responsibility back home for a closer look, does it not? At the end (or more accurately, at the beginning) the vessels can't hold the light, burst, and light is scattered everywhere. We then spend the rest of our lives gathering up the shards that claim at their center decay and transience, ruin and repair. Lucas's photograph reminds me of those shards.

CR: The poetics of *Tsim Tsum*, now I see — I didn't realize that the way you work, taking the reader to the end or beginning of time, had a name. It is interesting to see how the subject of your work also describes your sense of your own process. I wonder if that holds true for most writers? I am thinking about how Duncan's poems tend to unfold toward illumination and then be lost in that glare you mention. You know, as I am reading the Nabokov quote, I am thinking about Celan. This might be why I have such a hard time arriving at the dancing bear. It is difficult for me not to see the spectrum, not to be absorbed by the darkest bits, not to be caught by the shrapnel. This is not such a good thing—"oh Lana Turner we love you get up."

SOM: I think the reason I cannot properly heed Césaire's caution is because, for me, the dancing bear is the one who leaves the tufts of fur I must follow to get to the wailing man. Without distraction I cannot see what I am being distracted from. Distraction (in my head) organically comes first. It's as if the cymbals I imagine between the bear's paws make the sounds that prepare me for the wailing. And what is that bear wearing, I begin to wonder? Why is he dressed in men's clothing? What has become of the man? Maybe the bear and the man are of the same presence. I do believe that nothing can really be revealed unless it first was hidden and a little forgotten. I am realizing, as I say this, how positively mournful this sounds. Maybe this comes from my yeshiva background. When I was a girl I remember learning that in Genesis the first words spoken are "Let there be light." And there is light, and as soon as God makes this command it is God who divides *between* the light and *between* the darkness, so that the original words mark an illumination that depends on a division that depends also on darkness. It is so absolutely chilling because God's first words make a line that cuts him in two. It is the original act of metaphor. And this, I believe, is why your *Plot* speaks to me with such depth. In *Plot*, utterance births a hide that is the skin of the body that keeps the body hidden. It is like that moment in *Plot* where "a black log of soaked bark like floating fur" is not a log, but a woman. Could that woman have been there had it not been for the log?

CR: The short answer to this is yes. If Virginia Woolf had not drowned herself in the River Ouse, the kids who found her body would not have confused it for a log . . . a log to sit on during their picnic. You see, the body is there already again and again. And sometimes the body is so there you don't give a damn what the bear is wearing, if you get my drift. I think in your work the history of the Holocaust stands behind every turn in the collection. There are over five million bodies, exterminated bodies, in conversation with *The Babies* for me. It's hard not to see those bodies, that dust, as the trail of breadcrumbs to future genocide. Charles Bernstein has this poem that I love, it's called "In Particular." Every time I hear it I feel as if the world is being populated in its particulars, or not populated but recognized. It is the most generous and hopeful thing I have read in a long time. Existence and being, being, the space the body takes is privileged and privileged and privileged again and again. I want to be the kind of person who can write that kind of poem. Césaire was that, I think; that is why I listen to him.

Here is a question for you. Is the poem a performative space or a place of experience? If a place of experience, what should be experienced? What is it that you want awakened in me?

SOM: I do not imagine the poem as one or the other. It is, at its most successful, a third state. The poem should feel as far-fetched as if the call is coming from inside the house. The trail of breadcrumbs you speak of is actually (for me) about return and hope. What makes this trail terrifying, perhaps, is that it's a vertical trail, not a horizontal one. The box, or the prose poem, facilitates this movement. Because all the words are trapped inside the exterior borders of a box, all movement turns marsupial. Any exit strategy is plotted through the interior. I do this because I believe containment surfaces the visionary. The figures, among the crumbs, pace the chamber into a repetition that makes a transformation. This is not a poetics of annihilation, but a reminder (in the words of Paul Celan) that we must "pass through [our] own answerlessness" and emerge "enriched by all this," "stricken and seeking."

The third state is also about reconciliation. It is about things that have nothing to do with one another belonging to each other. Maybe more than anything that is what I want to wake up to. The Israeli novelist Amos Oz speaks of this third state as a place where dissonance becomes harmonious, where for example you are offered *either* herring or marmalade. And you decide you will have a little of both. The herring and the marmalade taste so strange together, but now (in the mouth) they suddenly belong to each other. Perhaps the breadcrumbs complete the meal. I don't know. I'll ask the bear.

from *Don't Let Me Be Lonely*

Or Paul Celan said that the poem was no different from a handshake. *I cannot see any basic difference between a handshake and a poem* — is how Rosmarie Waldrop translated his German. The handshake is our decided ritual of both asserting (I am here) and handing over (here) a self to another. Hence the poem is that — Here. I am here. This conflation of the solidity of presence with the offering of this same presence perhaps has everything to do with being alive.

from *Don't Let Me Be Lonely*

Or one meaning of here is "In this world, in this life, on earth. In this place or position, indicating the presence of," or in other words, I am here. It also means to hand something to somebody — Here you are. Here, he said to her. Here both recognizes and demands recognition. I see you, or here, he said to her. In order for something to be handed over a hand must extend and a hand must receive. We must both be here in this world in this life in this place indicating the presence of.

from *Plot*

of course. of course.

Here is a log . . . a black log of soaked bark like floating fur.

"What kind of log is that?"

"No log . . . a woman."

"A woman's body? Oh, right."

This in an instant . . . less than a minute . . . and yet, now, something
out there, out of sight, rapaciously frowning at life. We can't
shake the natural course of things. It's our own problem — the
damming in the human condition. We are, after all, well aware.

CHRISTIAN HAWKEY | TOMAŽ ŠALAMUN

Fräulein, can you

        sometimes, when I can't sleep, I drag my sleeping bag
into the meadow's precise center
& crawl inside, head first. Fräulein, there is the stars'
ceaseless drilling. I close my eyes. Somewhere below me
a star-nosed mole cuts its webbed hand
on a shard of glass. I close my ears
& over my body the current of a young doe
eddies, ripples across the field, a low-lying midnight fog
swirling after her, falling back, suspended. I know you are close.
The scar across my cheek burns. I think of reentering
        your atmosphere,
        your long, burning hair

Don't move. The slightest motion

        & this landscape, erased by floodlights

There is a Queen inside

                she cannot speak — with a yellow sponge I wet her lips
but only slightly, I am terrified
of her voice, of her enormous, rolling body
& the groans that move through it as if through rooms — when someone
    knocks
I simulate her voice *gravity is a dwarf factory, how light a caterpillar steps*
by her soft, trembling stomach I know she is laughing
& withdraw, closing door after door after door
until I can barely hear her, rain
outside an open window, a cigarette quietly glowing, *I am an arctic flower*
my Queen I can barely hear you, I am standing on my toes
                at eye level
                an electrical socket

Two faces,

                one above the other

Unhoused casements

        snap of tongues on a teeth-ridge, alveolus of the. Or,
out of boredom searching my face in the mirror I found a vein,
and searching the vein I found a scar, smooth as slate,
and searching the scar I found a name, an old name — there were serifs —
the name of a city I'd forgotten, which I whispered,
I don't know why, I was alone,
and the Whispered City unfolded a map of streets I once traveled
        wet cobblestones, *contradas*,
        a horse led through the doors of a chapel

To the pleasure of hundreds

        a sacred, steaming manure

CH: Tomaž, I thought I'd start by asking about your own influences: What writers were important to you as a young poet? And how did you first come to the practice of writing and reading poems?

TŠ: Christian, to answer this question I have to go way back. I grew up sheltered in a happy family as the firstborn among four. We lived in a small town Koper-Capodistria, then Zone B, run by the Yugoslav army, next to Zone A, Trieste-Trst, run by the American army. My mother was from Trieste, and being Slovenian, her family had to escape to Yugoslavia from Fascism in the '20s. She taught me piano two years before a musical school in town opened, which gave me the advantage of being the local "Wunderkind pianist." Music and art in general was something that filled me with awe and immense respect; I was precocious and was given very special treatment from my professors. At 12, when my father prohibited me from twice-daily training in our rowing club, I protested with a very dramatic gesture. I never again touched the piano. I suppressed everything "artistic" — despised it, especially poetry. Until I was 22, I only sailed, was a boy scout, or played basketball. I was impressed only by Rimbaud, since we had a very good French teacher, and by Oton Župančič, a Slovenian poet influenced by Whitman.

As a student I found myself studying history, art history and architecture in Ljubljana, had some "Lectura Dantis" in Perugia, altogether an overambitious plan (I had to enroll in two different universities at the same time) and I flunked a history exam. Since I always had only the highest grades, this was a complete debacle. I was existentially crushed and lost. In that moment, it was in 1963, the great Slovenian poet Dane Zajc visited our seminar and gave a tremendously charismatic reading. Also, my then-best friend Braco Rotar, now a famous semiologist, started to write poetry, and in my eyes changed from a civic person to a half-god. These two influences triggered a day of trance: my first five poems came in half an hour, and felt like stones falling from the sky. All my childhood memories, awe, and feelings of "greatness" came back. I jumped from Dane Zajc's shoulders. The next influence was Eliot, translated for the first time into Slovenian (there are two million Slovenians), then Pound, Ginsberg, and Blake, which I read in Croatian translations, and Khlebnikov, who I read in Serbian translations, and W. C. Williams and Stevens, in Italian translations. I was also under the spell of French poets: Nerval, Lautréamont, Cendrars, and Michaux.

In 1970, I was invited to New York to participate in the Information Show (MOMA) as a conceptual artist, a member of the OHO group. My English was still almost nonexistent. When Kynaston McShine, the curator (who gave me Kenneth Koch's book), proposed an interview with the editor of *Art News*, I said, out of fear, "I don't want to talk to journalists."

In 1972 I was a guest of the International Writing Program at Iowa. Anselm Hollo introduced me to Olson, Creeley, Basil Bunting and Ed Dorn; a student at Iowa, and a friend and poet I admired the most among students, Bob Perelman, introduced me to O'Hara, Zukovsky, and Coolidge (we visited him in California). But the most magic and definite influence for me (I still very vividly remember and feel the process: rapid melting) came from a book I discovered by chance, *Three Poems* by John Ashbery. To my amazement, I discovered that he was the editor of *Art News*, "the journalist" I had not been interested in talking to. At the end of my stay, I drove coast to coast, was accepted at Yaddo, and on the way back to Slovenia called up Ashbery who invited me to lunch. Immensely generous, he was obsessed by Raymond Roussel, and I became grafted to him as well. Luckily, I already had four published books before I came to America; otherwise I would have been swept away by your strong culture. These were definitely high points in my life and with this energy I was able to survive the politically horrible '70s in a small Slovenia. I felt blessed.

What about you? How would you answer the same question?

In (loving) haste (to borrow a phrase from Ashbery), Tomaž

CH: Dear Tomaž, Graft. Like that word. Immediately I looked it up: "1a: to cause (a scion) to unite with a stock; also: to unite (plants or scion and stock) to form a graft. b: to propagate a plant by grafting. 2a: to attach (a chemical unit) to a main molecular chain. 3: to implant (living tissue) surgically." Webster offers amusing illustrations of grafting techniques: a cleft graft, a splice graft, a whip, a saddle, a cambium. I'll scan it for you.

The word derives from the Greek *graphein*, which means "to write" or "carve." I feel like my grafting technique is somewhere between a whip and a cleft — a weft. And it's not authors that are grafted with or onto other authors, but poems. They graft themselves. Use authors to rewrite themselves. Languages sometimes feel like a self-propagating, palimpsest-like code that uses writers — moves between writers — to stay alive, to hand itself down between pages, the covers of books, lips. I've been reading a book called *The Botany of Desire* which argues that plants, in order to maintain genetic diversity and ensure their survival, use humans — a Dutch tulip dons a bright red hat, which makes someone come along, pluck it, and carry its seeds to Brazil — as much as we use them. Burroughs's idea of language as a virus from outer space is uninteresting to me, but I am drawn to what such figures of speech imply: that language is smarter than we are, that it operates beyond a rational, structuralist system, that it is, if approached the right way (receptively) what programmers call a "self-exciting" code.

When I read, I read as openly — and as widely — as possible. Never understood the various theories of influence, or friends who would refuse to read someone out of fear of being influenced. I have no anxiety! For me, the only way to learn is to open up, fall heels over head in love with a given author, surrender, surrender with intent, with attention, with focus. Keats's letter about the poet as chameleon comes to mind. When he described the feeling, upon walking into a room, of losing himself into every person in the room, he was also describing a way of reading. Poets I have become lost in? Stevens, Dickinson, Hart Crane, Bishop, Hölderlin, Vallejo (above all), Mandelstam, Trakl, Lautréamont, Nijinsky, his diaries. I am also intrigued by how each of these authors led me to other authors, but not in any linear sense: Ashbery led me to Hölderlin and Bishop, Bishop led me to Herbert, Hölderlin led me to Celan, Celan led me to Mandelstam, Mandelstam to Dante. Tunnels leading to other tunnels. At some point, a labyrinth. One that loops forward and back, turns in on itself, sets out again. Everyone gets lost in their own way. This is why I distrust stable, neat packagings of poetic "traditions." More interested in an endless, unfolding curiosity. Benjamin, in this regard, is a hero: there's a perceptible tenderness to his sentences, his prose style, his critical intelligence. He treats thoughts as if they were tactile bodies, as if he's writing while blindfolded, touching his way through an argument, ideas as dimensional objects, and then, finally — this is his genius — he touches the blindfold to remind himself of what he's seeing. But occasionally I land on a poet who leads me into oblivion, a dead end, a style so terminal I simply sit down and rest and rest my head against them — Stein, Vallejo, Dickinson, you.

I've been reading your book *Blackboards* this week and came across this line: "History shapes itself into little spheres, it / forms like a new mutant animal species." And then another poem, from *Feast*, begins with the line "By the way of all spheres" and ends with the lines "Along this window, in this window / there are innumerable other civilizations, / innumerable other cosmological systems. / Thus suffering does not matter, / layers do." "Spherical" comes close, for me, to describing your compositional style — or maybe a column of rings, stacked up, with no center. Mutation. Accumulation. You seem to be open to everything or refuse to privilege one thing over another, one experience over another, internal (memory, abstraction) over external experience (memory, abstraction). Why is this important to you? Is this important to you?

TŠ: Dear Christian, Please try to forgive my long silence. I was reading in London. I devoted myself to my son, David, in Berlin, who received a kidney transplant. And I was, for the first time in my life, in Tokyo. But the main fear for me in our conversation is that my English is so rudimentary that I cannot express anything of interest, although your poetry deeply moves me. Our poetic bodies are built and made with some similar food we've eaten on our way. I'm transported to a place where I breathe deeper, I'm blessed, and I start to scribble. Not at my physical home with Metka in Ljubljana, not when I am with my son in Berlin (too much poetry is so dangerous, it can empty out life into powder), but immediately when I move, when I travel. For example: sitting in the Tate Modern, staring at Rousseau's painting, having the Priority Mail envelope with your manuscript on my lap. I feel like a cannibal, happily devouring the space around me with my admiration for the energy in your language.

In Tokyo, two weeks later, in a small hotel in front of the Imperial Palace Garden, pushing everything aside, remembering how golden leaves fell on my head in Meiji Jingu Park in the afternoon, scribbling.

When you quote my lines, "Thus suffering does not matter, / layers do" I shiver. There's a strange, painful transgression here that I'm suspicious of, afraid of. Why this tendency toward apophatic inquiry? Perhaps it's an effort to understand time, or an urge to reverse time in order to forget and be free? And when you quote those lines from *Blackboards* and ask me about a "spherical" composition style I also don't know. Still, whenever I touch Giordano Bruno (*l'universo e tutto centro*) I explode, immediately immersed in his violent, loud, lucid rambling. It's as if I'm thirteen: "You won't ever achieve anything, everybody can impress you, you're not critical enough" (my mother, who always had great ambitions for all of her children, said this over and over to me).

And many of the writers you mention as influences were also important to me. Nijinsky's diaries were a direct influence on me in Mexico. Hölderlin less so. I was too full of Heidegger, and Trakl was stronger. Strangely I really started to appreciate Herbert late in my life (I used to think of him as one of those poets my parents liked). If I'm one of those you mention as having a terminal style, this might explain my fierce longing for young Americans, young Slovenians, young Brazilians, as my way to salvation. One of my most dangerous vanity blows came with the news that fifteen young Brazilian poets (feeling neglected, poor guys, writing in the B language, "everybody reading Spanish and not enough Portuguese") included me in their anthology as the only non-Brazilian. "Don't you see I'm being ironic, but I have to tell this to somebody," I say to my wife Metka. "No, you're deadly serious, you're only thinking you're ironic; you're a tsunami, and it gets worse and worse," Metka responds, only half playfully.

What's important to me? To be alive. To be friends with people and the world as much as I can.

Christian, how do you sustain flying within the lines? Do you cut out all weaker sentences or words which usually explain or provide easy explanatory links? I try to cut everything that a philosopher could inhabit by his reasoning, everything which is not *Dichtung*. Abrazos, Tomaž

CH: Tomaž, I'm writing from Seattle, where my family is gathered for Christmas. My brother has a house outside of the city: a small square mushroom growing at the base of enormous trees. Out the window: two horses in a fenced-in pasture, a pasture that is mostly dirt, since they have eaten every possible blade of green. I was just watching one horse put his head between the slats of the fence and lean out — the whole fence creaking under his weight — in order to reach a few forbidden tufts. His horse-lips, at the very moment he seemed unable to reach the grass blades, actually *unfurled* to give him an extra two inches of reach. Got it. Earlier, when I woke and looked out the back window, a deer was standing in the trees, amidst the ferns, motionless, save for its fluted ears. Swivel and flick. Swivel and flick. Wish we could move our ears in different directions. I actually whispered "good morning" behind the glass and watched one ear rotate toward me. Then my nephew walked in and shot me in the cheek with a rubber arrow.

How does one sustain flying? I don't. For me it's more of a kind of reverse flying, or a willingness to give perception over to — surrender to — flightlessness. Spicer said that poets think that they are pitchers, when in fact they are really catchers. Crouch down. See what comes in, sliding, curving. One is exposed, open, trying to sustain a state of receptivity and therefore follow the poem as it unfolds, or folds you deeper into its folds, line by word, word by line. Everything depends on sustained self-forgetfulness. Often it feels dangerous, because, unlike a catcher, the poet does not wear a face mask. Once I have a draft I do excise that which interrupts the sublanguage coherence of the poem, or gets in the way of what Mandelstam called "the performing understanding," which is another way of saying that I edit my self out of the poem as much as possible.

Tomaž, I want to ask you more about your process. I'm fascinated by the fact that you write best when you travel, when you are on the move — in hotels, airplanes, cars, London, Tokyo, amidst foreign languages. This seems unusual; most writers are obsessive about having a stationary writing space. You, on the other hand, seem most creative when you are in motion — a global Frank O'Hara. What is it about traveling that is important to your writing, your process?

TŠ: Christian, Exactly! "A kind of reverse flying, or a willingness to give perception over to — surrender to — flightlessness." I remember, in 1979, on my third day at Yaddo, in the West House, I was "pregnant" but still only alert, waiting in expectation, mute, when a door slammed. David del Tredici left. Just this sound, the door slamming, transposed me (dipped me) in a kind of trance — a rarefied, concentrated light, the senses melting and mobilized, vivid happiness and pain. It was just as if a small brook started to flow from my fingers. The whole *Ballad for Metka Krašovec* was written in four weeks. The start of writing is somehow linked with the crucial moments in one's life. One, in my life, which I can't grasp or understand, is also linked with a deer. I was thirteen. As a kind of socialist boy scout (*tabornik*) I was waiting for the bus that was supposed to bring us milk at five in the morning. I was early and still had time. I went up into the woods. A deer stood in front of me. The nearness, the silence, the immobility, the grace in his eyes pierced me. It seemed to really happen, but it probably didn't, it probably happened only in my mind. At the time I thought it really happened. It was as if my brains and my eyes became one organ — sugar, not yet melted and traveling down my sore throat. Total bliss. I couldn't stand that gaze for more than a split second. I started to pick berries, and went slowly down to wait for a bus.

Yes, everything depends on sustained forgetfulness. For me, this sometimes forms itself into red bricks, and they come by themselves, wherever I am, even in the plane, usually when I am *dépaysé*, and offer themselves as the ground on which I can stand, happily, scribbling. The problem now is the easiness with which it comes, the joy with which I help my brain to evaporate, the madness. All my life I longed for this: to train and develop the muscles to be able to go to the utmost border. Nerval. Hölderlin. Jim Tate. Especially Tate (I also adored his picture). In the late seventies and the eighties I had to stop reading him. He was more daring than me, and if I tried to follow him, America would crush and explode the little Slovenian. I would really go crazy. I could only start to read him again when I met him in person for the first time in the late eighties.

I have experienced the best of America: its generosity, its economy ("the success of your friend is your success"), and the matter-of-factness (the texts are to be judged, not VIP lines). Raised as a Francophile, I was full of prejudices. But only America was vital and interesting enough to broaden my sense of home. I'm now saddened and scared of Bush's America.

It snows incredibly, half meter by now. I'm leaving on the 2nd, and hope my plane will be able to take off. I will think of you on the New Year, and will send you my Pittsburgh e-mail the moment I get it, hopefully very soon. On Wednesday, salute the marvelous Seattle clouds, the most dramatic clouds in the world, and all your dear ones. My question: do you think that the best lines from the best poets written now are the food for our survival? Sometimes I feel, even if we will have to leave the earth and settle in the universe, the best lines will be totally important, even as a manual or survival kit — sleeping bags, tents. At the moment we don't know yet how to use them, but when the time comes, we will. My warmest regards, Tomaž

CH: Tomaž, I'm back in Brooklyn. Christmas in Seattle was so relaxing I feel exhausted. Your last note raised numerous ideas, questions, thought-memories, vectors, coordinates — I had to take out a notebook and list them, one by one, as I read, afraid that I would forget something by the time I'd finished reading.

1. Hard to imagine you as a boy scout, let alone a socialist boy scout.
2. "The grace in his eyes pierced me."
3. Gaze. Grace. Martin Buber on the eyes of animals — a language of grace. Why *grace*? Something about the presentness of the animal gaze, its intactness. Perhaps not gaze but glance: the grace of unselfconscious, one-way sight. *Only humans gaze.*
4. What the milk must have tasted like, when the bus finally arrived.
5. "Crucial moments in one's life." Crucial words.
6. Poems as dissolved organs.
7. Poems as sugared throats.
8. My cat just loped up and definitely gazed at my ham sandwich.
9. The gaze of animals: smell.
10. Joy + Evaporation = Madness. Clare. Hölderlin. Trakl's "gentle madness."
11. Border. Border Xings. Invention of the Intruder. A face entering a

fire's light. A face brave enough to leave it. Readers becoming writers, writers readers.

12. Story of Tate putting on a duck mask and walking up behind Charles Simic in a bank . . .

13. Bush's America. Lines of poetry as survival kits.

Tomaž, these last two points are linked. I've been translating the late poems of Osip Mandelstam, the poems written while he was exiled by Stalin to a labor camp in Voronezh. What is striking about them, aside from their diamond-like compression, is their sustained articulation of joy. This astounds me. Mandelstam was living in horrible conditions, separated from his wife and family, and on the verge of physical collapse, suicidal. One would think that he would write poems raging darkly against Stalin, against a totalitarian state, and yet he sort of does precisely the opposite: he writes poems that celebrate, with unwavering joy, the fact of being alive, of breathing, using language, moving his lips, and his thought — swift, associative, bird-like — mirrors this joy. Maybe the purest form of resistance is to not let anyone or thing or preconceived idea negotiate the terms of your resistance. Mandelstam once said the role of lyric poets is to exchange signals with Mars. Which I take to mean the future, addressing an unknown future, an unknown reader, which is really a more true way of addressing one's self, one's self in outer space, as a future space. This was his survival kit — his gift.

Have a wonderful time in Pittsburgh. I have so many remaining questions, but I will settle with one: you mention that James Tate's poems were/are "too daring." How do you define "daring"? Christian

TŠ: Dear Christian, How do I define daring? I can't. I can only look at my scars which are material and spiritual products — great word — poems and sins, spots on my memory that still have some power to touch me, burn me, to put me in awe, to give me some pleasure. When alive and alert, writing — I cannot really say alive and alert because while writing I feel as if I'm at the edge of an abyss, but the abyss isn't something I'm able to fall into, it's more like a space (fog) (catatonic attack) (and at the same time, a lucid sleepiness) which numbs everything except the path, a path composed of lines, which again is not a path but more like a delta-time where everything can be thrown in my face, all my life, instantly. And in the center of it is the end of a thread, running itself out of the labyrinth, turning me around (I'm the spool of this thread or wool wrapped around nothing). I feel healed by and in the process. I'm breathing. I'm experiencing insane joy. I lose fat. But I also feel like a criminal. At the very beginning of poetry was a stepping out, a falling out, a jump into otherness with no purpose, with no moral reason, with no ethical balance or ground, with no sense, and yes, with all this, the hope of heaven. Maybe the closest analogy to this is when a beloved child throws himself or herself on the ground and screams: If you won't love me even more, I want to die. "Poezija je zato, ker clovek ni bog in to je, kar clovek najteze prenese." I feel like gambling for the highest stakes, for immortality, yes, and of course I don't give a damn for life here or there, if I am or if I'm not, if I was or wasn't. I want to burn myself to the utmost humility. I don't want to read this turning of the spool. Tomaž

19.IX.1982

I opened the fig and in it
squatted an angel bound with his own hair.
Axes threatened his honey,
I tore his eye, though it hurt him.
Out of red forest a deer sprang,
He came close to the angel, close with his snout,
and disappeared. Like a dark papyrus
a mass showed behind the crown
and started to spin.

O the name!
Ireneus, Elephant, Milchin, Wedding Guest, Parnassus,
Geza, Ahmed, Blood, Deer, Tempest
intertwined like roots and grew,
and kept shooting the folding fan of crosses
until they undulated like medusa's whips
in the lazy, agitated sea.

Let's the tree have blue heart.
Let's open the house windows around the blue heart!
Let's lure the sun into the windowpanes!
Let's hear the blue blast in the tooth,
let it resound, hollow inside the water.
The fig: the temple and the tempest,
the power which holds together the crown of Christ.

O climb, climb!
And he tore himself away like a cocoon.
With his palm he clung to my white neck,
because his body flew

much faster than mine.
But mine was larger and heavier, more guided
and it curtained the horizon.
We made a suitcase, from a shawl we made a bundle,
from a bundle a pueblo.

Eyes, a nose, a mouth, caves of ears.
First the city was built, then the man.
At first the city had more flesh than the man.
Give it back to him.
Give it back to him, I tell you.

So that the beak doesn't entangle itself in the moss,
so that the crown doesn't explode because of the horrible
pressure.
Or take the machine and make the nib,
Just as the ice-cream man makes the nib.

And this whish: the arch above the circle is heaven.
The blind window of the world.

(Translated from the Slovenian by Thomas Kane and the author.)

Spring Street

I had a sweet liver. Coasts to the sky.
Honking of the truck on Houston street,
the dark one.

The tribe demolished the layer cake.
The layer cake destroyed the seed.
Salt. Midgets. I bite your white white bridge.

You sleepy, softly turning wheel.
As a winch pulling a boat to earth,
you lift, you wreck my veins.

Let it flow into you, let it flow into you, my sweet juice.
You need me. If not, you wouldn't tear me apart.
You wouldn't move your warm

bread, wrapped in rags.
For you yourself are pinned together, for me you crunch.
The sea of blood is not aware of the heat of your heart.

And cunning. But you don't know how
rich. Carried toward your bite-mark.
Spend. You froth, you froth,

red blood breaks into a waterfall.
O leaf of my tree,
white fire of my grief.

You are seized, my son, you are seized.
You flow away on the path
from which you came.

(Translated from the Slovenian by Joshua Beckman and the author.)

CHRISTINE HUME | ROSMARIE WALDROP

Comprehension Questions

What kind of phantom is the ship?

Where does the girl hide her great distances?

Accordingly, what is the rate to multiply by to find the intense
sensitivity of minor characters?

How do the men abandon ship?

Why do they trouble the forest with their strange butterflies
and huge suns full of complete daylight?

What role does the dog play in developing catastrophe?

If the setting permitted biological time, would red shift through
the captain's mirage?

What dark authority lurks among unpruned spruce?

Whose foreshadowing crawls out and what sets it off?

Do you believe the wave is not a girl in furs?

Is this a comedy or a tragedy of secret motions?

Why should a zephyr so rarely intervene?

Does the stormy girl's beauty suggest something about
the captain?

Why do his arrows ricochet wildly just before the target?

Meanwhile, what does the girl's fear become when she turns around?

Which constellation best fits the story?

Though the captain arrests the ice horse, what fantasy freezes the
     dark around him?

When does it matter? When can you deceive?

Why do the men take the tusk and shank inside?

Does the narrator gain sight by his frustration, humiliation,
     torture, and debt?

Which prophesies help the girl court the ship?

Is anything more grotesque than the face of human ecstasy?

What Became of the Company You've Kept, According to One Who Left

Tourist: re-enacts her 91 days on a raft

Man Stabbed By His Wife: shows up later with deer on a leash

Blurry Swarm of Wind: remains attracted by dark clothing and
plagued by bad dreams

Pregnant Woman: checks the sky on the way back to the truck
and insists on moving the town inland before the sea
ambushes it

Surveyor: grows a tail to help get his body down a mountain
that night

Full Moon: left wandering the fiend fields and laughs her head off

Silence: tinkers with phlogiston inhalants until the town gets
fucked up

Deathcunt: ingests a giant cedar and inspires fear on the aits
among the jilted

Carpenter: after hearing rats, goes ashore with a disreputable
disease

Incipient Doxy: forks her thumb in an industrial accident

King of Infinite Space: makes time stretch out unbearably between
horizon and fire

Stranger-the-first: lousy with hootch, sings an affectionate
Communism song to a widow

Insomniac: suffers her fixed lights and mental horses by planning
        elaborate apologies; keeps warm by becoming a self-
        embarrassing machine

Mother: has a lacework of shallow shifting mists in an abandoned
        town named after her

Mad Captain: horses around to keep the magnet off; spots new
        personifications of god

Mallard Girl: insists it was a mistake

Dead Body: lost

Army Brat: plants large yellow poppies to hide a cliff

Mastodon: grows irresistibly infatuated with large yellow poppies

Replacement Crew: over-jacks the wind-chill then gambles it gone

Suspect-the-second: your touch replaces her with something realistic

Ice Queen: takes the position of postmaster 99783 and holds a
        broken mirror up to your correspondences   changing
        the words,   putting holes and opposition into them
        into the correspondences   that had been kind

CH: Growing up in an occupied zone in postwar Germany must have given you an uncanny sense of English as a force for occupation and incorporation. If language is a field or territory that you've "gap gardened" and explored the amorphous boundaries and ultimate foreignness of, then this occupation is a kind of possession. For you, at the age of ten, the English language really did take over! How do you see this early situation as informing (or not) your own attitude and attunement toward language? How do you think the structure and sound of German has influenced your use of English?

RW: No doubt all that you mention has had an influence, but I can't pin it down. I have the feeling that as a child I was a kind of sponge — just soaking things up without too much sense of what it was all about. Except of course the two radical changes of my world: in 1943 when my hometown was bombed and 1945 when all — well, a lot of — the values changed! But English at that point was simply part of school and what I knew the American soldiers about town spoke. I've always thought that it was the conscious change to English, my coming to the U.S., that not only made me a translator, but gave me a sense of being "between," and a sense of writing as exploring what "happens between." Between words, sentences, people, cultures. But maybe it all started in 1945 when I was ten.

CH: "Between" is everywhere in your work; for instance, from your autobiography:

"This became important for my own method of composition: the tension between clusters (lines or single words) scattered on a page and a temporal sequence."

"To accept the complete sentence (most of the time), but to do my best to subvert it from the inside, by sliding between frames of reference."

"It was a way of getting out of myself. Into what? An interaction, a dialog with language, with a whole net of earlier and concurrent texts. Relation. Between."

"Using Williams's book as a matrix allowed me to work out some of my own ambivalences as an immigrant: a "conqueror" of sorts, and yet irredeemably between cultures."

The way your speaking voice settled between German and English suggests your literary voice stands against absolutes and rigidly coded accents, landing somewhere between seriousness and irreverence, disturbing our settled relation to language.

Yet "between" is such a loaded word in our poetry culture, a word with a double edge: it's as often used to describe the opportunistic, professionalized "on-the-fence" aesthetic and politic as it is to describe an inclusivity. It can signal an inquiry into places that appear uninhabited or empty (like synaptic and linguistic leaps), but it might also imply a lack of allegiances and alliances. How do you distinguish your own sense of between from these possibilities? And as someone "between words, sentences, people, cultures," to what or whom are your most adamant commitments?

RW: I'm glad you see my voice "between seriousness and irreverence." It's maybe the biggest lesson of Dada that we can — and should — be serious and not serious at the same time. Passionately serious, but at the same time able to take some distance on ourselves — and our art/subject/ whatever.

My sense of between is a sense of relation. One of the first poems I wrote in English is called "Between" and places itself in the Atlantic ("not all here / or there"). But the water not only separates, it also connects the continents. Therefore the poem can end with "But when it rains I inherit the land."

I found it very exciting to discover how ubiquitous the image of the electromagnetic field is in the twentieth century. In the field, everything happens between; relation is everything. Whitehead posits the actual world as built up of "occasions" rather than "things" (which he calls "already abstractions from actual occasions"). Kurt Lewin describes mental states as balances of forces and vectors. Fenollosa examined the sentence and concluded: "A true noun, an isolated thing, does not exist in nature. Things are only the terminal points, or rather the meeting points, of actions, cross-sections cut through actions, snapshots. Neither can a pure verb, an abstract motion, be possible in nature. . . . Thing and action cannot be separated." W. C. Williams says, "the poem is a field of action." Pound writes, "the thing that matters in art is a sort of energy, a force transfusing, welding and unifying." And of course Olson: "At root (or stump) what is, is no longer THINGS but what happens BETWEEN things, these are the terms of the reality contemporary to us — and the terms of what we are."

This is perhaps also behind my changing from single word or very short lines to prose poems. Not that the words in a line are any less in relation than in a sentence! Or the charge between them any less crucial! So maybe this is balderdash.

"Adamant commitments"— hm. I don't think you want me to blather about the Big Values like honesty, truthfulness, love! In my work, I am committed to a questioning attitude, precision of language (and thinking, if possible), to poetry as inquiry. But almost anything is subject to being questioned, rethought.

CH: "Between" might, in other hands, be construed as reinforcing an ideology of binaries and dualities. To say you are "between" is to live with a mother on one side and a father on the other, or a father and a holy ghost, or a liberal and a conservative, or a past and a future. "Between" implies a bifurcation of the world into inner/outer, creative/critical, reading/writing, public/private, known/unknown, literal/figurative — all tidy symmetrical fantasies, false divides, that your work actively investigates and complicates.

Do you identify with Blake's notion of "contraries" as a force for "progression," or what you might call movement? Another way I hear your work is as dialectic between vulgar (with its various synonyms — vernacular, public, coarse, rude, barbaric) and refined. Your sense of humor, your use of deadpan register at once parodies and make use of the usual ways of making sense.

"Between" also is very much entrenched in a highly spatial imagination — something you highlight in your own poetics, especially "The Ground Is the Only Figure" and your primary technique, collage ("torn nature"). In such a discursive spatiality there is an affective topography of being excluded (*Lawn of Excluded Middle*), where identity is lost. Yet another way to think of being between is temporally, via rhythm. Rhythm is something you don't address explicitly in your poetics, which rely on spatial metaphors, though obviously you've had a long and fruitful relationship with music.

Dissonance: "Let us feel the magnetic field between the two dimensions, the horizontal push becomes dammed up, the vertical orchestral . . . "

RW: You're right about the binary and how ingrained it is in our thinking. But the really pernicious part of it is that usually one of the pair gets valorized over the other, or even to the exclusion of the other. (Even Derrida, who battles these dichotomies, seems to fall into this trap when he reverses the traditional valuation and privileges writing over speech, difference over identity, sign over thing, etc.) I think of the "between" more in terms of both, and of extending the gray zone between the black/white in the direction of multivalence. "The yes and no in everything."

Of course there's also neither/nor! Where exclusion comes in again. But I don't agree that in the "topography of being excluded . . . identity is lost." I would think it could, on the contrary, lead to a strong identity as other. As you know I think of the law of excluded middle as a "lawn," the empty center as fertile, playground, womb, the "empty" space in a flute, in a violin that gives body to the sound.

And yes, the positive side is that the tension between contraries is, as you say "a force for progression." That tension makes us think harder, makes the poem move, develop.

Tension is also one of the few ways we can talk about rhythm. As long as you write in a regular meter you can talk about rhythm in terms of the tension between the meter and "normal" speech. In free verse, in terms of the tension between line and sentence. But in prose poems? I've recently used periods as rhythmic markers rather than, or in addition to, using them as grammatical markers: "How the words are. Suspended around you." This kind of thing.

I haven't written much about rhythm (or the music of verse) because it is so hard to pin down. The sense of rhythm seems to differ widely from one person to the other. I remember trying to work with Donald Hall at the University of Michigan. He read my lines as if they were prose, very fast. Every time, I had to say, I don't hear it like this: I made the lines short to make them slow. But when I read the lines back to him my way he was not convinced. He was helpful on many other craft aspects, but I realized I could not pay attention to anything he said about rhythm.

The difficulty of talking about rhythm probably has to do with the fact that it is an aspect of time, which is also hard to talk about.

I've just started reading G. J. Whitrow's *The Natural Philosophy of Time*. Whitrow spends a good part of his first section on the scientists and philosophers, from Archimedes to Helmholtz and Poinsot, who, for this very reason, tried to eliminate issues of time and to reduce science to spatial laws like constancy and uniformity. He quotes Einstein: "It is a characteristic of thought in physics . . . that it endeavors in principle to make do with 'space-like' concepts alone, and strives to express with their aid all relations having the form of laws." You noticed the spatial nature of "between."

CH: The day your last e-mail came, I also received a new issue of *Aufgabe* in the mail, the John Cage issue, which includes your response to a lecture Norman O. Brown gave on Cage. It was also the day Barbara Guest died.

These Cagian coincidences and congruencies keep resonating:

I opened Guest's *Forces of Imagination:* "The Infancy of Poetics" says only "The poem begins in silence." An uncanny correspondence with Cage's pantheon of silences. Your "Form and Discontent" places the two side by side: "Barbara Guest: 'The dark identity of the poem.' / John Cage: 'The importance of being perplexed.'" And further down the page, we come back to the topic of rhythm, which reiterates, though in her characteristic "invisible magic," something along the lines of what you were saying via the Donald Hall anecdote: "Guest: 'The poem enters its own rhythmical waters.'" The difficulty of talking about death — like rhythm — probably has to do with the fact that it is an aspect of time, which is also hard to talk about: "Our time not calculable by stopwatch or plucked string."

Guest's poetry too alchemizes time: "On track, the unknown with such sharp clarity."

I want to ask you about Cage, but I'm more immediately moved by Guest's death and have been wondering about your particular response; as a woman who has made her way in the same male-saturated scene, how this death might be different for you than, say, the death of Creeley or Mac Low, who own the same immortal dimensions as Guest.

For all the quotation in Brown's lecture, not one woman makes her way into the conversation. Many women reply to it in the tribute, but to me Brown's unspoken omission marks a certain blindness or tone-deafness.

"Is every tone virgin?"

As someone who never met Guest, I can't imagine her ever dying; I just go back to the work. At the same time, her death seems like a passage (from modernism?) or a call to introspection and abstraction. The way you describe Guest's use of literary allusion, for instance, seems emblematic here — to "poke fun at our expectations," to "jolt logic," "to direct our attention toward and introduce" something surprising (movement). "The poem notes the entrance of greenery, a green vision with a voice," Guest writes in *Imagination* ("The Voice of the Poem").

In the index to your *Dissonance (if you are interested)*, there is a small list of Guest pages, in the first of which (12–22) I could not find a Guest reference. This absence of course made the connections between what you are discussing in pages 12–22 — mysticism, abstraction, "similarity disorder," exploration of the limits of language — and Guest's work all the more potent. Because I kept looking for her where she was apparently not, she was always all the more present, "a turbulent presence." It seems like a game fitting to both of you, who, in your writing, can be perverse and mischievous with a poker face.

In writing, you and Guest are both riveted to absence, but ideology and methodology seem to part ways. Your normative surfaces, Guest's fragments. Your blocks of prose, Guest's "painterly" line. "Can't we discover the ground of sound, and let life be both on land and in the air?"

As you say of Albiach and Royet-Journoud's work, "Here" and I'm applying this now to Guest, "the stress is, rather, on what disrupts the flow, on the lines against which the words have to define themselves." The persuasive textures of your works take radically different readerly strategies and pleasures, yet your ideology of collage and metaphor seems very much simpatico.

What is your relationship to Barbara Guest's work?

RW: How awful, this error in the index; 12–22 should have been 121–22! I hope there are not too many more like this! But Barbara Guest. It seems there is no catching up with mourning. As you say, poets don't die. They live in their work. It's the death of the person, the friend, that makes me grieve. But with Barbara Guest, Robert Creeley, and Jackson Mac Low dying in short succession — three poets equally important in their very different ways — I do have the feeling it's the end of a world.

I discovered Barbara with the book *Moscow Mansions* and fell immediately under her spell. I soon after wrote a sequence that uses phrases from her "Byron's Signatories" (it's "Kind Regards," a chapbook published in 1975 and reprinted in *Streets Enough to Welcome Snow*), and have gone back to her poems again and again. I've always admired her combination of lightness and passion, her sudden veerings in unsuspected directions. In talking with her too, the sudden whimsy that in no way diminished her passionate commitment to poetry and art. But in the poems, the infallible rhythm, the purity of her line . . . It is a great sadness that we won't get any more of it.

CH: You often use at least two dominant rhythmic modes in your work — juxtaposing prose against lineated poetry or against lists, two voices in conversation, etc. In the case of "Music is an Oversimplification of the Situation We're In" — your tribute to Cage — the prose paragraphs are set against a stream of "key" words, which I imagine as a kind of rhythmic murmur under the main text, or the extraneous noise that got picked up in the "recording," in a manner appropriate to Cage, or simply a visual rhythm. It's like a through-writing of Cage and Brown, a verticality set against a horizontal instinct. How do your rhythm choices interact with your ideas of literary or generic hybridity?

You say that you fell under Barbara Guest's "spell." To me that implies a kind of rhythm, a magical incantation, a rhythm of perception just outside of conscious apprehension, one that arouses affective response and engorges our senses and sense of our world. It is a deeply physical experience. Our senses of time and rhythm are cultural; yet rhythm also seems to be an instinct. Do you think there's such a thing as an American rhythm?

RW: In "Music Is an Oversimplification," I thought of the list less as a rhythm than as a palette, the way some painters, like Tom Phillips, put a strip of colors down one side of the painting. The words are all from Cage's *Silence*, which I worked from (rather than Brown's lecture). Obviously nobody is going to read that list (alphabetical!), but it does make a contrasting murmur, as you say, and a visual rhythm.

On the other hand, in *Reluctant Gravities*, I began with the prose "conversations," but felt those blocks of prose were so dense that there needed to be a bit more "air" from time to time. Hence the "interludes" in verse. Here I really wanted to juxtapose two different rhythms and speeds.

To "hybridity" in general: my experience is that heterogeneous elements produce the kind of tension that is fruitful, that stretches my ideas in the process of wrestling them together. Of course, not all juxtapositions work; it's a matter of finding those that do.

I don't think rhythm is an instinct, but I agree that it is physical, based on body rhythms like breath and pulse. In language it also relates to everyday speech rhythms. And here your "American rhythm" comes in. At this point, I suspect we still have a Southern rhythm, different from a New England rhythm, etc. But radio and TV have begun to level those differences and will probably continue the process to the point where we may indeed get an American rhythm.

But even while I'm spouting this I get suspicious. We can't really abstract any one of the elements in writing. Remember when Housman was raving about "the furies and surges" of Blake's rhythm in "Tyger, Tyger, burning bright / In the forests of the night." Pound countered with "Tiger, Tiger, catch 'em quick / All the little lambs are sick." In other words: the meaning of the words changes the rhythm. And so we're back with rhythm as cultural. I don't think I can sort it out!

CH: The relationship of semantics and sound also finds itself in a similar conundrum, where context and somatics collide and corrupt each other. Why do you think audiences of other artistic fields, say visual art or music, seemingly have a much easier time with abstraction and the conceptual than audiences of poetry?

RW: Atonal music and abstract painting also had a hard time at first. However, it's true, poetry audiences lag behind still. It's probably because the medium is language. Everybody thinks they know the language and would be competent to write poems if they wanted to!

CH: As a result of your editorial advocacy, your translation projects, and your own maverick writing, contemporary American poetry looks and sounds much different than it did twenty years ago. I'd love to hear how you characterize that change of weather, if you agree. What do you find most exciting about contemporary poetry? Or not?

RW: You're obviously in overstatement mode. What I've done is a small part of the change and ferment that seems to have begun with the small press explosion (plus Beats/NY School/SF Renaissance) in the 60s and gotten new impetus with online publishing. And let's not forget, in between, the Language poets whose radical statements (nonreferential poetry!) riled even the people who didn't read their poems. Outrage is a ferment too.

I think we've had a great opening of the field. There are many more poetries getting a hearing/showing than before. And while there is of course much that I find dull, there is lots of energy — and surprises.

I've been trying to write a prose poem for Barbara. I'll put the current state below.

BARBARA GUEST, 1920–2006

Where language stops matter begins. Of words. The simple contact with a wooden spoon. I don't easily give up on the uncertainties that might, if only for a moment, alleviate grief. But time is perishable. I believe. A sense of consciousness comes precisely. From the flow of perceptions.

Relations of warfare and polka dots. And you cannot twice capture the flash of identity between subject and object.

The poem begins in silence, you wrote, mystery, wild gardens, pitch within the ear, chalk, rivulets, shifting persona, shuffling light.

As long as we've not reached, as in a dream, the fibrous, woody substance of words. We are prisoners. Of narratives in the room. Sprawling to consider an emphasis falls. On reality. Neither thick lids nor vowels inclement can obstruct the transparency of the dragonfly's wings. While the brain establishes consciousness through stimuli occurring not more than a twenty-fourth of a second apart. You occupy the lotus position.

The poem is fragile, you wrote, the contour elusive, ropes sway, heavy violets, galactic rhythm, sibilants, solitude edged, upward from the neck, provokes night.

When approaching death we cannot go into the matter of darkness. Viewed on the screen of distance, your shadow rephrased. Forbids the instant disclosure. The necessary night entangled in the folds of preoccupation until the next bold seizure of dawn. It is the connecting between moments — not the moments themselves — that is consciousness. Field broken by low running water, dour sky, the earth in twists moving like the water into the body's memory of self.

The poem is a résumé, you wrote, of impalpable vision, the clair-obscur of thought, a brown mouse, twilight soup, the figure appears, adoptive day, scorched tongue, the edge, always.

After your death we find matter. For many fine tales about your life. And work. The speculative use of minerals, like beryl, to prevent attachment to words from overflowing. To catch the fraction of a second when the seam of present and future is visible in the flash of the lizard's flight. Loss requires restructuring all of our consciousness, our relation to sunrise. And giving way to the emotions.

The poem draws blood, you wrote, kicks away the ladder, rose marble table, folds of skin, mirrors, fans, nimble wind, multiplied by frost, the rage of night.

CH: I didn't mean to suggest that you'd single-handedly changed our contemporary context, but I did want to point out the myriad ways in which you have contributed to this sea change — perhaps to find out what you think most needed to be rethought in poetry of the last three decades. Also, for me, what you identify as problems or inadequacies of language use (initially outlined in *Against Language?*) and your responses to those issues really distinguish your work and have made a marked difference in what I can take for granted as possible in poetry.

I've been reading board books to my ten-month-old daughter, and I've noticed that many, many of them have a mirror somewhere, asking "Where's the baby?" I'm not sure how long the mirror-in-the-book phenomenon has been around, but I find my own students often still read this way. The tendency of readers to identify themselves in the text, to literally look for oneself in the text (and conversely, to look for the author too literally, autobiographically within the text), is disheartening. Your approach to "character" often frustrates this impulse and focuses on a hybrid voice, the voice of language, or the "not I."

The way you use pronouns (I-you, he-she in the trilogy and in *Love, Like Pronouns*) is grammatical, relational — and it's often very humorous the way they play with their own rhetoricity. In *Reluctant Gravities*, the songs between the conversations draw on the vocabulary of those conversations. The song "voice" feels like a collaboration between the he and she, a hybrid of their voices. You've said elsewhere that when you collaborate with Keith, the result is a third voice altogether.

You are clearly drawn to vocabulary lists and collaborative voices — *A Key to the Language of America* also uses lists to show the conflicts between two cultures, Native American and Colonial American. In the Guest and Cage tribute lists are asemantic through-lines of respective authors set contrapuntally against larger blocks of text that adopt the rhetoric of exposition (though not its goals).

The Guest poem particularly is interesting in terms of pronouns — the I-you relationship that begins the poem becomes we-you after the first stanza, perhaps to sharpen the distinction between the two terms, or to give the "you" more equal footing, or to represent the loneliness of death to those who are still alive. In any case, the interludes in this poem — lists structured around what "you wrote," drawing words and phrases from

Guest's writing on writing — seem a hybrid voice, a collaboration with Guest's writing. In the final stanza, "kicks away the ladder" (a phrase I would associate more with you, via Wittgenstein, than with Guest) makes this most obvious.

More importantly, these list-interludes highlight your capacity to leap between abstract and material language with alacrity and alchemy in both of your works. The fast cuts between fragments of abstract and material language, of Anglo-Saxon and Latinate words, admit the incompletion of one "system" without the other and suggest a more complex linguistic ecology, one that reinstates the physical in language but also creates a language that manifests itself like a spell. This list takes on the materiality of "matter" by creating movement, like a flip book or film frames, "stimuli occurring not more than a twenty-fourth of a second apart." The whole poem exists as "the flash of identity between subject and object." The question of reality and the "authentic" identity is replaced by the possibility of rupture, artifice, and distortion — and the plurality of "shifting persona." You (and Guest) force an oddness and an otherness that asks the reader to interact with something outside themselves.

The lists' relations are democratic, and their fragments play against the completeness of the sentence. They are also sequential. The process of making them is meaningful, as you tend to use them as a kind of through-writing of other texts. The Guest and the Cage tributes both address the subject, but they also manufacture atmospheres. The German philosopher Gernot Böhme locates atmospheres as the "in between," straddling environmental quality and human sensibilities, which provokes a dramatic awareness of transitions and relationships. The transition is the emptiness, the white space — in the poem itself, and at a micro-level in the list.

Emily Dickinson: "Nothing is the force / that renovates the world."

Rosmarie Waldrop: "thinking develops / out of the negative // the vacuum abhorred / by nature / is fertile."

Before I spiral out any further, I'll wrap this up with a simple question: Do you have any future goals for, or projects involving, hybrid voices and collaboration? How do you want your future or current work to develop these approaches?

RW: I'm very intrigued by the mirror in the children's books. Looking for oneself and for vicarious experience in a book is, I suspect, the way we all start reading. It takes some sophistication to go beyond it. You are an exceptional reader. I've often gotten my pronouns taken literally and the I-you interpreted strictly as a woman talking to a man. I can't imagine working without some counterpoint. And it usually comes from other writing. But I don't have a plan or even a strategy beforehand. Some writers do — Marjorie Welish, for instance. I read around until I come across a text that sets off sparks, and I know I can work with it. Unlike Cage, I'm also not sure "what needs to be done." Though I have a sense what must be avoided! But then both Cage and Marjorie Welish believe in "progress" in the arts, and I don't. There are too many glorious eccentrics. I'm now winding down a sequence that bounces off a semiotic text about zero, as vanishing point and money. This got very difficult because of the material's level of abstraction, and developed into a kind of enactment of my ambivalence about abstraction in writing. But now I feel once again faced by a void. Or, as Jabès called it, I'm entering "the Book of Torment," the space between projects.

Music Is an Oversimplification of the Situation We're In

THE SILENCE OF THIS GREAT NOISE. Sounds take place. The noise of this truck. Wherever we are. My mother's fury in my heart. This truck at fifty miles per hour. A voice out of hell. Or an open door, quartet for explosive motor, wind, heartbeat and landslide. Hair standing on end to harmony. Bury yourself in sound. It warms the body, forfeits the horizon. Wide-eared. Notated or not, sounds eat space, a means of rapid transportation. Not written down they appear as silence. Is the ear behind glass, like the eye? Suppose I found grains of sound in my pocket, should I brush off chromatic proximity?

a abolish about absence acceleration accordingly action admit against all almost ambient ambiguous American among anechoic animal another anxiety any art at atmosphere atonal attention audience

CONSTANT CONNECTION TO THE PAST BY THE PRINCIPLE OF FORM. One person's harmony is another's brick wall. To beat his head against. The past everywhere is preying on nervous systems, methods of fingering. What a night, I said, what a night. The piano hammers its felt into stellar space, a synonym for submersion. We don't need to destroy the past: it's past. Shaken. Echoes on track. Depending on whether you are born deaf, a sonata may be conceptual escape, absence of gesture, or a horse galloping along horizontal evolutions. To spread, to resemble nature, to rush out of sight. Lit-up overtones. Spontaneous anxiety. We dream forms of fire, scorched fingers on the keys.

avoid awe babble banality bang beach beat beautiful become bed Beethoven before benevolence bill-board birth bizarre blackbird Blake blind blood blow body bone bouquet breathless brick broken brush

THE IDENTIFICATION OF POISONOUS MUSHROOMS. In a matrix of war, color drains from the inquest. The habit of scales, counterpoint, harmony concerns discrete steps. The high-pitched nervous system. On stepping-stones twelve. Overtone structures. Frequency of blood in circulation. Bizarre and exhausting in the night. We open our fears, drum our fists. Stare holes into our eyes: phantom weapons, flower-bullets. Frequent pitch, maximum loudness, overkill structure, the sound of fury. At any point, along any line or curve one has a choice.

Buddhist bullet burn bury but by call candle casualty cemetery chair chamber champion chance change charge chest childhood choice chromatic circulation city clap clean clear click cluster

INCOMPLETE EXPLOSION OF LIMITS EXPLAINED. The empty space in the heart is reserved for Kansas. There is no empty space, as there is no silence. Kansas like nothing on earth. I do not fear for the future of music or mourn the sound that dies away. A hedgehog interrupts my being lost at the edge of the tape. March night crescendos into desert. Oil on fire. Try to imagine a music free of imagination. Frequencies free of memory would open the total field of possibilities, all dawn above magnetic ground. Even before we add to imperfections in the paper. If we retraced our steps to where positions are not inter-changeable, we would need to light a match.

code co-existence coins cold colors combustion common compare compendium competitive composition conceptual concern concert confusion connection consequence constant constellation contemporary con-

HAPPIEST OF COMPOSERS. His waking expression, is it not a smile? The sleep of his reason gives birth to rhythms a far cry from horse's hoofs, to mushrooms that outgrow both rain and explanation. Is he not a bit lost in his too large suit? He twitches his nostrils, stretches his eardrum. As for nature, he carries it from the edge of thought into his body. An error of localization, say his detractors, juggling extremes of joy and pain. See

integration of opposites, compare Dionysus. Why will he not separate art from life? What is his purpose, his lack of, his thought, his ought? Horrid heavenly interpenetrations. A piece of string. A sunset.

nental control convention correct cough counterpoint cow-bell crabgrass crescendo curve cut danger dark
ay deaf death declare denominator denouement density desert desire destroy devotion dice Dionysus

THE DANGERS OF CONTEMPORARY MUSIC. We might never know them. A sound as sound does not require we hear it without feeling. Or camp near a cemetery. Pitch is not a matter of like and dislike. See how he picks shells on the beach, a curve away from ideas of order, day unending in the burning sun. At the corner of the square full of potholes, a sudden horse bucks the rider and the sound of words. Do you flatten yourself against the wall? Strings are instructive, voices too, and sitting still anywhere. On track, the unknown with such sharp clarity. To listen or not to listen. Do you try to grab the reins? As if by habit, the potholes fill with rain, and bodies stand on their heads.

irection disappear discover discrete discriminate dislike disparate dissimilars dissolved distasteful
ivision doing dollar doubt dream drift drop drown duck duration dynamite each ear earnestness earth

INDETERMINACY. At each structural division, a toss of coins, a music of changes. A vertigo where your childhood could have dissolved had your mother not pulled you back to human savings. Error beside the point: once it happens it is. Structure unnecessary, though of interest; even indeterminate, it remains present. Crabgrass. Kudzu. Transparent weddings. Two inches of silence on track one. Hold watch to mike. Stretch membrane. The ear you won't lend will forego marvel for His Master's Voice. In its nest, bags are prepared for your body or others, a long safety without tightening in the chest or late clouds.

echo ecstasy edge elastic elbow electronic element empty encumbered engine enough eraser erotic error escape Esperanto essence European even evening every evil evolutions exclusions exhausting experience

CLOSE ATTENTION TO CLOSE ATTENTION. The worn out sounds are not worn out. Beethoven as surprising as a cowbell if you listen with ignorance. The points of fusion are many. From one of them, you may invite clusters of jazz, wingbeats, billboards, combustion engines, and wildflowers. The warm vigor of a horse. The air shivers timbres toward the tympanum, though without denoument. Yes, I'll enter your ear, like any mother, no need to hold it open. Lolling tones gather no mushrooms. While even mossy patience gradually wears away, fear leaves scars on the retina. We're left among electrons, atonal, aching.

explanation explosive expression extremes eye fail faithful fall family father fatigue feeling Feldman field fill fingering fire fist flatten flimsy flourish fly fold foot force forego forfeit forget fork form forth

"IMAGINARY LANDSCAPE NUMBER IV." Shock of the new and awe of mastery fail before the silence of a 500-pound bomb. In a city of 150 mosques, there are no longer any calls to prayer. An eraser is used wherever necessary. The air trembles at the sound of a plane. Somebody's church celebrates napalm Sunday. The mind may be used to ignore ambient sounds that are unmusical or distasteful. Look for clean walls to put bullets in and whistle three times at the stench. I have not yet told any stories. Or the mind may give up on improving the world and function as faithful receiver of experience. Small pieces fall from the air with long tails of smoke. We've broken the backbone. We've destroyed everything. We've provided the chance for a new start.

found free frequency friend Fuller function fungus furniture fury fusion future gallop gamut gargle gather genetic Geneva gesture give glass glory glue go good grab gradually grass great ground guts habit hai

INCUMBENT MIDDLE. Every day is a beautiful day. Every beautiful day is like every beautiful day. Sunrise. A child is born. A piece of music. Perspective becomes orderly, radiating from the needs of the child. This is a lecture on composition. Structure, method, form. Why do we rush along the road like magnetic tape on fire? Form without spontaneity brings about the death of all pigeons and magpies in the skies. In the coexistence of dissimilars, pitch leans away from purpose, and urgency is implied. Inward, to a point in dream. Outward, to the tips of fingers and toes. Let's retire to an open window instead of the woods, including tables and chairs. Is every tone virgin? If repeated? Masterpieces are the most frightening monsters. Whereas night gets dark by itself.

ammer happen happiest harmony hard hat head healthy hear heartbeat hedgehog hell helmet hep-
at heroic high-pitched hip hiss history hold home hoof hope horizon horse hot huge hum

OBSERVATION. Is there such a thing as silence? And do I have to listen to it? To something? To a stream babbling, if in the woods? I've buried the horse. Its gallop so faint silence couldn't but absorb it. Provided that clumsy bones are no obstruction. Thickly instrumental. Almost breathless with continental drift, encumbered by "radios twelve." Let us consider contemporary milk. At room temperature it sours. Unless we protect it from life by placing it in a museum. Then it is art. Which affects ear, nose, throat, tongue. And all you can do is suddenly sneeze. This observation is not profound, but against loss.

uman ideas identification if ignorance illusion imagination immense imperfections impertinence im-
lied improving in inches include incomplete incumbent incurable indeterminacy inevitable inquest

THE IMPERTINENCE OF EXPLANATION. Immense field of possibilities divided by square roots, the travel through micro-macro rhythm so unpredictable. He obtains oracles by toss, surprises constellations by disappearing into history. One does what must be done. Before death cuts in. Our time not calculable by stopwatch or plucked string. Shadows by falling. The soul, gatherer-together of disparate elements, goes out, brief candle. Ambiguously tonal state of affairs with twelve bricks, but no plan. Can't we discover the ground of sound, and let life be both on land and in the air? While ecstasy pulses to every point of the labyrinth and night comes due to change of weather?

inspiration instant instead instep instructive instrumental integration intelligent interest inter changeable interpenetration interrupt interval inward iron irresponsibility irritate italic itself jazz jo

SRIKANTH REDDY | MARK LEVINE

Evening with Stars

It was light. Whoever it was
who left it under the gumtree last night
forgot to close the gate. This morning when I stepped
out on the breezeway I had to shoo off a she-pig
& three rag-pickers before I could tell
what it was they were carting away
through the leaves. I had the houseboy bear it
into the sunroom. After attending to my & my employer's
business, I returned sometime after midnight
to examine it. A pair of monkeys
were hoisting it over the threshold
toward a courtyard of fireflies. When I shook my fist
they dropped it & I settled down at last.
It was gilt. It was evening with stars.
Where a latch should have been, a latch
was painted on. Over the lid, a procession.
Chariot. Splintered tree. Chariot. Chariot.
In the lamplight the hollows
of the footsoldiers' eyes were guttering.
I'd say they looked happy.
Tired & happy. Their soil-flecked boots
sank down to the buckle in weeds
& lacquered nettles, six men to a burden.
It was light. I could see
in the middle distance a bone priest
picking his way through crop rows
toward the wreckage of an iron temple.
Scarlet clouds moving out. Jasper clouds moving in.
Here, on a cistern, a woman
keeps nursing her infant.

She is unwell.
The workmanship is astonishing.
You can pick out every lesion on her breast.

Mostly, I am alone.

Hotel Lullaby

No matter how often you knock
on the ocean the ocean

just waves. No matter
how often you enter the ocean

the ocean still says
no one's home. You must leave

her dear Ursula. As I write this
they polish the big

chandelier. Every prism
a sunset in abstract

or bijou foyer depending
on where you stand.

They take it apart every Fall
& call it Spring cleaning.

They bring me my tea.
They ask me my name

& I tell them Ursula,
I don't even know

how to miss who you left.

Corruption (II)

In one of Grimm's stories, a little tailor defeats a giant in a throwing contest by lofting a bird in the air. Happily ever after arrives, but the bird never lands. She flies straight out of the tale. Tonight, a vessel catapults through the heavens with a gold-plated phonograph fixed to its side. In less than forty thousand years this craft will drift through the nearest system, bearing greetings in fifty-seven languages, including the encoded song of the humpback whale. By then our tongue will have crossed into extinction or changed utterly. Lately, I have taken an interest in words like "here." Here was a chapel, for instance. Here is a footprint filling with rain. Here might be enough. Could not the same be said of elsewhere? Yes, I suppose. But I know precious little of elsewhere.

SR: In the title poem from *Enola Gay,* there's a moment when the speaker, surveying an absurdist apocalyptic landscape, suddenly announces, "I am with child." For some reason, I find myself thinking of that line often. It always struck me as totally bizarre, and yet somehow utterly appropriate for the occasion of the poem. Well, it's years after the publication of that book, and I hear you're going to be a father pretty soon! (Applause.) But I'm still puzzled by that line from long ago. When you wrote that, were you anticipating fatherhood way off on the distant horizon, or worrying about how having a child might affect your writing life someday, or somehow testing the limits of what could be said by your presumably male speaker? What on earth could you have possibly meant at the time?

ML: Your sources are correct. At this advanced moment in the process I am positively *big* with child. (You should see Emily.) And, as I wrote on the next line of that poem, "This time it's a child." It does seem — not having read the poem in about five years, until your question inspired me to take a look (with one hand over my eyes) — like an outlandish thing to have said. I know that I have always found the phrase "with child" to be wonderfully weird, as though "child" were some abstract, mystical form. (Which, to be frank, at this point, for me it is.) Where else but in poetry, or in an asylum, can a sort-of-grown man not only say such a thing, but say it and mean it — and feel it to be true? I have always adored Sidney's line toward the end of the first sonnet in *Astrophil and Stella*: "Thus, great with child to speak, and helpless in my throes . . . " Is there any one among us who didn't come to poetry out of the urgent discomfort of being "great with child to speak"? It's surely one of the hallowed tropes of the self-effacing, self-regenerating labor of putting words on a page. Now that, for me, it's a literal condition — well, almost — the metaphor only gets enriched. One doesn't need to have had a child — only to have been one once, I suppose — to recognize that "The Child is father of the Man," and that we often hang out, simultaneously, in overlapping chronologies (no more so than in poetry), and occupy roles that would seem to be mutually exclusive. Perhaps I just have womb envy.

SR: And do you think that, on some unconscious level, you *knew* that you were in some sense writing about your future child?

ML: It always surprises me (and sometimes worries me) to realize, long after the fact, how obscurely aware, or even ill-informed, I am of my preoccupations at the time I'm writing, and how very partial is my understanding of what I'm saying. I would never have believed that, in some ways, I could have been thinking about "paternity" when I wrote *Enola Gay* ten years ago. The title poem of my new book, *The Wilds*, was called "On His First Son" for several years until I made the change recently. Yet I certainly had no sense that I was, to some extent, addressing myself in that poem to the unforeseen prospect of my own future son. I don't know what I thought — whether I was trying to write as my own father addressing me; or as myself, "giving birth" so to speak, to a kind of reckoning with my father; or writing to my own former, lost self; or none of the above; or all. It may not be very respectable to admit to being a touch clueless about what could be considered very fundamental questions of subject matter in poetry, but that's how it is for me, and willfully. It's possible that I would have imagined that to say "mother" and "father" and "child" in a poem was doing nothing more than designating "figures." I probably had a well-rehearsed abhorrence of the "personal" in poetry. I was kidding myself, though.

SR: It sounds to me like you're very wary of thinking too much about — or "theorizing" — what you're doing as a poet while you're in the act of writing.

ML: It troubles me a bit that, as poets, we seem to feel put on the spot to pretend that everything we put in poems emerges from a very supportable rationale. Maybe we've been successfully cowed by those who are hostile to poetry, and have internalized their suspicion that the whole thing is a sham, an "elitist" attempt to befuddle and mock the guileless reader. And so we apologetically, or pompously, give in to this rather recent expectation that artists are supposed to talk a good game about what they do. I'll tell you, I once spent a week interviewing the skateboarder Tony Hawk — a bit before he became a multinational industry — and here's what I liked best about him: great skateboarder, not a great interview subject. Every time he got on his board it was magic; every time he opened his mouth it was, well, pretty ordinary stuff. His intelligence was thoroughly absorbed in what he did, and to him, talking about it was not only irrelevant — it was almost a violation of the spirit of his sport. This seems appropriate. By now, I've spent enough time around young people writing poems to recognize the common anxiety, even embarrassment, about simply "being" a poet, rather than pretending to be a poet and an eager A-student rolled up into a single very polished package. But why, with all the hand-wringing poetry talk out there — our own, no doubt, included — are there some matters that, it seems, are very rarely aired, even in the supposedly brass-tacks environment of the poetry workshop? Confounding questions like: How much do you know what your poem is about when you're writing it? Do you know "who is speaking"? Do you know "what the situation is"? Do you know what your "themes" are? When you get right down to it: do you know what is "happening" — what is "going on" — in your poem when you are writing it? I don't know about you, Chicu, but I'd often be lying if I answered most of these questions in the affirmative. I don't even want to be able to say "yes." If I could, I'd wonder why I was writing a poem.

SR: Maybe we need *others* to tell us what we're doing as artists (or skateboarders) in order to understand, ourselves, what our concerns may be?

ML: With any luck, the only kind of understanding we really need is the one we get, and that eludes us, in writing our poem. Still, a student of mine, a very intelligent one, once pointed out to me at a party that my conversation seemed to be returning frequently to questions of childhood — my own, hers, those of others, not to mention the status of childhood generally. She wondered if I was obsessed with the subject. I was really taken aback, because I always thought of myself as someone who was deeply and distinctly uninterested in childhood, and who would certainly never write poems about childhood — indeed, there was a type of "poem of memory" (what an awful phrase) that I felt I had actively scorned since I started writing poems. But after the student made that remark to me, I took a look at the poems I was writing, and poems I had written in my previous books — and I even thought about some nonfiction I had written, which tended to be on topics that were assigned to me, like skateboarding, and were rarely of my choosing — and I thought, good god, I'm someone who is preoccupied by childhood and memory, and I had thought of myself in completely the opposite terms.

So, if it's not too late to return to a question you posed so long ago you may have forgotten it: I have no idea what the effect of having a child will be on poetry for me. I have been very lucky to spend a second childhood (years twenty through forty) writing poetry, it would seem, out of the first childhood. There's something about that cusp of consciousness that a child is perched on that is powerful to me, much as I'm drawn to the sensation of undocumented, or unconfirmable, memory. Like any parent-to-be, I guess, I'm really, really curious about what I can learn about human beings by watching one develop in front of me. The process seems like poetry to me, though I'm not thinking about it in terms of something as menial as "getting material" for poems. After a while, the only reason I can see to write poems is out of personal need, and it's very hard to know what the need will be once the little guy arrives. But I probably say that only because I am currently so full of terrified anticipation.

SR: As a former baby myself, I find the subject endlessly interesting. I thought it was pretty fascinating (and deeply weird) that you'd been thinking about calling the title poem of the new book "On His First Son" for years before the proverbial twinkle in your eye. And I vaguely remember hearing somewhere that you'd once thought of *Debt* as being in some ways a book of the father, and of *Enola Gay* as being a book of the mother, which makes me feel like *The Wilds* (a book of the child) might complete that family logic?

But what I want to focus on is what you described as "that cusp of consciousness that a child is perched on," and how it shapes your sense of what poetry is. That cusp of consciousness seems a lot like the threshold between knowing and uncertainty that Keats described as negative capability. And I'd agree enthusiastically that this cusp or threshold is the most productive space for a poet to inhabit. But lately I've also been worried that uncertainty lets one off the ethical hook — it lets one, as it were, refuse to "grow up." I guess my vague feelings of guilt about not speaking up more about the political situation over recent years has something to do with this. In the lead-up to the war, for instance, I felt "uncertain" about whether or not there were weapons of mass destruction tucked away somewhere in Mesopotamia (among many other things), and my general reluctance to forcefully decide matters for myself mirrored, I think, a broader failure of liberals to dissent from what our nation is perpetrating abroad. That's a detour, I know, but what I'm getting at is a sense that there is a danger to uncertainty. I'm definitely not advocating a more "political" poetry — Lord knows I find most overtly political verse to be fairly dreary — but I'm wondering what you think about the ethics of uncertainty as a poet writing today?

ML: Let's see, how can I best avoid your question? Do you remember when you were younger and some snide kid told you to "grow up"? I think I can still hear that voice. I hated that kid. What he was really saying was: Don't be yourself. Don't have an imagination. Behave. I'm just not interested in growing up in those ways. (On the other hand, I already find myself in mourning for a certain kind of bygone civility — the days when people could disagree about poetics and politics in respectful and civil ways, without needing to assault each other from the safety of their dreary blogs.) I was once involved in one of those dreary discussions on "the state of poetry," and one of my interlocutors was an ambitious and quite accomplished young critic, a guy then under thirty, who complained that poets in America had abandoned the duty of being "judicious and authoritative" in poems. I was taken aback. He struck me as one of those people in college who wears a bowtie and carries a pocket watch — as someone who has gotten over-invested in a certain model of "maturity." You know the type — the miniature Bill Buckleys of the poetry world, on a mission to set the rest of us straight? (I can't say I'm much fonder of their confreres on the Left.) I don't know, there may be a lot of things wrong with poetry — now and always — but the reluctance to speak with the kind of "authority" this guy meant — confident, knowing, absolute — doesn't seem to me to be one of them. In my mind, one of the services poets perform, intuitively, is to hold up the authority of poetic and imaginative tradition against other claims to authority. My suspicion is that the recurrent charge that poets are not sufficiently "engaged" is typically a symptom of one of two things: the right-wing interest in trivializing poetry, or misplaced left-wing guilt. I'm not proposing a Peter Pan model of the poet, but my guess is that "not growing up"— if it constitutes a willingness to remain, as you say, "in mysteries, doubts, and uncertainties"— is much preferable — poetically, ethically, politically — to being prematurely pickled.

SR: So it's this cusp of uncertainty that you find to be fundamentally poetic somehow?

ML: That cusp — I think the desire to be there must in part be temperamental. I like basketball games that go into overtime; overtime drives some people crazy. I don't really care about how books or movies end. I like the unresolved. I've always been drawn to the moment "before"— the moment when you have a heightened awareness that you're in the presence of something real, something meaningful, but when the meaning hasn't yet been captured. To me, that's the "intensest rendezvous." In Bob Dylan's terms, it's the refrain of "Ballad of a Thin Man": "You know something is happening, but you don't know what it is, do you, Mr. Jones?"

But I understand your uncertainty about uncertainty. (Your meta-uncertainty?) It's something that the uncertain ones among us must grapple with. Doesn't it come down to a question of the authenticity of our uncertainty? If uncertainty is a posture — something we adopt in an effort to make cool poems — it would, indeed, be frivolous. But true uncertainty is a beautiful thing, aesthetically. It's the outcome of a brain overwhelmed by emotion. And my guess is that those (like Mister Bowtie) who adopt a pedantic posture of certainty are far more "dangerous," morally and politically, and, of course, artistically, than those who have fewer answers, less of an agenda to promote, and who try to use their work as a way of shedding a little light on the darkness.

My glib, reflexive take on this problem would be that of an aesthete:

that the ethical task of a poet is to write as well as we can, as accurately, forthrightly, and courageously — to be as uncompromising as we can in relation to poetic truth. But that is a tall order, an ideal against which one always falls short. Also, of course, "excellence" is not value neutral: is the "ethical task" of a nuclear bomb-maker to make the best bomb he can? Um, no. But in that case the problem is that the medium itself — nuclear bomb-making — is morally corrupted from the start. Whereas I have cast my lot with those who believe that the poetic tradition is, at its height and in its impulse, noble, resistant, and self-scrutinizing. So, yeah, I think the world would be a much better place if we all listened to each other the way poems listen to us.

SR: I do think you've got a point about misplaced left-wing guilt motivating the politicization of poetry today. In fact, one could probably write a whole book about the hidden role of political guilt in shaping American poetry from Whitman all the way through to the Confessional poets. But then again, who except Mister Bowtie would want to read it?

I'm also mulling over what you said about "the authenticity of our uncertainty," which seems to me like a useful way of thinking about the special kind of knowledge poetry might have to offer. Maybe poetry is where we can weigh our uncertainty, to make sure it's "earned" and not just an easy way out of (political, emotional, or philosophical) problems. This is pretty abstract, but it leads to the even more abstract question of what secures or grounds that authenticity? I mean, how do we know if somebody is just playacting their angst or whether it's the real deal? One answer, I think, is the very un-abstract answer to be found throughout your poems — namely, embodiment. A person who physically enters into his or her poetry seems to me more vulnerable, more exposed, and therefore more authentically uncertain than somebody who writes from a disembodied perspective. After all, I'm much more likely to believe that somebody falls upon the thorns of life if they actually bleed. This question of embodiment is one that's always struck me as a major concern (conscious or not) in your poems. Peculiar things happen to bodies throughout *Debt* and *Enola Gay* — the speaker's head becomes a zipper, a woman's breasts are replaced by stone — as if you were desperately trying to bring the human figure into representation, and somehow discovered that the most authentic way to do this might be by wounding, burning, breaking, or otherwise damaging it.

Anyway, we're a long way from babies now, but I did want to ask you about this focus on the human figure, because it seems to me like the body enters into language in a different, maybe gentler way in the new poems: "watched the kneeling girl / twist upward into shape / a stem twined round her / she is out of milk / that flows from her in the song of spring."

ML: Well, I have a hard time believing that authenticity doesn't lie near the root of what many of us — despite having been reared in the strange pieties of postmodernism — really value, whether we are talking about authenticity in poems, or in friendships, relationships, politics, most everything. I do believe, as you're suggesting, that poems provide us with an incomparable medium for discerning authenticity, and for helping to locate and hone the authenticity in ourselves. (One of my favorite nuggets from Dickinson: "Microscopes are prudent / In an Emergency.") Maybe this sounds flaky. I'm not talking about "absolute truth." I really don't know anyone (in my small circles of intimates) who is a believer in that oh-so-easily-reviled construct. But just because it's easy to make a hash of "absolute truth," once one has overheard a few phrases of theory, it seems to me ridiculous to pretend that it's not possible to move toward the genuine, the true, however elusive it is, in ourselves and in poems. And I guess I wonder what we're doing with ourselves if we're not doing that. Of course I'm aware that poems, like everything else made by human beings, are "artificial," but I don't believe that excludes poems from approaching authenticity and partaking of it — as far as I'm concerned, poems routinely do that, and that's a big reason that we read them.

One thing that's so moving about poems is that we "know" they are "artificial," but still we invest them, and their materials, with the force of the "real." We need to do this, because we need to feel the reality of our lives. When I write the word "tree," I don't just see a word or construct — I see a physical tree. And if I'm not being particularly lazy as a writer, I'm going to do more to specify the reality, the tree-ness, of that tree

— not only as a way of writing a "nice" poem, but of specifying, and thereby sharing in, the reality of reality.

SR: So, "no ideas but in things"?

ML: It's easy to talk in abstract terms, which always makes me uncomfortable, because I'm drawn to the physical experience of poems, not their "ideas." You asked whether, in reading poems, we can begin to distinguish between the appearance of "authenticity" and something that smacks of the real deal? Don't you think we rely on being able to make that distinction, however provisionally? I have to believe it can be done. The poem makes a claim — "My heart aches, and a drowsy numbness pains my sense," for instance — and, after submerging ourselves in the poem, we can ask, "Do I feel the truth of that claim, or does it just seem like a convenient or clever thing to say? Does the poem, in its rhythms, syntax, imagery, and so forth, struggle with, and in, drowsiness, numbness, and pain, or not? Does the claim feel abstract or, as you say, 'embodied?' And how does one embody the experience of one's poem?" There must be as many ways as there are authentic poems (i.e., not that many). First off, I suppose, one believes in the reality of one's own imaginative event. One orients oneself to a position inside the poem — one lives in and through the poem, rather than hovering above it, using it as a way to "say something," or as a vehicle for producing "nice poetic effects," which, once you've read enough poems, are not as rare or interesting as they might first appear. I've found, myself, that focusing in particular on imagery has helped me to "feel" the poem by employing my (generally underused) senses, rather than trying to direct the poem with my often enfeebled brain. I've always been puzzled by the relative thinness of imagery in the English poetic tradition, by the way in which sensory experience has tended to get subordinated to "rhetoric" or "theme," for which the imagery is expected merely to offer support. Only with modernism does the situation begin to change, and not in a lasting way. Perhaps because I came to poetry as a way of getting outside my head and its limitations, I've been inclined to enter a poem by drawing some broad strokes of imagery, believing in the provisional physical reality of the image, and then believing that, since it's real, I have to deal with it, explore it, be respectful of it. The function of the image, for me, is not to serve my "purposes" in the poem, but rather to allow me into the poem, to provide the site for an action to take place. It doesn't mean I'm going to write a "good" poem. That's not really what I'm after. As my three or four readers may confirm, it's entirely possible that I may not, personally, have the stuff to write a "good" poem. But I've still got to try to live as richly as I can.

SR: One artist who comes to mind in hearing you talk about representation and reality is Francis Bacon. Maybe it's simply because of the violence brought to bear on the body in his painting — which, in a way, reminds me of the startling deformations of the human figure in *Debt* and *Enola Gay* — but somehow I often think of Bacon's images when I'm reading your poems.

ML: Bacon's work and process is exemplary to me. I love the way he deploys traditional values — of form, structure, line, color, modeling, and subject matter — to explore what he calls his "nervous system." He also talks, in his interviews with David Sylvester, of using traditional techniques and materials of painting to capture, even trap, the "real." Reality is the outcome of his process, not a known quantity that he enters his process wishing to depict. I really think that's why his work seems so alive, so "authentic." Then of course there is his sheer skill. And his genius. Last year a student gave me Deleuze's book on Bacon. (You can guess who is educating whom in my classes.) I thought Deleuze had some fantastic things to say about Bacon's capacity to produce the sensation of a variety of forces impinging on our bodies. You could tell Deleuze really felt the sensation, himself, in Bacon's work. To me, he was approaching the paintings like a poet (or a painter), allowing the work to overwhelm him. And he suggested beautifully that Bacon's ability to express force in paint was the result of feeling those forces operate on him — that, at his best, Bacon was painting out of his body, and crossing over into the canvas. In that way, I'd say, every Bacon painting is a kind of self-portrait. And of course I believe that to be the case with forceful poems, too.

SR: "Reality is the outcome of his process"— I like that a lot. In fact, what I like most about Bacon's painting — which I don't know well enough to speak about at all, really — is the way it exhibits the trace of its own process. (Somehow the blurs and smears on his canvases seem to me like a document of perception, or rather, a document of the "process" of trying to perceive an unruly subject that won't stay still.) One thing that I often think about from those snows of yesteryear at Iowa is your emphasis on process in the classroom. And, though I know you're wary of terms like "ethics" in talking about poetry, it seems to me like there *is* a strong ethical component to your way of thinking about the writing process, which to a certain degree involves relinquishing "control" over one's material in favor of a more exploratory or unpremeditated relationship toward one's subject. To my mind, this way of thinking about how to write also opens onto a way of thinking about how to treat other people. But I'm willing to drop my ethical hobbyhorse in favor of looking a bit more deeply into this process question. Could you tell me a bit about how your own process as a writer has developed?

ML: When I started writing, what I was looking for was a way to be wild — to say the things that seemed forbidden (by school, family, girlfriend, etc.) but true. My first poetry teacher, Philip ("no relation") Levine, was a great inspiration to me. He told me I could write poems without being polite. So I practiced being blunt and, in my terms, literal. Even if the landscape of my poems was "surreal," I was going to treat that landscape as something real, and try to be genuinely affected by what went on there. No more metaphor for me. At an extreme, this meant that instead of saying something along the lines of, "I am like a zipper" (i.e., I open and close, I get split and reattached, etc.), I would say, "I am a zipper" and mean it, and try to inhabit that sensibility in the poem. A lot of my first book is comprised of poems in the mode of "I do this, I do that, I see this, I touch that." Lots of action and, as you said earlier, a nasty, sort of punkish aversion to "thinking," even a stance of ridicule toward "emotion recollected in tranquility." I thought tranquility was the enemy of poetry — who knows, it might be — and that recollection was a form of fraudulence. I wanted everything to be present tense, and present.

It's hard to imagine now, barely twenty years later, but a lot of my peers found those poems in my first book to be not just "daring" but almost incomprehensible, and in violation of the protocols of poetry. Of course, I enjoyed being an enfant terrible for a minute or two. I believed I was participating in a great avant-garde tradition by building my poems on a series of exclusions — expunging anything that might reek of explanation or self-justification, including the syntax of logical connection, and the rationality (A equals B) of metaphor, and the cohesiveness of "theme," and the authority of narration, and the consolation of any rhythm that might seemed modulated. Thus did an otherwise well-behaved twenty-five-year-old write a book of poems.

But here's the thing about prematurity: I was ashamed of that book right away. (I would be lying if I didn't admit that these days; I've made my peace with it, and am sort of impressed with its audacity.) Over the next several years, I tried to figure out how to avoid imitating myself, and how to avoid writing poems that felt dictated by a stance toward poetry that became stale quickly. I moved to Montana for a teaching job and two things happened: first, I discovered the natural world; second, I began reading the English poetic tradition in a completely different, less disinterested way — the result, in all honesty, of being required to teach a course in traditional prosody to the writing students each semester. Previously, I had been a single-minded protégé of modernism; but I began to feel — no doubt through a misguided and idiosyncratic reading of the tradition — a deep and personal connection to Shakespeare, Wyatt, Donne, Keats, Hopkins, Dickinson, many others. It struck me that for daring, for density of language and thought, for true "modernity," the tradition had a whole lot more to offer than whatever one might find in this month's poetry journals. I began to read the tradition for insights on poetic process and technique.

Gradually, I came to write longer sentences, to use syntax that I had forbidden myself, and, above all from my point of view, to introduce diction that I would have rejected previously as "poetic" or "beautiful." I wanted something that was located deeper in what I took to be the "lyric core" of the experience of consciousness, so I made an effort to strip away the scaffolding of "story" and "incident" that I used to rely on to get myself into a poem. I moved toward a poem that was distinctly more honed, more "crafted," than those in my first book. My other objective was to disallow myself the privileges of the ironist: I didn't want to use tone as a way of interpreting and narrowing the experience of the poem. So my poems became both more traditional and, I suspect, harder to get a handle on. I also imposed on myself — in reaction to my first book — formal variety. I already knew that my work was not going to develop by artificially changing my "subject matter" — I really believe that one's true subject matter is given, not chosen — so I was going to focus, instead, on changing, and improving, my technique.

SR: It does seem to me like there's a kind of quiet but forceful shift in your process with this new book. Process seems more apparent — more "on the surface" of the poems — in *The Wilds* than in your previous collections, I think. This means, on one hand, that the poems feel more raw and less resolved than before. (The endings of the poems, for example, often seem to question or trouble the gestures of literary closure found in many other books of poetry today, or, for that matter, the senses of ending in *Debt* or *Enola Gay*.) As you say, this seems to have something to do with grammar — one might think of it as a new grammar of feeling that wasn't apparent in the earlier collections. And on a technical level, in *The Wilds* this new process becomes visible through the edgy, peculiar, and utterly unpredictable unfurling of syntax across poetic lines, as in the opening of the poem "Triangle":

> If not for
> the triangle accompanying
> my newborn to
> his father's mother's
> scheduled excavation I
> would have spilled
> him mistakenly down
> the banister where
> I ought to
> belong having squandered
> my grip elemental
> as my syntax
> was.

Reading these poems, I feel like I'm watching the syntax feeling its way toward a destination without any sense of predestination. I know that sounds awfully pretentious, but allow me to adjust my bowtie and elaborate. It's like the grammar unfolds — in "real time" — a sense of what the poem is. Does that even come close to making any sense? And if it does, I was wondering if you might be willing to talk about the role of syntax in the process of composing a poem like "Triangle," and how this process differs from your earlier methods of composition. And for extra credit, could you say something about the role of lineation in "staging" the grammar of the poem as it was written?

ML: In my third book, which is very new to me, the process of working out what the "next stage" of poetry might mean for me developed over several years. And as you say, the major shift in these poems involves the relationship to syntax. I don't know why or how it happened. Maybe it's because I had started writing so much prose over the years, and I am perpetually frustrated by prose's demand that we say one thing at a time, one thing after another, when what our bodies really want to do, I think, is to experience conflicting states simultaneously. It may be, as you say, that the process in these newer poems is more exposed — I certainly hope that's so — but on the other hand, this process is rarely referred to, as it was in my first book. In the poem "Triangle" that you mention, I suppose the most basic way in which "process" is invoked is that each line is composed of three words — a triangular, and always-shifting, syntactical fragment, connected to those surrounding it. It seemed interesting to me to measure a line based on the quantity of words — trying, somehow, to have something "happen," in some way, in each trio of words — rather than on the basis of rhythmic stresses or counted syllables: I thought there might be a lot of possibilities for variation within the sameness of each line's measure. But to be honest, that decision didn't emerge until I was well into writing a draft of the poem, and was chiseling away at it. I believe, surely, that I had in the back of my mind an old favorite poem, the "Little Triangle" series by Vasko Popa, but I also know that at the time I was trying to figure out a way to write entire poems in a single sentence (a very different shape from that of the closed geometry of a triangle), and was exploring how far I might be able to stretch the materials of a sentence and still keep the sentence intact. In the interest of full, self-contradictory disclosure, I would tell you that the months in which I was making this "single-sentence" effort were those that involved the buildup to the war in Iraq and the beginning of that war, and in my mind the desire to keep speaking without interruption felt somehow connected — in conflicted ways — to the politics of that moment. A few of those one-sentence poems survive in my book, but some became collections of fragments that sort of drift into and collide with each other, and others simply start and stop without syntactical boundaries. "Triangle" is one of the more tight-assed poems in the book.

SR: So what is the "triangle" that's being referred to in the poem?

ML: In retrospect, it would be easy to assign it an identity — the Third Party, the Other, the Alternate, and so on. But when I wrote the poem I think — I know — I had in mind a walk I took with Emily on a dirt road through woods in Maine, which passes a beautiful salt marsh before going over a hill and dropping to a secluded beach — and I had the image of the two of us walking with a triangle around us, around our waists, like a big belt, if that makes sense. Of my 435 favorite lines in "The Waste Land," my most favorite might be, "Who is the third who walks always beside you?" That third term, in this poem, is the point outside our pair who makes of our pair a triangle, and it is the triangle itself, which includes us, and is invisible to us but present, and points both to ground and to sky, past and future, and which is a real thing to us, a being, a shape, something we made in the course of our walk, something like a poem. In that way, the poem is entirely autobiographical, like all my poems are these days, autobiographical and also full of made-up stuff.

Work Song

My name is Henri. Listen. It's morning.
I pull my head from my scissors, I pull
the light bulb from my mouth — Boss comes at me
while I'm still blinking.
Pastes the pink slip on my collarbone.
It's OK, I say, I was a lazy worker, and I stole.
I wipe my feet on his skullcap on the way out.

I am Henri, mouth full of soda crackers.
I live in Toulouse, which is a piece of cardboard.
Summers the Mayor paints it blue, we fish in it.
Winters we skate on it. Children are always
drowning or falling through cracks. Parents are distraught
but get over it. It's easy to replace a child.
Like my parents' child, Henri.

I stuff my hands in my shoes
and crawl through the snow on all fours.
Animals fear me. I smell so good.
I have two sets of footprints, I confuse the police.
When I reach the highway I unzip my head.

I am a zipper. A paper cut.
I fed myself so many times
through the shredder I am confetti,
I am a ticker-tape parade, I am an astronaut
waving from my convertible at Henri.

Henri from Toulouse, is that you?
Why the unhappy face? I should shoot you
for spoiling my parade. Come on, man,

put yourself together! You want so much to die
that you don't want to die.

My name is Henri. I am Toulouse. I am scraps
of bleached parchment, I am the standing militia,
a quill, the Red Cross, I am the feather
in my cap, the Hebrew Testament, I am the World Court.
An electric fan blows
beneath my black robe. I am dignity itself.

I am an ice machine.
I am an alp.
I stuff myself in the refrigerator
wrapped in newsprint. With salt in my heart
I stay good for days.

Counting the Forests

We had little to work with. That was his plan.
He was out until daybreak or nightfall or until
the reappearance of his servant who had fled
to the mountains during the ice storm.
He was out; he was out and his voice
was gone too. We heard streetcars scraping
down the hill outside his room; we heard drills
pressing the walls of the blue quarry.

He was counting the forests. That was his plan.
He carried a sack of dried fish
prepared by his servant and cured
in sea-salt. His servant was near; he could hear
the rasp of his servant's breath.
His servant was making the vigil in a mountain
somewhere in the ice-country; and the ice-country was vast
and blue and full of death-forms. So was the forest.

Here in the red forest: a forest of birds.
Birds and dark water and looming red leaves
brushed with murmuring voices.
They swept towards him, the voices, like tensed wings.
And he ran from them; but the red
forest was glazed and the trees were vast
with ice-forms. And at the edge of the red forest
he could see into the stone forest and could see

the voices rinsing over the stone floor.
He had been there already and had taken count.
And he had counted the animal forest and the
smoldering forest and the weeping forest and the forest
of the forgotten tropics and the God-forest.
What could he say to his accusers?

He set out in darkness. In darkness
we waited at the corner of the forest
for his reappearance. So many forests!
Somewhere was a silent forest. Ice above, ice below.
Somewhere was a coldness with a rope in it
like a memory-braid or a pair of braids.

Triangle

If not for
the triangle accompanying
my newborn to
his father's mother's
scheduled excavation I
would have spilled
him mistakenly down
the banister where
I ought to
belong having squandered

my grip elemental
as my syntax
was. I soaked
my feet preemptively
in the salt
marsh while a
heron done symbolizing
tumbled toward grass
at low tide.
Then switching cadences I
fastened an additional set
of footprints in yellow
snow as though you
followed documenting our deeds
beneath the awning of
the pale green farmhouse
by the sea where
we did him in.
The three of us
made quite a pair
of anxious experts forcibly
removing his gills and
other primitive appendages like
feelers we pulled out.
Do I understand you
diverted onlookers with your
talents for song-speech?
Your meal lay wasting.
A horse would approach
you nuzzling wood chips
from this year's
tree or cadence
or memory-shrub.
We recall you.
As you were.
Of our making.

KAREN VOLKMAN | ALLEN GROSSMAN

Sonnet

I asked every flower I met
had they seen my palest friend.
The chant of the roots will beget
petals that blazon and bend

and erasable eyes to forget
the sun and the storm and the wind,
the sky which wheels in its net,
the black of the blurrest portend.

"We see in the sheerest clair
the nothing that vitals and vides.
No friend of your night and your debt

will blight our murmur with seeds
of the mortal flower, regret,
which roots in the arc of the air."

Although the paths lead into the forest, we are bitter with the bodies of days that end too early. All things tend to a darker dissolution. In a pond, the green flecks adrift, the ducks are dimming, murk preserving rust brine and the fish with a marl fin. We may be guided by grieved grass, the workless, mossy flesh, which tufts the dumb stones in their staunch sleep, awake.

Women who tend the brown days can only listen, it is this that quivers — the no-time, the nothing — which birds have swallowed like lucid beads of sight. If you dig in the earth with your fingers, with your stick, what to do with the blameless accruings? You strike lack. You slap the long oblivion of a blank alive with harm. If it is morning, why are we dying? There used to be so many stories we could sing, the tongue of luck, the dreamwork. And how the days fall like random raindrops, and leave no stain, beside the quiet streams where time is seeping, bone, blame.

And when the nights, the May nights, the moan nights, when they come. When they come, the wrong words will follow, glancing sorrow. My idiot Spring, with its hot heart and figures, the flowers lame laws in a weatherbane wind. Where is my silver harrow, my ore-waif strewing pierce-bits with every skip? (In one story, she plays the accordion on the Traumplatz, a tune, a veiny tune, that wouldn't please a monkey.) Where is my inkblot midnight, full of eyes? Yawn, I would say, gall-mouth, fertile fallow: a driblet, a teacup, a chalice, a reeking wave.

And when the morning, the bruise morning, the brine morning, when it *thens* — cracked alphabet of revelation — stitch and line — *then* the foot marries the forward, the fall the toward. Then the null and the next are cousins, in high-noon hammocks of incestuous list. Then what should I do with my waver, my very war, my sky-blue exigency, bloody with minutes? Which extremest west will swallow all this tending?

KV: I'd like to start by discussing one of your first ideas to influence me, one of your best known, which you discuss at the start of *Winter Conversations*: the poem as an act of "magnanimity toward the beloved," and the interactivity of the poem with the reader via this relationship. My generation of poets is much concerned, if not obsessed, with the instability of the lyric "I" and with the role of media in constructions of the self — how do these concerns complicate that relationship? In what sense can a mobile, mutable self affirm continuity and cohesion?

AG: Karen, I have before me your question and also your new poem beginning "One might start here." Your question asks how I can say (or can I still say, as I did say some years ago in a text called *Winter Conversations* — a text made in the '80s of the last century) that "a poem is an act of magnanimity toward the beloved." In my view *now, a poet can intend* only what I said then. Nothing has changed, even though the words of mine that drew your attention are old. I say to you, as you say in your new poem: "Kiss the question, it's your long lost sweetheart."

The "lyric I" you speak of (you say your generation is worried about it) does not exist. It is a recent academic fabrication which seems to allow a mistaken identification of the natural social person with the person who speaks in a poem. But the poet's "magnanimity" is funded by the fact you have forgotten: namely that the "I" who speaks in the poem is radically other than the "I" who makes a poem. The "I" who speaks in the poem is not personal and can (as a result) do the work of our humanity — express our "magnanimity toward the beloved" (teach and delight as Horace reminds: *aut prodesse, aut delectare*).

The lyric "I" beginning (let us say) with Sappho is a made thing on an ancient model. The media does not "complicate the relationship" — cannot possibly do so, is not on the same channel. There was never a natural self who was not, in your words "mobile, mutable." Indeed, why should your "generation of poets" think so? The American poets from Whitman to Crane (and before and beyond) were working at one magnanimous gift — a self with which the reader of poetry could ally and rise and cross over. The poem is "an act of magnanimity toward the beloved"— *the beloved,* not the beloved as a reader (or a maker-writer), but as a will that comes to poetry to participate in the self that poetry knows, which is not a natural "myself," but as you wonderfully write: "All quiet, all sweet, all needle-bright and bleeding."

KV: Okay, let me respond to all this. First, to clarify, I don't see the lyric "I" as a confusion with the poem's maker "I"— simply referring to it as the lyric "I" implies that it's a constructed thing, separate and separable from the poet, existing in, and largely created by, lyric conventions. The conflict comes with the imperative that this constructed "I" and its movements within the poem serve as a model for consciousness, and that it embody the new pressures and expansions brought to bear on consciousness in the age of media and mass culture. Your response seems to indicate either that you feel media has made no relevant alteration to our state of being in the world, so compels no adjustment to that ancient model, or that the model is in itself capacious and fluid enough to absorb such a change — or that it has no such obligation to reflect changes to our merely "social" selves.

There is also an increasing concern on the part of many poets over the last decades that this modeling has an ethical imperative to assert freedoms rather than affirming what can be viewed as a falsely consoling cohesiveness — instability, indeterminateness, lack of closure representing a consciousness in action, a model of the self as open, exploring, and dynamically engaged rather than a closed, determined model guarding its boundaries against contradiction and incursion. Maybe you feel you've already answered this, but my question is whether that ancient model of an "I" going back to Sappho can still exist within these altered terms, or whether the imperatives of this changed mode negate the possibility of that traditional "magnanimous gift," replacing it with some different, perhaps harsher form of magnanimity — whether such a model of consciousness can in fact console, or whether it prefers to provoke and trouble.

AG: This question of the relation of new media, which you bring up — by new media you mean something concrete, right? Television, etc.?

KV: Yes, and just the fact of media's ubiquity, constructions, received language, received words, and the part they play in forming the complex relations explored in current poetic making.

AG: And the question is, does that make a difference, and does that compel an adjustment to the ancient model. Okay, that's an interesting question. Now what you're asserting is that we live in a world that has brought about radical changes in what one calls a person, or a person's awareness of a person's self, and that this, you're proposing to me, compels an adjustment to the ancient model that poetry, for example in Sappho, or for that matter Shakespeare, implies. The alternative would be that that ancient model, you're saying, is in itself capacious and fluid enough to absorb such a change, or that it has no obligation to reflect those changes. Now what I think you are affirming in a way is that there is something about the present time which requires that one change one's conception of poetry, or that one indeed produce a poetry that is by its nature novel — and the nature of this novelty would be somehow a congruent response with the novelty of where we are culturally as a consequence of electronic and other instrument means of mediation.

There is no alternative to writing poems except as they have been written. Whatever goes on in the sophistication of mediations between persons in a post-electronic culture has made no difference. I do look at virtually all the poetry that comes across my desk — I see a lot of it — and I see no specific, viable or interesting response to electronic mediation. In fact, I don't think electronic mediation makes any difference to mediation; that is to say, whether I'm talking on the telephone or whether I'm related to the other by mechanical means doesn't seem to make any difference — it's the *same* conversation. If it is not, then I need to assert — I wish to assert, I wish urgently to assert — that I see nothing in the poetry printed, written today, admired, acknowledged, taught, that in any way responds to that state of affairs. If there is something different about the relation of the *I* and the *thou* and what can be said between them, then it has not registered itself in anything motile, linguistic. If we talk on the telephone it is still the same talk.

KV: I don't mean so much the phone . . .

AG: I understand. Then what specifically do you mean?

KV: Being, or at least feeling, a part — and a weak, helplessly programmable part — of mass culture, trapped within received narratives — which, for a poet, would certainly include the coded gestures and conventions of lyric and the relation to culture they imply. And what this increasing consciousness of being contained within and shaped by these structures (and strictures) does to the situation of the speaker within a poem.

AG: I think people live in the same relationship to one another whatever the novelty — if there is any — of the structures in which they come into relation. The most *extreme* deformations — concentration camps, the relationship between the man on one side of the rifle and the man in front of it, the possibility of explosions so enormous that whole cities can be destroyed — I don't know what else there would be. Now, there may be something deep in electronic culture about which I know nothing, but this would be expressed in some other way than language — and so long as we're talking subject-predicate, so long as we're addressing one another appositionally, so long as we have to call one another up, so long as it's a matter of translatability into sentences, it won't have changed.

KV: But I think it's a kind of horror for my generation that our private lives have been programmed by Hollywood, basically. And our private conversations and desires are in effect no longer private or personal.

AG: Well, that is something simply uninteresting. If it's been programmed by Hollywood, then the business is to work with that. But that has nothing to do with . . .

KV: Poetry has nothing to do with the fear that our most basic desires have been plotted and determined?

AG: Yes, nothing to do with that. Nothing to do with when you're in a satisfactory relationship with someone else — when you're making love, having serious conversation as we are now — is intruded upon by that. It may be that the movies are so persuasive that you or some others or your students have nothing to say but what they saw people say to one another in the movies, but that would not have been much different from what people saw one another say to each other in stage plays from the time of Sophocles on.

Indeed it is probable that Sophoclean drama and all other drama following it tended to make greater difference between, for example, common tragedy and comedy. Now it has often been said — and there would be nothing novel about this — that the reduced person in Aristotle, described as the comic person — which means the person in human scale — has been imposed upon us. What we have been deprived of is, in effect, tragic stature. But then our poetic tradition never really dealt in tragic stature, particularly in the lyric tradition. The lyric tradition was always a comic tradition, whether they were sad poems or happy poems — Shakespearean poems in their massive multiplicity of subject are a good example — it's all *speakable* and it can only be known as speakable. In other words, as long as we're doing poetry I think we are doing some mimesis of social language, which may be language internal to the self, it may be between selves, it may be between a self and a multitude, but it will be the same. And it is, it would seem to me, really a way of abandoning the issue to suppose that there is some difference we might find. I don't see it.

The thing that might come to mind is to really use the knowledge that sticks to poetry when describing the world that we now live in. There is no poetry of the Holocaust. I'm quite interested in that. The fact that everyone keeps trying to say something about the Holocaust — they can tell the story over and over again with greater and ever more terrifying documentation, but there is no motile shift in the communicative discourse. I think everyone who works with the Holocaust feels that there must be some way of recording it. The idea that the scream is the delineation of an expressive limit — and the question is, what lies on the other side of that expressive limit? The fact that we can do no more than to talk, to sing, to scream, to mutter — but we could do that in the fifth century BC. So your sense — which you and I ought to pay a lot of attention to, on your nomination — is in fact that the world that finally determines our lives is one which not only we but no one could incorporate, or the descriptions of that experience are not adequate.

Poetry now is subjected, as is all human discourse, to an urgency of which one law would be that we can blow up the world at the present time, and I think poetry has nothing to say to that. So one has to abandon one's idealism, one's sense that poetry is really important, because something else has become more important. I think it might be quite reasonable that what could be stated in tragedy was really important, was as it were the outer reach of what is really important, embraced everything that could be understood to be really important, responding to it — but at present tragedy has been disqualified. The end of the world will not look like that. The end of important lives or any lives don't look like that anymore.

So poetry becomes less interesting, less claiming of one's concern; it is probable that there is something now imaginable somehow that claims our concern that has no discourse. And was not this always true? I think it was not always true. I suspect we still, from moment to moment, live in a world in which indeed everything that happens is includable in discourse, but perhaps there is something that you are pointing to in poetry that has a heuristic that requires that it go one step farther. And maybe there's a kind of idealism of poetry that it is the discourse that goes one step farther — might that not be right? In other words, whatever goes on stage or whatever has been published in poetry down to the modern period is not to be cancelled — but your experience, or our experience, requires something else. And our enormous commitment to poetry, our sense and our admiration of poetry, a high indispensable admiration, seems to makes us want poetry to *be* something, and that I think is something radically the way it is. That is to say, poetry is not up to requirements. And you say, Oh this can't be true; we teach poetry because it offers truths about the world. Well, it may very well simply offer such truths as what are true. It seems to me very clear that if poetry has to be truthful about the world in which we now live, there is no such poetry. Or poetry can't be. So, about that, it seems to me you have to take, I have to take, a radical position — one does one's best to give an account of experience. But I think at present it is unlikely in poetry. There is a desuetude, something not completely right about the admiration for poetry at the present time. One teaches poetry, but one just teaches *poetry*. One has in the back of one's mind this sense that poetry is not as important as one thought because it does not touch the world. It may be just simply that we've come to the experience at the edge of the discourses we possess.

There is nothing that we do that has any significant reference to the world in which we live at present, if significant reference means crises which make the difference between yes and no, or existence and non-existence. Can you see what I'm saying? It's a much more radical problem than an engagement with the idea of poetry permits one to consider. Now you can say, well he's crazy, but my feeling is that anyone who really thinks that, rather than that the arts refer to the world in which we now live, will say, What's the difference? We live, we die, we love one another or we don't, and so forth. Well, there is a difference, and I think the difference encoded is just exactly what is encoded in our excess force, beyond the imaginable.

I'm very struck by the fact that it's not obvious to everybody that our languages — poetry being a language, prose being a language — just don't reach to the state of affairs in which we live. As I say, the Holocaust was terrifyingly indescribable. When one reflects upon it, one reaches simply the end of what one can say, and that might be taken as a point at which what occurs cannot be, one might say, *honorably* accommodated by discourse.

KV: Is this a kind of broadening and diffusion of "the nightmare of the shattered face" that you spoke of years ago?

AG: That might be what I mean. Somehow or other it seems to me some part of my consciousness that I carry with me out of some past, but I think part of the problem of finding ever more elegant accounts of what poetry does or can do, if one thinks hard — and I guess I'm vain enough to suppose that I do, at least in these matters — may be that, insofar as poetry is new knowledge, we've come to an end of it. Some professor might say to me, Doubt is new knowledge; there's no new knowledge. The oldest writers — the tragedians, the great comic and wise persons — they all knew about the world, and we've learned from them; my feeling has always been that we learn something from them. But insofar as we learn by our own experience, we do not learn *enough* from them to make us wise. So my poem about wisdom would be that it is something other than we thought. My last book of poetry will be about this matter of wisdom, which would have to be finally about the fact that wisdom simply is no longer wise. Or truth is no longer true. Not because falsehood is true, but because truth and falsehood don't make the difference. If I were to really write a poem that I thought were true, I don't know what it would be. That's what I'm trying to think about in my old age.

KV: This question of wisdom — whether it is still possible, what form it can take in a time of unstable meanings, in response to nuclear culture and the other extreme perils and terrors of our current situation — is one I am exploring in my new project, the book-length poem *Aurora*, which begins with "One might start here . . ." And it's a question I think of often in relation to your poems, in their acts of offering knowledge through multiple voicings of the dead and imagined as a magnanimous gift. I think this is a somewhat different, though related, concern than the one you characterized many years back as "the nightmare of the shattered face," but I wonder if there is a sense in which nightmare and shattering may be terms more relevant to our current state of being, which in my perhaps extreme view is one of psychic shock — the attempt to encompass an excessive degree or breadth of consciousness as an essential or necessary expressive risk. I've noted in your most recent work — including the poems of *Descartes' Loneliness* — a greater transparency and simplicity of statement than in the dark musicality of your earlier books — which seems a move away from the implosive inwardness that tends toward shattering, and a move instead toward a limpid exteriority as a gentler tendering of that magnanimous gift.

AG: On wisdom, I have a new poem responsive to your text, "One might start here."

KV: And a poem seems a wise close to our conversation.

Rain on a Still Pond

She's come. — Suddenly the room where I sit
feels emptier than before. If I look up now,
I will see her standing in the open door
gazing in toward me with her question.
And I am less because she's here, not more.

It is as when, on a summer afternoon,
raindrops begin to fall in utter silence
on a still pond. And a canoeist out there
lifts up his eyes and sees, looking at
the water, how water is falling into water.

A new solitude, until that moment
not known — it is the empty universe
of her voice — passes into my heart,
like water vanishing into water. She says,
"When you return to the shore, canoeist,

and are rested from your journey, remember me.
Among the histories of rain I linger to hear,
I linger to hear your answer to my question:
How do you merit to live so long?"
Then I say to her "*Dilectissima*, it is as when

the sky darkens imperceptibly and a wind
moves slowly, as great things do, high up in
trees at the shore, not yet touching the surface
of the still pond. And then one raindrop falls
on the still water, without sound, and makes a circle.

First one drop falls and makes a circle. Then
another, at a distance. The first circle is
larger than the second at the moment of
the appearance of the second, and lingers.
Then the pond is stricken by the third raindrop.

The second circle grows large. But the first
raindrop of the shower has disappeared.
A big wind descends upon the pond.
Time is told telling of our lives, each of us
appearing and disappearing." Once more

I hear her question. Or is it the wind.
"But how do you merit to live so long?"
And then she vanishes, water into water.
Turning from the door I sit alone
once more. But this time taught, as by a daughter.

"Warble," Says the Bird

"Warble," says the bird. "Waters are many."
"Warble," says the bird. "The light is one."
On the waters the light skips and prances,
but the east *is* the face to which we turn.

Wounded, wound, draped and thrown
over the thin scum of persons, living and dead,
is a low cloud of thought, birdsong in
the half-dark at the end of our time,

and, over that, the sower's scattering hand,
or the arc of the sower's shovel swinging low
above the threshing floor of ocean
where the seed reaches its end, and stops.

"Warble," says the bird. "Earth is not the only green.
The scum is green between the air and rock.
I say the east is a face to which I turn,
but sun without color is not the sun."

I Am That I AM

Better a deceiving god than no god at all.
This is experience in a certain mind
— not any mind — but one specific mind
with a particular history *like* yours
or mine, but other than yours and mine
— distinct, utterly unknown to both of us,
entirely other, and yet of the same kind
as your mind, or my mind, or any other.

Here we meet who are otherwise nothing
to one another, neither brother nor friend. . . .
Our minds wander off. — Look! This piece of wax
has not yet lost all taste of its honey.
It retains some odor of the wild flowers
from which it has been gathered by the bee.
It is hard. It is cold. It emits a sound
when stricken. It may be any shape.

But it remains still the same piece of wax.
No one denies that. And I perceive it.
It is *not accidental* to the mind
to be united to the body. Yet how
prone to errors my mind is. If I had
not now looked out the window and seen
a human being going by in the street,
I would not believe it emits a sound

when stricken. Yet I am. I exist. I have
a body which can act and also suffer.
As your highness is so clear-seeing, there
is no concealing anything from you.
— *You are not one of those who never philosophize.*
The piece of wax is moved toward the fire.
But the piece of wax remains, because
this wax is not perceived except by mind.

But my essence consists wholly in being
a thinking *thing*. Right now, in bed with Helene,
the natural light of reason makes known
to me what is to be known. So I say
"Helene! You are a pure spirit. You represent
truths such that they bear their evidence
on their face. As for me, I visit the butcher
to watch the slaughtering of cattle. There

I dissect the heads of the animals
to learn what imagination consists of."
— Francine lies beside me in her box. But
whether she sleeps or wakes I don't know.
"Francine! Here are my dreams. Pay attention,
Francine/machine The world is light, light-rays.
Love is a theory of light which intends light."
I know what I am for. But do I exist?

Although nothing imagined is true,
the power of imagining is real.
Certainly I *seem* to see. I seem
to hear. I seem to be warmed. To imagine
is nothing other than to contemplate
the image of a corporeal thing.
That is what you must assure me of. What
you are for. But you do not assure me.

SAWAKO NAKAYASU | CARLA HARRYMAN

9.19.2004
for Nada and Gary

Whenever I meet new people I want to touch them first and find out their texture. I do this in stores when I am shopping, too, so shopkeepers hate me. I turn to the person on my left and ask very gently if I can lick his or her eyeball. The food arrives and I place a slice of raw cow tongue in my mouth, because someone once told me that this is absolutely the sexiest food item in the world. If you like kissing cows. I get up to go use the restroom, but the person on my right, instead of moving out of the way, offers to me his or her arm, with a large gash from last week's motorcycle accident. There is an awkward moment, and then I sit back down so that I am more stable. I clean off my right hand before I touch, insert my finger inside and then further, some asshole at the other end of the table is making stupid sound effects, but in any case I am soon unaware of everything oh no everything at all, and if I were not myself at the moment I would probably have to avert my eyes, unable to watch as a certain virginity is lost, and then lost.

Texture of a conductor. Or rather this is more about density; let's say you press yourself up against your favorite conductor, take an analog thermal-image of his body and all the flesh there within contained, which carries the physical memory of every symphony every concerto, well every damn piece of music ever conducted by this body. No it is not muscle memory, this, but a memory of every single morning after, of birds making a choppy break for the imagined loosening threat of blue, of every score that took him down, killed him, of the joy that came from being nourished, not by food but by a mouthful, a bodyful of music, and cavities, yes you will feel each cavity in his body as well, an honest press and you will find yourself faced with the distractions of the give in his body, variable just like any other indeed, this very give being the real source of that thing called music otherwise known as love, as we continue to press and press up and press in, against those stolid firm and tender maestros in order to experience the give in our own tender bodies once we get past the daily commute. And when that conductor turns out to be not one of music but of trains, and his familiarity with a different sort of give in the body, as it finds itself faced with the pressure of a speeding vehicle or even that of an angry nation. Two days ago a man and his wife strung themselves from a tree, finding no other way to face down the unbending fact of their negligence.

6.21.2003

Danger as a texture.

Which appears first at the back of the mouth and I think about
swallowing, or the inability to swallow it away. A dark alley of the body.

Or was it a sound, danger music, and does the texture take its actual place
in the dark corridors of the ear.

Places that remain dark in the middle of any day. There are corridors, and
then there are refrigerator shelves. Fear of the kitchen. A cooked body.
How to rid boxes of darkness. How to wake up clean. How to rid a body
of its darkness. In order to step out. Into the bright and shiny danger
called day.

Dear Carla,

I just came across some of our older correspondence, which reminded me that our conversation goes back a number of years, and that besides having been an "influence" to me through your work, you've also been an important mentor, especially during times of uncertainty (and how uncertain I've been, at times!) — in between my bouts with formal education, leaving and returning to the U.S. (an ongoing process, apparently), and as I began to publish — all border-crossings of a sort. You were inspiring to me as an example of a writer who I found amidst the poets, inhabiting a terrain of literary art-making that felt wide open and juicily mingling with other arts and genres. It was exciting to have you (and the artists you referred me to, including Fiona Templeton, Guillermo Gómez-Peña, and Adrian Piper) as precedents, role models, and companions.

Dear Sawako,

I want to talk about all that you mention — writing, performance, collaboration, — but also to find a place to reestablish contact. I have the impulse to find a word or phrase or stanza or sentence from your current work to suggest or provoke a conversation, the context of which is yet to be determined.

Like you I've been traveling, even if differently, and perhaps this is also a potential topic of discussion. Is your traveling related to displacement, desire, difficulty, dancing, drastic circumstance, desultory, dice throws (throes?), dunno, divorce, divine prospects, doing the right thing, damned if you do and damned if you don't, drill, discount bookings, diving head first into god knows what? And so on ...

*Re: an instance in your current
work — how about a Steinian
moment:
More and more Needing Yellow
and the end result of an explosion, which is yellow or is it not
needed.*[1]

So, I'm very interested in the
range of your collaborative works
with musicians, visual artists,
theater, all of it, all of those intersections and communities —
"a colossal collaboration between people and nature was
underway."[2]

*

David Antin, 1976: "if robert
frost was a / poet i dont want to
be a poet if socrates was a poet /
ill consider it"
Sawako Nakayasu, 1995: "If Carla
Harryman is a poet, then maybe
I want to be a poet too."

(I think you've expressed elsewhere your ambivalence about
being called a "poet." This is
something that I've vaguely
struggled with, and might ask
you about later . . .)

*Ooo, flagellation, ma
Mulerie*[9]

Baby *was* good at collaborating
with nature, perhaps better than
I. There is so much to engage in
regarding ideas from outside.

Collaboration reprocesses "influence" as a dynamic something,
between and amongst people.

*Yes, dynamic. Collaboration:
reprocessing "influence" as well as
"dialogue," multi-directionally —*

*

I think I have always been a
"Language writer," or whatever
a Language poet would come to
be in respect to an approach to
writing in which the tension in
poetry between construction and
expression, materiality and embodiment, external and internal,
perception and category, narrative and non-narrative, genre

No, it's only that poetry had no identity, but experience sees innocence otherwise

*

Influence: I read your work, and then chose to study with you as an undergraduate at University of California, San Diego. Before that, I had studied poetry with Jerome Rothenberg and Rae Armantrout. It was in Rae's class that I first found you, via your poem called "Matter" in the Sun & Moon anthology *From the Other Side of the Century*.[3]

I am now looking at *Memory Play*,[4] which I am very drawn to, particularly as it might relate to *Baby*. It seems that people often write sets of books (trilogies, Silliman's *Alphabet*, etc.) and I like the idea of book-to-book conversations. There's a wonderful scene in a Godard film where a couple conduct an argument by thrusting books in each other's faces. But I feel like that kind of intertextual conversation (not always fighting, but communicating) is often happening in your work.

interrogation, and reflexive language and critique are paramount concerns of the work overall. This is of course an absurd statement. A "baby" wouldn't think these things.

So a baby wouldn't think these things, but would you say that a baby, or the concept of a baby, might enact these things? Or, do you see a child's frame of mind in approaching, exploring, discovering the world as having some connection to that of an artist or writer?

I do not privilege whatever one retains of "a child's frame of mind" as a special attribute of the writer, although this is a privilege that writers sometimes do claim. Yet, our understandings of childhood are partly formed by literature, and our understandings help shape the child, whatever their sources. As for Baby being a concept that enacts a critical relation to language: yes, this is partly the case. But Baby is not assigned a particular position within such criticality. She can be an object, subject, or porous medium. She can be a powerful observer, or a commentator, or a parrot.

Yes, that's so, the book to book
condensation

And that they accumulate atop
one another in a similar way:

> Baby knew that someday she
> would be a child and then a
> teenager and then an adult and
> that child, teenager, and adult
> would never be able to live
> without her. . . . Babies lived
> longer than anybody . . .

And that *Baby* seems to point
to both an accumulated wisdom just as much as the childhood state of being-knowing,
which seems to resonate with
the way *Memory Play* makes
memory both accumulative and
regenerative.

*

In The Grand Piano (Part 1),
you talk about your experience of
working at the American Poetry
Archive and the Poetry Center,
reading Robert Creeley, and then
a later experience of reading him
in Paris — and through what you
discovered in his work, you discov-
ered you were a writer:

What I find useful, though, is
thinking about the "baby-state"
as one that exists before the ac-
quisition of (socialized) gender,
language (which in Japanese is
quite genderized), and genre. Even
in college I was a little fuzzy as to
the distinctions between "genre"
and a "course title," (they both
seemed somewhat arbitrary), and
was exposed to hybrid (or what I
consider genre-less) texts by writers
like Samuel Beckett and Nathalie
Sarraute under a still different
category, "French literature." But if
I were to write in that pre-catego-
rization "baby-state," I might feel
more freedom in writing without
feeling or noticing the thickness of
the genre walls.

*

As for "then and there" perceiv-
ing myself as a writer in 1971 after
reading Creeley's *For Love* in
Paris, that's another story. I was a
writer "then and there," but that
doesn't mean I hadn't seen myself
as a writer before "then," even if
The Grand Piano entry might
give the impression that this was

Can a man poet of my generation imagine a woman reading this poem and loving this poem not because she identifies with it as an object but as the person who makes?[5]

I love how you say "person who makes," partly because it reminds me of the Japanese word *sakka*: person/family/house who makes. This word is used for artists and writers in general, an umbrella term that encompasses all the specific labels like poet, novelist, painter, etc. But I'm also interested in the fact that part of your "becoming" a writer involved this process of identifying with, or self-identifying as, the "person who makes" (in this case, "The Door"), instead of identifying with the poem itself. While much of the project of Language poetry challenges the notion of a closed authorship, I wonder if your relationship to theater, music, performance played a part in this kind of thinking as well. With writing, the collaboration is not nearly as explicit (and physically necessary) as it is with the performative arts. Did you feel like you were bringing these

an initial kind of self-recognition. But a subtle reading would perhaps indicate that the way I recognized Creeley's work was the way a writer would read it "then and there." That "then and there" is also an ironic extension of Creeley's "here now" poetics.

A sidebar to this would be that at that time in Paris I knew a poet (somewhat older than the very young me) who had experienced a terrible accident and consequently the loss of her fiancé who no longer cared for her after the trauma. The story as told to me was that his rejection of her caused a kind of breakdown and she became schizophrenic. Her family also was embarrassed by the indiscretion of her accident and injury and her having been jilted. They owned a small apartment on rue de Fleurus which may have been in the courtyard of Gertrude Stein's apartment, but maybe I'm making that part up: "then and there" are a bit fuzzy, in more senses than one. I feel confident that I know the story, or a version of the story, but do I know the place where I heard the story?

elements from elsewhere to writing, or that writing, as you saw it, inherently possessed these collaborative qualities?

*

But for now, I'd like to ask about your own beginnings, your "youth" (or even babyhood) as a writer: How, when, where did you become a writer, of what kind, and how did you turn into a writer of such various genres? What or who were some of your earlier influences? What were you reading, seeing, hearing, doing?

I'm a little envious of people who had early exposure to great poetry. But on the other hand, what I got instead was the foreignness of language (at age six), dinner table arguments about what certain words meant and how they were pronounced, and music — who knows how "influence" got played out, but my dad was always blasting opera in the house during the weekends. (I myself didn't learn to appreciate opera until a few years ago.)

*

Okay, so who were my influences? I was fascinated by (but really if one could say "fascinated in" that would be even closer) poetry as far back as I can remember. My mother had a few volumes of poetry; one was *Light and Humorous Verse* and I don't know if it included Blake's *Songs of Innocence and Experience* or if these were in another book. It definitely had poems by Lewis Carroll. I loved the Blake *Songs* and Emily Dickinson who was mysterious and difficult and some of the Shakespeare my mother would recite to me. (She'd do the "Out out brief candle life is but a walking shadow" monologue when she was trying to get us to exit the car, an army green Hudson.) At one point I memorized an awful poem by Arthur Guiterman called "The Legend of the First Cam-u-el."

Forgive me for quoting you again:
What calls itself a glimmer hoists itself slowly into my mouth, which wasn't even open.[6]

The desire, intention, will, ability, capacity to speak. At the specific time I was writing these "mouth"-pieces I was actually in intense pain, my jaw being clamped down by the pressure of impacted wisdom teeth. And yet all moments of writing are in some way a negotiation of my reluctance to speak through the open mouth, and the still-persistent and physical desire to say something that would or might be inappropriate otherwise. Propriety is big where I come from. Certain things are easier said in one language over another; my Japanese friend prefers to read Kant in English rather than Japanese translation. Another friend speaks to me in Japanese except to speak of love, in which case she switches to English. In English I have a potty mouth; in Japanese I have a higher-pitched voice. For most of my life I've spoken Japanese like a middle-aged woman because it was based on my mother's speech, my linguistic influence.

So when you talk about "baby-poet," that's what I think of. Although, I didn't literally think "I am a poet," in fact that was an impossible thought: poetry was poetry, not a poet writing. Shakespeare was poetry. Blake and Dickinson were poetry. And a poem was less an object than a particular manifestation of poetry. Writing and reading poems were completely connected even when I was writing something other than poetry. So I suppose this fascination "in" poetry develops into something else. The issue of poetry's object status becomes an object of fascination and interrogation for the later writer.

Right now I'm thinking of the first phrases of *Baby*, "These were words she would learn someday. She was fire in the womb with a skirt." "Baby," "she," and "poetry" could possibly each interpenetrate the other or, conversely, spring forth from the same linguistically animated place.

I want to play with this "baby-poet" thing a bit more and think about the question of genre, where writing in a sense is

*

And that paragraph continues, "Then a shirt which she pulled up through a small door that people on the other side called a cervical opening." I think that these phrases invoke Judith Butler's gender-as-performance, but also mark the baby-poet's arrival (though she is already present) in a context where gender acquisition and language acquisition happen simultaneously. When I look back on my own "baby-poet" days (let's say in my early twenties), it strikes me that writing poetry, in a way, allowed me to reacquire (or reinvent) my own gender and genre as something that had not previously existed for me. (Did I have a genre before I was writing?)

*

I used to believe that I "fell in" with poetry because whatever I was writing didn't quite look like a particular genre and that poetry, then, seemed to be the least "bounded" of genres — but perhaps I mistook "poetry" for "poets." (And then mistook "poets" for people like you . . . ?)

something less bounded by genre than what poetry as a genre (as opposed to poetry in the largest sense of the word) appears to be under the aegis of the conventions of poetics. Genre is destabilized in my writing for a constellation of reasons, including a mix of language experiences that would put me under a kind of spell: hearing and reading poetry; hearing people speak in artful ways, tell stories, preach. There were a lot of people in my family — grandparents, aunts, uncles — who had individuated, contrastive, and eccentric ways of communicating, and I was tuned into this: my Aunt Waneta's and father's tales of life in Oklahoma before and during the Dust Bowl, my grandfather Fox's melodious philosophical ruminations, my grandmother Fox's sociable conversation, my mother's concise analytical style of speech. I have retained this attunement to the styles of speech of my childhood. So this would be an example of the ways in which the aural intersects with the written.

I suspect there are just as many people who would say that I am a poet as those who would say that I am not. When my first book came out I felt strongly that it was "not poetry" (and hence should not say so on the back cover), but the publisher talked me into it by saying that this book could expand the range of what could be considered poetry. That isn't my aim exactly, and yet if something can't count as poetry, an already marginalized genre, that leaves even less of a space for work that doesn't neatly fit in — or conversely, more work to be done in making space for such things?

But perhaps I'd rather latch onto the "poetry in the largest sense of the word" idea, which allows me to consider: poetry-hockey, poetry-music, poetry-game, poetry as collaboration. My interest in hockey is almost not at all about the NHL, almost completely based in particular moments within the moment of play that suspiciously resemble moments of both reading and writing poetry. Poetry as sport. And hockey as improvisational performance.

But another influence would be Mr. Ball's high school history class. We studied twentieth century American history from a Marxist economic standpoint. What had a huge effect on me in terms of language was the dialectical logic of history this approach revealed. This interceded in the storytelling and fact-specific modes of learning history.

To begin again to answer your questions, it may be that this constellation of early influences, where analytic knowledge and aural experience meet in the psychologically and socially vivid spaces of the most immediate childhood environments, has a lot to do with the performativity of the writing.

Somehow, I think these instances add up as "baby-influences," and in discussing them here I have taken a somewhat different tactic than I have thus far in my *Grand Piano* entries, or even in other interviews. Yet if I were to name a corresponding teacher influence to those you mention it would be Ronald Sukenick, who I studied with my first two years of university at University of California,

The commonality is in a real-time processing of events and conditions and rules, and history and memory and skill and grace, and individual plus collective plus opposing forces. But poetry can also become physically manifest, in the visual, aural, respiratory sense. Of course it doesn't have to be hockey; it just happens to be so for me. I'm a terribly unathletic person in general, by the way.

And while I was linking hockey-as-game-as-poetry-as-sport, you had another take on "game" as being like "collaboration." This is from the first issue of *Factorial*, where I had published part of *The Games*, your collaborative project with the artist Amy Trachtenberg. In the comments at the end of the book, you (in a collaboratively written note) say:

> "To varying degrees and when taking the existing work as a whole, the mutual exploration of the game as a concept involves a fundamental engagement with pre-existing materials (idiom, artifact), chance events (imagination, accident, materials at hand), and indeterminate (unfixed and un-

Irvine. He not only pointed his students in the direction of the tradition of the avant-garde, new wave, postmodern fiction, Black Mountain and New York School poetry, but he also imparted method, in the most open-ended of ways. Method would have to do with the site where the present activity of writing, argument and analysis, psychology, and linguistic inventiveness become co-constitutive in writing acts. So here also is one of the early sites of the performative for me. But this truly would be only one initial site of the performative, which would eventually, I suppose, lead to the game. In going back to childhood, and situating "influence" there, the distinction between identifying with the poem and the person who makes it is almost not what's going on: a binary has yet to be vividly encountered.

And I wonder if somehow Kiriu Minashita's reference to "mediation" in her essay "Titles, Or the Conversion Plug of the *Anima*" [10] might not suggest something about how difficult it is to speak about identification with the poem-object versus identification with the "person who makes,"

categorizable) outcomes. The concept of 'game' and values of collaboration are closely linked in this ongoing work."[7]

*

And collaboration — this, too, seems to play a part in Language poetry's critique of authorial hierarchy, forging a social inter-action within the work itself. I know that you've worked on a great number of collaborative projects with people from all genres. Could I get you to talk more about your processes in collaboration? What are some of the physical and intellectual pro-cesses involved? How do they get initiated?

With the exception of *The Wide Road* with Lyn Hejinian, it seems that most of your collaborations that I know of are with artists in other genres rather than with other writers. Am I just not aware of this work?

when one approaches the prob-lem of naming and titling from a critical perspective. The "person who makes" is in a sense a con-cept, one carefully chosen to in-terject a critique into the question of identification with the poem: the poem in the case of "The Door" is hyper-masculinist; I cannot identify with the content of the poem. Disidentification in this case may become a feature of the not-spoken in Minashita's sense. Disidentification may seem like a very specific response, but it leads to the softening "of the hardened social," in the words of Rodrigo Toscano, if one doesn't simply stick oneself with it.

But I leave it to you to let me know if it is possible to apply her use of "mediation" in this way, or is this association strained? By the way, your volume of transla-tions *Four from Japan* is an amaz-ing book and I'm quite excited to talk to you a lot more about your encounters with Japanese poets and poetry.

I wonder if, even within the realm of your own, single-author writing there is a different kind of collaboration (meta-collaboration?) being suggested. In the poem "Matter" you write: "Love was alone with love. And there was nothing I could do about it."[8] Or more recently, in *Baby*, how the baby and teenager and adult are one: "She would always be part of them. And each one now also had a baby in him or her."

So then the collaboration might be one of perception, a collaboratively perceived universe, or of characters (not limited to humans) at play with each other within your work?

Additionally, I am thinking about your poem "Force" in your forthcoming collection *Hurry Home Honey* and particularly the lines:

> To enter a room or make room
> In a mouth or to mouth

Is it okay to leave it here for now and to simply open the conversation-mouth to you at this point without suggesting further direction?

Dear Sawako,

Collaboration can be a marvelously additive *and* subtractive activity. There are so many agendas for collaboration, and perhaps that consideration has made me a bit slow in responding to the questions you've posed about my engagement with it. The interpersonal aspect of collaboration can be (although it isn't always) its most seductive and pleasurable feature. When one is privileged enough to engage with another's (or others') process and mentality, one's sense of the world becomes transitional: one can actively see the way one accepts or doesn't accept change and new information, or any information that is or is not similar to that which one drifts toward in one's own practice. The collaborator(s) and the emergent work (text, theater piece, image text, sound text) make appear some of those things that one senses may appear but can never get to on one's own. This is rather odd, because in saying this I'm not thinking of individual works as completed things, but rather I'm thinking about the additive processes that make things appear for the collaborators within a work's development.

The subtractive aspect of this has to do with the sense that something else beyond or other than what one can do on one's own has appeared, is appearing. "It" has vacated the frightening mass of hidden potential of reality and imagination. It has left the thickness of such a world a little less overwhelming to the mind.

You know I was wondering about your interest in what you call "potty" words and the bicultural content of your use of them, although what I'm remembering right now is more your use of vomit, snot, swallowing, eating — visceral rather than necessarily potty. In any case, when I think of your use of such words, whether they be vomit or shit, it is as if the body has announced itself in a surprising manner. Conventionally one might associate visceral words with convulsive writing, or self-fascination, or revulsion — but you have a comical treatment of language which I associate with a style of drawing, a kind of spare line drawing. Although the total effect of your works is not comparable to drawing, but rather, again, something more performative, laid out, shifting, mirror-like, and layered. I think of the early work you did in my class and your interest in sports, dance, rules, layouts, plans, shifting formations — and also the relationalities that constitute such formations.

In fact, your thinking about space, activity, formation, and perspective seems to inform the way you've formatted our conversation. Even as you were inspired by Lyn Hejinian's and my approach to the last section of *The Wide Road* to lay out the conversation this way, you use the parallel form quite differently than Lyn and I, because of the white space and the playful way you place our words in relationship to one another. I was surprised by the effect — it really started to take on qualities I associate with your work — as if words and strategies and persons were gliding around on a surface meant to support their glides.

Love,
Carla

Which reminds me of a whole other subject I wanted to bring up, the intersections between the actualities of domestic life (marriage, children) and your writing life. How do your various identities inform your work?

Or rather, I've always been interested in the feminism of your work, and how it shifts the conversation back toward underlying issues, an inherited hierarchy of literary values. These issues were important to me in my early twenties as I was coming to age as an adult and as a writer, but now as I begin to notice marriage, children, and parenting on the imminent horizon, I am also faced with an inherited hierarchy of social values which ask to be questioned.

Note: I am assuming that "inherited hierarchy" here has to do with the position of women within gender-based and class-based traditions? What are the features of the bicultural overlay you find most challenging or difficult to question? Does your interrogation of the hierarchy of literary values in any way affect how you think about the hierarchy of social values?

I'm going to pick up on the beginning of your last letter and try to say something about actualities of domestic life and writing life. I seem to know quite a few women writers grappling with childbearing and rearing at the moment. For many, the actualities entailed are domestic, writing, and job(s) — that's how it has always been for me. However, what you are asking is not how do you do it (which is a frequently asked question) but how do your "various identities inform" the writing. Now that's an interesting and challenging question, one that my thoughts immediately skirt around. A little voice in my head says "it's not about identity." And then the next thing I think is "interpellation." Why?

Interpellate ← Appellate One of the first things I learned in French: Comment t'appelle-tu? Je m'appelle Sawako . . . What do I call myself?

I was six and we had moved to the U.S. and no one could pronounce my name — perhaps this was my first instance of being

It's easier for me to interrogate certain hierarchies in literary values, because those in my immediate general public (outside of certain communities of writers and artists) are uninterested in what I do artistically. But if I were to live out my personal and social life to the same degree (as much as they can be compared) of experimentation, weirdness, and eschewal of tradition, I would probably have a hard time getting along with many of my friends, family members, and coworkers (sometimes I do). In Japan it's worse: my "values" as a Japanese woman are far from the norm; my femininity itself is probably much more American than Japanese. Similarly, as soon as I write a "story" or a "play" I am subject to the reader's expectations of a story or play. But I love the sensation of being in an airplane across the Pacific: I may have a very specific seat on the plane (23A), but I am culturally and linguistically *nowhere* — which is perhaps a state I am able to replicate in writing.

*

"interpellated"(correct me if I'm wrong), when my name got Americanized: "sa-WAH-ko." Soon enough I was introducing myself as "sa-WAH-ko," too.

*

It was not long ago that the representation of the domestic sphere in literature was largely demeaned. Yet, we can see today that it is a profoundly political work, one that observes the oppressive smallness of the world for many ordinary people while it also illuminates "the big picture" from the perspective of a discrete sensibility.

*

Between such history and this moment and its practicalities where/how do you see yourself? I would love to hear more about what's behind your question, what you imagine, don't imagine, foresee, can't foresee. My life situation typically has a bearing on my writing. This doesn't mean the writing reflects the situation, but that it influences how I go about writing what I write. My

While in Japan I tried to read up on some Japanese literature, especially poetry by women. In the 1980s, Hiromi Ito, although heavily criticized for some of the shock-value effects of her work, broke a lot of ground in bringing explicitly female content (of childbirth and motherhood), much of it eroticized, into the contemporary poetry mix. She also wrote unabashedly about taboo subjects such as infanticide and masturbation. Ito's work was heavily grounded in her own readings of Cixous and Kristeva, and it carved the way for a whole wave of younger Japanese women to explore such issues. Yosano Akiko is well-known as the original feminist poet from the turn of the twentieth century, but as the Japanese literary canon undergoes yet another round of revision, it seems that they are now beginning to seriously consider the importance of poets, such as Chika Sagawa, whose contributions as women move beyond what was or is easily recognizable as "women's poetry." Whereas it used to be that one could only be lauded for, or ignored because of, their femininity, it seems that the conversation is opening up to include more possibilities now.

most recent book-length poem, *Open Box*[12], is a good example. The U.S. was about to invade Iraq. Like so many, I was enraged, flummoxed, politically active, and sometimes speechless. I had to stop listening to the car radio and the news because, like others who had the same response, I was literally incapacitated by the banality and lies we were being subjected to by mainstream media. Often, I found that music was the only thing coming from a box that communicated anything real to me, and I listened to music a lot. *Open Box* was written in this context in which listening to music gave me access to listening to the poem as it developed. And I was able to connect the immediate sense of living and listening in an open way with political, intellectual, and aesthetic concerns and engagements. *Open Box* would not have been written if the U.S. had not invaded Iraq. Of course contingency is in general important to what gets written. *Open Box* as a work emphasizes this in its four-line irregular stanzas and the way the predictability of the form is undercut by the unpredictability of the improvised moves made in the writing.

It would be interesting to have a discussion (but maybe some other day) on the impact that writers such as Kristeva and Cixous had on Japanese and Americans, comparatively, in the 1980s. I often think of American feminism within the traditions of innovative writing to be somewhat aversive to the French theorists of this period — although the use of Kristeva's formulation of the semiotic was pervasive. And as Rachel Blau duPlessis states in an interview:

> *Some of the most fruitful moments of women poets' exchanges on these issues came during the twenty-plus years from the 1980s to the present under the rubric of "innovative." American writers who come to mind whose works directly engaged Cixous and Kristeva in the 80's include the poet Beverly Dahlen and the novelist Kathy Acker.*[11]

*

So you see, I see writing and living as vividly contingent.

*

Open Box worked with a constraint that required an instantaneous response on the part of the writer to the lines — there was almost no editing. Both novels, *The Words: After Carl Sandburg's Rootabaga Stories and Jean-Paul Sartre*[13] and *Gardener of Stars*[14], are based on various improvisational strategies — from the performative monologue in *Gardener* to the use of repetition in *The Words*, in which repetition has to do with listening to "the invention" that precedes it. The works by no means devote themselves to these single strategies; these are just examples. I would consider some of the games to be based in structured improvisation as well. Sometimes a structure is a concept, or involved in some kind of instruction like "make up a board game now." Or "imagine a theory of social action that entails imperceptible or barely perceptible actions, then make it up on the spot."

What you say about *Open Box* — about music being able to communicate something real — makes me also feel a parallel in children, that for better or worse they are often more capable of communicating openly and honestly than "adults." And in fact, the cover of *Baby* (created by your son) features an open box on it,

> Such that the box is equally present
> From the perspective of any
> Side and its open
> Distance

These "improvised moves" you made in the writing of *Open Box* — would you say that they borrowed from improvised music or dance in terms of compositional approach? Normally I tend to think of your work as precisely controlled and finely tuned, but I would love to hear what "improvised writing" means to you.

*

Or even before "mother," what if the genre is "woman"? The genre changes somewhat from country to country, and if I am in a foreign country, I take on "foreign" in addition to being "woman,"

And now to return to the question of identity:

In a sense I take your extension of the use of this word into the quotidian of public / private life frames as entailing a kind of politics that assumes the social subject as one with a multiplicity of identities.

One assumes these labels *and* makes a relationship to them. If one has a child, one is immediately turned into something like a genre, so for the fun of it let's call it that. The genre is "mother," or "parent," or "father," though "mother" carries with it often oppressive assumptions that "father" counters. Therefore, even though I have embraced this description wholeheartedly within the society of my friends, I resist it to some degree in larger social contexts. This does not mean that I hide that I am a parent, not at all, but rather that I don't go along unquestioningly with the role assigned to me as a mother in certain specific situations that I encounter. I am now the parent of an adult, but I did not and

and the force with which the labels are imposed gets mitigated by the new addition.

Wanting to exist, and write, in hybrid states, hybrid genres . . .

I am reminded here of your translation in English (from the French I presume?) of Ryoko Sekiguchi, the Japanese poet who lives in France, writes in Japanese, and sometimes translates her books into French. Do you converse with her?

I got to meet her for the first time last fall when we had the Japanese poets in New York for a Belladonna/Litmus Press event. When she read her work from *Heliotropes*, the audience received it in three languages all at once: Ryoko herself read in a fluid combination of Japanese and French, while Tracy Grinnell read the English translation (which was translated from French by Cole Swensen).

would not become obedient to expectations of what a mother should do, unless I need to for some reason involving the well-being of the child. That said, this latter circumstance, the well-being of the child, is always a caveat and entails negotiation with others, which can be very difficult as well as pleasurable and illuminating.

If you have a family in the United States, part of your encounter with parenthood involves living in a country that by and large hates children. What I am talking about here is the state/nation, which is a different mechanism in many regards than the communal relations we are part of in daily life, but the state does affect those relations and sometimes quite significantly. For instance, when a child is having trouble in school (let's imagine it as public school at the moment), often blame starts to be cast around. Sometimes single parents or divorces in families or unconventional family situations are blamed for the child's problems. Or in turn, the teacher or the school is blamed. Or the parent is identified as overbearing, or

There's a comment she makes in her statement of poetics, "Self Translation, or the Artifice of Constraint," in Four from Japan. In it she states, "One must consider that a subordinate translation is not being made, but that two versions with the same status are." Hybrid writing often engages questions of subordination, sometimes by a critical refusal to subordinate. I see this query in regards to resistance to subordination in your translation work, the way you devise the literal as well as linguistic spaces of your Factorial *journal. For instance, you'll place a sequence of writings in English next to an untranslated sequence of works in Japanese. Also in respect to your own writing, I think about your interest in "game," again literal and figural and linguistic, and certain properties of games including rules, outcomes, and what occurs between rules and outcomes. These would have a rather mingled status within the "play" of your writing. Yes?*

Yes! I love all the connotations of the word "play." There is so much joy, theater, flexibility, chance,

accused of being a parent who doesn't care about the child. There is often no time for the teacher to truly understand the actual circumstances of the children. The school is under-funded; class sizes are too big; teacher training is an educational weak link. Regardless of the headlines and news reports, very little has been done economically, analytically, educationally to offer children a reasonable childhood when they are at school. Note that in today's *New York Times* it was reported that No Child Left Behind policy allows states to set their own goals for percentage of high school graduates. Three states have goals of fifty percent! The majority seem to have goals between sixty and ninety percent. I believe California's goal is sixty percent, an outrage. When one becomes a parent, the details of this outrage become palpable. It goes without saying but still I feel I must say it, behind this is economic interests and policies that support the economic greed of the private sector.

If one is in a relatively privileged situation, whether that is due to economic privilege or a solid

imagination, and uncertainty (thus possibility) loaded in it, and it is, essentially, while much less result-oriented than most other pursuits, enough in itself. My interest in hybrid writing overlaps with my interest in the process and practice (and of course results) of translation, as well as my inclination toward "game" — which includes a bias toward process over product. "Game" is interesting partly because the very interest in "product" (often, winning) can lead the "process" to be engaging and ever-changing. *Factorial*, too, while it is a "product" of editing (though I am unsure of what it meant to "win"), has shifted focus over the years from collaboration to translation, and I am now thinking about making an issue featuring the notes, cribs, ponies, drafts, and questions produced in the process of translation.

Also the issue of subordination Sekiguchi brings up is similarly a concern of mine in regards to the bilingual performances I've been doing using German and French, variously. Although I use translated text, the performances are not presented as a translation

community or beneficial cosmopolitan circumstance, then sometimes it is possible to send your child to a school that satisfies their interests in learning, offers a solid educational foundation, and creates meaningful community. But these good situations are always compromised by the absolutely unacceptable conditions of education for many. That I have a child who has what would be considered an exceptional and even "elite" education is an unacceptable fact. Don't let me get started.

So the child is paramount: your whole being vibrates to the new and the young life to which you are also responsible. The love of the child is also a challenge to certain notions of identity — at its base, love for a child has no identity, but it reforms one's entire relationship to the world. Having a child initiates a shift in consciousness (in both parents, but differently in each) that changes everything and that entails, sadly, an initiation into repressive conventions and institutional norms and the failures of social and cultural imagination in the most vivid way. This is why "identity"

of English into another language. People interleave the languages. This means that both performers and audience are focusing on a diversity of features of language and sound, from semantic meaning, to rhythm, to noise. This stresses the activity of listening while replacing or displacing dramatic action (another system of subordination).

I didn't know you had done this — it's something I've been exploring as well. I was in Japan when my first book came out, and had some opportunities to read/perform, though I felt awkward about reading an unconventional text in English to a primarily Japanese-speaking audience. So I started playing with a form of half-improvised simultaneous self-translation/interpretation kind of reading. The original intent was to give the Japanese audience some kind of foothold or point of access, but I started doing this in the U.S., too, and grew more interested in the continuum between the languages: that English/Japanese wasn't either/or, but between vocabulary, homophones, accents, syntax, and rhyme, they comprised a much larger continuum of in-between ground. Again, a lot

is somehow so inadequate to what actually occurs at the intersection between "domestic" life and society's interpellations of "child," "mother," "father." From this perspective, identity is less something one owns than something imposed on oneself and others. From a literary perspective, Denise Riley's *The Words of Selves* is a wonderful source for such considerations.

I imagine you are aware that much of my work dating back to the mid-eighties is entwined in considerations of childhood. These works would include *Vice*[15], *Memory Play, The Words: After Carl Sandburg's Rootabaga Stories and Jean-Paul Sartre, Gardener of Stars, Baby*, and several essays. *Vice* was written in the first year of Asa's life, and writing a book in that year opened up a new writing space for me, one that engaged the irregular temporality of being a young mother with a job. I was working at the University Art Museum in Berkeley. Sometimes I would just close my office door, leaf through a Sotheby's catalog, and start jamming on the typewriter or in a notebook. I also used office

of "play" in there. When Bill Berkson came to Tokyo he gave a reading at the Yotsuya Art Studium, an institution that I see as an experiment in the "art school" genre. His poems were translated, interpreted, read bilingually or as simultaneous bilingual interpretation, and the whole thing was quite interesting — and something I would like to explore further, as I continue to live and write in both cultures and languages.

(Also, some Japanese rap will rhyme English words with Japanese words. And students who attend international schools in Tokyo often speak a hybrid language with each other.)

A visual analogy to such a listening experience would be in the example I gave of your Factorial *editing. The graphic qualities of the Japanese works and the visual forms of the poems, some of which look conventional and others which look similar to concrete poetry, stand out to a non-Japanese speaker such as myself in the way verbal sound might stand out to a*

memos, postcard images, radio news, and whatever I was reading (always in fits and starts) to generate material. This is not an extremely illuminating description of process, but the important aspect of it was that I used anything at hand to write whenever I could write. And that activity, combined with the urgent experience of time, of having time or stealing time, had consequences — including that I wrote a longer work, one that, through improvisatory tactics, constructed a new way of working with fragmentation and duration.

You've written elsewhere about how this country hates children. I also think I remember hearing or reading somewhere that your interest in games arose out of a dissatisfaction with the games that were generally available for American children. I don't know if they are available in collected format but what I know to be your "games" pieces — beginning with pieces like "Matter" — were striking to me because they presented the game as an abstractable, universal concept. I found it useful to think

*non-German speaker in one of
my bilingual plays. Thus difference engages the reader/audience
emphatically but not within a
structure of subordination. Does
this make sense?*

Yes — or, it goes back to Ryoko's
quote about avoiding a "subordinate translation," which you created in the bilingual performative
space. Which makes me think
about the possibilities of a work
to resist this kind of subordination in multiple planes at once:
interpretation being subordinate
to translation, improvisation to
composition, process to product.

*of us as players in a game, bound
and not bound to the rules of the
game, with some defined objectives
as well as surprises in the process.
American education is a poorly
designed game, but the greater
picture of parenthood has so much
potential.*

Yes, and the revelations of parenthood in combination with
the fresh encounters with social
negativity give one a lot to think
about and to rethink in respect to
writing, in my experience. For instance, and very quickly as I feel
I really must end, I have always
been interested in the subject
of "mimesis," but when I had a
child and I began to perceive the
mimetic inventions of the child, a
whole world of wonder and question opened to me. *Baby* testifies
to this.

Dear Sawako,

You have asked me several times about performance and collaboration,
and I haven't answered some of the more specific questions. I have col-
laborated with quite a few visual artists, musicians, and writers. Lyn
Hejinian and I have yet to finish our novel *The Wide Road*, a book we
have a complete draft of but that needs revision. We began with an idea
that we would go on an erotic journey, modeling our excursion very

loosely after Basho's *A Narrow Road to the Deep North*, but of course this reference is also comedic, if not satirical. The work was largely written through the mail. We would add onto the piece, then send it off — even as at the time we were living only a mile from one another. Sometimes we would do readings from it and, in order to make sure our audience wouldn't be able to tell who wrote what, we would rearrange some of the text. Then, the work has also incorporated these performance-oriented decisions. Someday, we really do have to finish it. I have also through the years, though not too recently, done collaborations with Steve Benson, some of them quite ephemeral. A favorite, however, was also written partly through the mail. Steve had just returned from Mexico and, although he was in Oakland, he and I exchanged letters as if he were still there. The collaboration, "Dialogue: Museo de Antropología, Mexico" discusses travel — and this brings me back to another theme I'd like to hear about from you. But for now I'll leave you with a passage:

> SB: I think when you're home you feel like you have more say over what temperature you subsist in, so that you exercise your preferences, you make adjustments in your circumstances. You can feel and consider the relative merits of various temperatures and fictionalize yourself within them. But when you're on the road, your disguise repertoire isn't so complex, you submit to circumstances without making them up, you assume they're more powerful than you are, they have a more imposing charisma than you. Am I right?

> CH: When I'm traveling, everything that makes a striking impression on me seems to have, not a symbolic value or the implication of an omen, but . . . it seems to open a door through which I disappear, so that keeping tabs on myself becomes a matter of remembering what I would think in an emergency — an emergency of confrontation.

> SB: But how do you ever remember? Do you write it down?

> CH: I can't say. Somebody who didn't know me very well might say that I make it up afterwards. I don't remember writing anything down.[16]

So that's the extract, and I can say a bit more about collaboration in more than one medium the next time.

Yours,
Carla

* * *

Dear Carla,

I love the way Steve frames "what temperature you subsist in" — a more elegant way to frame my own rough variation on the theme, that when I travel, my foreignness trumps my gender. Which means that in France, I felt more "foreign" than I felt "woman," which bought me a certain freedom, whereas in Tokyo, where I look and talk like enough of a Japanese woman, it was too easy for everyone to expect me to behave according to feminine norms and ideals. I envied the "true" foreigners, who were excused from social expectations (though at the cost of some exclusion, too), and I felt tempted to shave my head again, though I haven't done that since I was twenty-two.

But perhaps this is a different kind of travel. I've lived in many places in my life, and have traveled fairly extensively too. Another distinction I would like to blur: I like to take long enough trips that they might border on living there, one or two months, or longer if possible. My parents lived in the U.S. for twenty-something years and then just packed up and "went home," back to Japan — apparently it was their intention all the time, as if these years in the U.S. were just another long trip.

* * *

Dear Sawako,

I'm interested in how your experience of trips that "might border on living there" as well as the problem of interpellation affect your writing. Both physical movement and travel seem to be sites of social gathering, of desire, and of comical concatenations related to displacement. At least that's what I think when I read these lines from *nothing fictional but the accuracy or arrangement (she*:

pulls a family and a barbeque on the the back of a motorcycle,
why not why not have a family and move around a little too,
to be here, a queue here, a speed, oh lovely breeze[17]

Speaking of displacement, when Steve and I wrote our dialogue, he was
in Mexico for quite a number of months and I was home in Berkeley,
California, attempting to make a living and be a parent. I quote Asa at
some point saying, "Mommy when I was in your tummy it was dark and
white." The "tummy" becomes another virtual museum, like the museum
of our exchange, the one that Steve actually visited and the one "we" pre-
tended we were touring in our exchange of letters. This pretense is laid
bare, it's as if we're doing a magic show that exposes how all the magic
tricks are performed, so there's no illusion that we're traveling together
in Mexico. This then shifts the meaning of travel to a different register
in which writing is an entailment. In displacing a museum scene that
includes artifact and cultural context I say, "No matter how determinedly
my thought/breathed lived words are poured into this object, this writing, what I make is not me and the words are not exactly mine either.
This writing is separate, banal, and more than me. Through its condensation of information, of words, it can communicate more than I can speak.
And yet it is dull, indistinct, a speck absorbed into culture."

When Steve returned from Mexico to Berkeley, we edited the work by
editing and revising each other's sections, and then editing and revising
our own. So the piece in that sense messes with identity. C and S are and
are not C and S. Here's another snippet from "Dialogue":

CH: The marvel of travel is it reduces one's ability to view anything
else as strange, since oneself is the stranger. I think you're right about
seriousness — that we look for its cues in the other. It also might be
thought of as a value-neutral state of finding one's way with an un-
cluttered use of one's intelligence. An intelligence that's not used to
please but to do research without a dependence on effect. It is good to
be left with little. If I were home right now, I would be distracted by
questions such as, do I need to add more soil to the flower bed? Was it
that I tired before finishing? How much experience must I have to be
confident of what I've produced? Will my labor be wasted? Oh, good.
You've returned.

SB: Yes.

CH: Well, what I've been wanting to ask you is this: what use is there for you in "ruining" the places you're in by finding your way through them? Once again I've returned to this fascinating identification with destruction that you carry . . .

SB: . . . This harrowing of the world may be a key pivotal factor in my "identification," as you put it, (not to mention my "fascination") with the world. Maybe it's my yearning or clinging to an obsolete identification with the world, a resistance to splitting with off, that mobilizes this will toward "destruction." To identify with the "other" becomes, given knowledge or experience, a violation of its nature, its "otherness," no? To "come into contact" with it I think I have to release myself from this will to identify, and perhaps to destroy, and I have to accept a limit — my fascination has been all too much with the relentless and hypnotic dance of my efforts to assimilate and contravene the other through interpretation.

The form of the façade of the temple seems to be a face, like a giant Moloch, bodiless. Inside it's dark and plain; there aren't any paintings in this reproduction — or, I forget, is it real, imported? Imagine a tiger tearing through these woods. Are there tigers in the Yucatan?
    Is it ever safe?
    As you are interested in hearing about other kinds of collaboration, I'm now trying to think of a good segue to an example. In performance I like to resist the use of mise-en-scène and props as illustration or static interpretation of text. Thus when I work with visual artists, as well as with musicians, I prefer to spend a lot of time with them at rehearsals so that everybody involved is responding to the particular performance situation, the performance environment itself, and to the textual language. Everybody in a sense participates in improvisation that resolves in performance. This is the ideal situation in any case; there are many variations depending on the actual performance situation. When I was asked to do an exhibition as a writer responding to the permanent collection of the Cranbrook Art Museum, I wanted to avoid illustration as well. I was not interested in constructing a coffee-table book on the museum wall, with

text situated side by side with visual works "speaking" to them. With the help of the museum I was able to enlist a wonderful designer, Peter Hill. I had decided that I would use obvious rather than obscure objects from the museum and chose their modern chair collection. I rendered the shadows of the chairs cast onto walls on butcher block paper, then variously composed language sometimes on the gigantic sheets of paper and sometimes on the computer that would then become the chairs' shadows. I also interviewed high school students from Cranbrook about the famous dining hall chairs they still use there, and composed pieces with their words — so another aspect of the collaboration involved site-related interviews. Once I had composed the works that were to become the flat-surfaced chair shadows applied to the walls, Peter worked on the word-chair design. Thus much of the collaboration was based on conversation around a concept that I already had in mind. It was really a wonderful process, but it's a bit different than ensemble work where the performance itself is more collectively realized, even if the text in a sense serves as a foundation, just as the shadow-chair concept was the foundation for Chairs of Words.

I'm looking forward to your responses to any of this.
Carla

* * *

Dear Carla,

The "identification" and consequent destruction-violation that Steve refers to seem to resonate with forms of cultural appropriation, itself a form of travel, travel through art. But not all "travel" leads to identification; there is probably a level of empathy which comes before that — and this empathy, in art and writing, would feel closer to collaboration and improvisation. By being implicated in the making of your performance, the "otherness" between writer and performer (traveler and local) gets diminished; a group improvisation is necessarily empathetic.

(On the other hand, what do I, as a relatively-Japanese writer, think about Basho being a loose model for *The Wide Road*? What is contained or implied in this *wideness*, as opposed to Basho's narrow path? And what is the difference between explicitly framing the books in relation to each other, versus implicitly (silently) regarding something as "influence"?)

And then, going back to collaboration: your descriptions of various projects, and especially your blending of composition and improvisation, lead me to another distinction I am interested in blurring: that between translation (composition) and interpretation (improvisation). But perhaps this is a conversation to save for later, before we get carried away on yet another topic . . .

Yours, fondly,
Sawako

Notes

1. Sawako Nakayasu, *Texture Notes* (forthcoming from Chicago: Letter Machine Editions, 2009).

2. Carla Harryman, *Baby* (New York: Adventures in Poetry, 2005).

3. Douglas Messerli, ed., *From the Other Side of the Century: A New American Poetry 1960-1990* (Los Angeles: Sun & Moon Press, 1994).

4. Carla Harryman, *Memory Play* (Oakland, CA: O Books, 1994).

5. Steve Benson, Carla Harryman, Lyn Hejinian, Barrett Watten, Kit Robinson, Tom Mandel, Rae Armantrout, and Bob Perelman, *The Grand Piano: An Experiment in Collective Autobiography, San Francisco, 1975-1980* (Detroit: Mode A/This Press, 2007).

6. Sawako Nakayasu, *Hurry Home Honey* (forthcoming from Burning Deck, 2009).

7. Sawako Nakayasu, Mark Tardi, and Sarah Ruhl, eds., *One Factorial* (San Diego: Factorial Press, 2002).

8. Carla Harryman, *There Never Was a Rose without a Thorn* (San Francisco: City Lights Publishers, 1995).

9. Carla Harryman, *Toujours l'epine est sous la rose*, trans. Martin Richet (Paris: Ikko, 2006).

10. Kiriu Minashita, Kyong-mi Park, Ryoko Sekiguchi, and Takako Arai, *Four from Japan* (New York: Litmus Press/Belladonna Books, 2006).

11. Rachel Blau DuPlessis, "Blue Studio: Gender Arcades," http://wings.buffalo.edu/epc/ authors/duplessis/blue.html.

12. Carla Harryman, *Open Box: Improvisations* (New York: Small Press Distribution, 2007).

13. Carla Harryman, *The Words: After Carl Sandburg's Rootabaga Stories and Jean-Paul Sartre* (Oakland, CA: Institute of Physics Publishing, 1999).

14. Carla Harryman, *Gardener of Stars* (Berkeley, CA: Atelos, 2001).

15. Carla Harryman, *Vice* (Elmwood, CT: Potes & Poets Press, 1986).

16. Carla Harryman and Steve Benson, "Dialogue: Museo de Antropología, Mexico," *Poetics Journal* 8 (June 1989): 47.

17. Sawako Nakayasu, *nothing fictional but the accuracy or arrangement (she* (Florence, MA: Quale Press, 2005).

from *Baby*

Now. Word. Technology.

These were words she would learn someday. In the meantime she was fire in the womb with a skirt. Then a shirt which she pulled up through a small door that people on the other side called a cervical opening. Oh hallowed name and jittery shirt. She listened to a tiger reading files. She wanted to know what a tiger looks like, first. Before she wanted to know what anything else looked like. Someone, had that someone known anything about what baby wanted, would have said authoritatively it's the sound of the parent's voice you anticipate desire and suck in all at once through those perfect mitten ears and translucent and batted at things pulled red then formed into conch spindles then later shielded by hands from undesirable noise. The tiger opened a file claiming, this is the beginning of a long story. Which is everything baby wanted except the shirt she rolled up and over and in and by with for her skirt. The corner of everything was smitten with attentiveness. The difference between a womb and a room lies in such corners of attentiveness. Or the technology of listening.

Fish Speech

In the beginning, there was nothing. No cattails, no wigs, no paws. There was no doom. No lavender or shirt sleeves. No burn no yellow or rest. Neither was there beginning. No light went out. No one held her own against an army of misshapen events. There were no chains. There was no writing or speech. There was nothing to shave, nothing to swim, and nothing to cut. Clouds were not clouds. Silence was neither dominant nor peaceful nor silent. There was no salt or smell. No twisted seaweed. Or any buoyant flowering possibility of an ambiguous growth. There were no killers and fleeting lives. There were neither chains of events nor metaphor. There were no stories or bones. No mulch or cocoons. No lizard, pelicans, or fish.

In the beginning, there were no instructions and nothing was abstract. There was nothing to identify. And no revision or modification of the description of the thing identified. Neither were there eyes nor touch. There were no millipedes. Earthworms did not nurture the soil. There was no nurturing, no soil, no worms of any kind. There was no inferno.

Sound, word, rhythm, pucker, loss, organization, and signature were nothing. There was no distance. There were no tornadoes and no change in the atmosphere. There was no atmosphere and no alteration. There was no heat, or hint of the future, no possibility of Dante. For hints, futures, possibilities did not exist. There was no extinction.

There were no keys or clues. There was no DNA. Nothing squeezed. There was no singularity or multiplicity. There was no red.

In the beginning, there was nothing to hold and nothing to hold in mind, since there was no beginning, no nothing, and no mind. The end also did not exist. Nothing stopped. There was no gender, no extremes, no image or lack of image and no money. There were no pencils. In the beginning, there were no names.

In the beginning, there was no apoliticized moment of the absolute and no political critiques. Neither was there the hibiscus flowering bearded orchid cunt juices or a male suspect. Neither black nor brown nor white. No maiming and nothing to maim. No future and nothing to preserve.

Membership

They placed their demented musings outside themselves, and called the displacement society and public space. Therefore, society and public space were the projected fantasies of individuals onto the ground we once occupied. A room in the "public realm" looked like a demand in a very loud voice, with a hidden threat waiting behind its vocalizations. "Public" structures were indeed the facsimile resulting from fantasies of demented fanatics with excess power: the institutions all had to be negotiated around, within, between this way and that in a continuum of daily maneuverings. Most negotiations involved avoiding the institutions as much as possible. Why should a few fanatics absorb the wild fantasies of the *rest-of-us* was a common complaint against "public participation," as defined by the institutions. But some, like electrons, struck the projected wave of institutionality at the right moment, just as a door had opened, or a window of opportunity. This was counted on by the handful of creators: 10,000 in a million would bounce at the right moment into the projected wave and be welcomed inside as participants. What did they do inside?

Sometimes news from these institutions bounced out as if quantums of energy given off during a hidden event. Because of the dearth of information surrounding these leaked quantums of news, they became significant. The news became huge, magnified as it was in the field-glasses of silent fears. Through magnified fear, the "outside" got a glimmer of what it was like to be entered into the institution. The pieces of news, once leaked, became giant spectacles, hurling their flag-torn and lock-ridden bodies into tea houses, book stalls and other randomly concocted enterprises.

How could a quantum have provoked such a break in the routine life, which consisted of avoidance of the "public good" as prescribed by the projections of a handful of lunatics who think of their creations as the determinants of society?

Because there was no other way, no other realm than this realm of negative positivity and positive negativity, all were always already gathered around these projected institutions, even in their avoidance of them. Those who had been institutionalized and those who had shirked imprisonment, all made up a reciprocating form of knowledge.

Now that we have achieved happier circumstances, we can tip our hats in gratitude to those ancient ones who could only act on their knowledge of imprisonment and freedom by doing something together that pleased them within and without the institutional walls. From them, we learned the sacrament of specific pleasures, such as tease parties, and other things the smallest unit of measurable energy has not been known to be able to achieve on its own.

Matter

Love was alone with love. And there was nothing I could do about it. Love was alone with love. Why make another move? Why move? It's your turn over there, someone said, and I thought I'm going to open my legs and see what happens. Hurry up, lay down your cards. The cards were in my hand. I put down the card to see what would happen while I opened my legs. You open now, I said. And love responded quickly. You are a good player. Have you been playing long? I learned from an expert, said love. Is the expert still living? Yes, she is. A she, I said. Love was impatient and wanted to know if I had another move. I closed my legs up to see if that counted. Look at your hand, said love trying to be patient. And you, I said, prefer these cards over other forms of excitement. If you can't play, you'll never meet the expert, love replied. I didn't really care, but my body was standing on end at the thought of fucking. When I saw that I and my body were not the same, I knew what card to play and played it as soon as my turn came without second-guessing my opponent's position in the game.

PAUL FATTARUSO | DARA WIER

from *The Submariner's Waltz*

I opened the brushed steel box
and took my dinner wafer.
There went another chirp.
The dark wafer was instantly heavy in my stomach,
and I looked out the window to see
if I could see the boat chirping,

if I could see a ripple move out from the boat
from where it chirped, if I could look where the boat
was about to chirp. No one had seen

or felt the boat chirping, but everyone
knew the sound of metals rubbed
together, or apart, by playing
ball with a boy with a metal patella in school,
or moving a key across the door of a brushed steel
box, or by a sticky shower door, so that

when the boat chirped, in my periphery
I could see the hull opening apart at the seams
and my nasal cavity expanded
and my palate sank
to get ready to
breathe in the
pliant water.

There was nothing to see through the window
except the immediate film of low gravity,
which dilates the pupils,

when Pavel tapped my arm
to show me a black, silky cricket with violet eyes and hair.

The cricket was long and thin, and huddled in a crease
of Pavel's palm. Pavel found it in a fissure in the wall
of a torpedo tube, and mistook it for just a spot of something
in his vitreous humor, until he noticed its smell.

The cricket was black and violet,
long and thin, had a smell like chlorine,
glassy wings, and when it chirped,
our ears buckled,
and Pavel spit up the color of melon skin.

I used one of my pins
to remove one wing
to test it.

For a long time it was quiet, just the humming of our systems,
so I took my wing and struck it to the other wing like a match,
and each time it made a clipped, broken, machine noise.
I held the cricket while Pavel carved it a cage out of candle wax.
I held the cricket and watched it look away,
and when I looked where it looked, it looked somewhere else.

I offered it a strand of yellow tinsel,
and without looking it took it up in its forelegs.
The boat had been decorated for the Day
of Saint Christopher, and never undecorated.
The tinsel came gradually undone
and spread everywhere,

into the corners of our pillowcases,
the stitching of our buttonholes, into gum foil,
woven into our beards so tightly we could

not clip it out, under our nails,
in the works of the periscopes,
in the wheels of our watches,
and still the watches did not pause,
nothing altered in function, except it glimmered
habitually, kept us up at night, watching
its inverse glimmer on the backs of our eyelids,
imagining the same glimmer threading our gums
as we smiled in the dark.
The cricket's wing was strong,

and looked like a black glass oar.
As a teenager I canoed.
I canoed into the middle of the water,
brought in the oar, and lay on my stomach
with only my eyes peeking over the boat,
scanning the surface of the water —
reflections of the daytime moon, or
I held out an orange to watch its
image in the surface of the water.

Now just the idea
of the surface of the water
disorients me.

I kept the cricket's wing
as a tiny article to identify me.
Nearly everyone had a tiny article
to identify them. Pavel had
a collapsing knife he caught in the belly of an eel as a boy,
with Saint Christopher painted roughly on its handle,
nipple-deep in water with a baby in his left hand, a palm tree
in the baby's left hand, under pale blue sky
and clouds white like eggs, and Pavel
painted the same scene large to hang

on the Day of Saint Christopher,
and it never came down,
and Pavel used the same knife to carve the cricket's cage.

For then, I put the wing in the cuff of my sleeve.

PF: What influence do sleep and dreaming have on your writing life?

DW: A lot. Almost nothing? I can say, aside from a few direct hits, there were a few dreams that were too realized and remembered, their stories too good without my intervention, to not take into account the demands of their good stories, and so I did go ahead and sort of (sort of being very literal) record them. So no, not too many times have dreams figured in (but I liked it when they did).

And you know how sneaky dreams are, they do what they will. I think there's a poem or two in *Blue for the Plough* related to this (or hypnagogic states just prior to regulation dreaming).

And isn't that what's so good about dreams? Defying regulation, making a mockery of silly fights people have about narrative this and narrative that. I love how disorderly dreams are. And so demanding. And to think, all over the planet people are dreaming in their time zones of dreaming. They are having one dream right after another. Are there places where dreams are regulated? Where you are not allowed to dream this or that? It's a wonder how little we have to do with our sleeping dreams. I guess there have been/are some who think controlling one's dreams is a fine objective. Now that is frightening.

PF: I don't know; I had a dream the other night that I was rinsing out a soup can. But it was terrifying. That can't be right. That's got to be a regulated dream. But then, there are those moments when I awake completely unhinged by some dream that appeared like a stranger, and yet it's mine. I sit up in bed and think, *What have I done?*

DW: I've often enough felt guilt following a dream, or occasionally I'm out of sorts with someone who's been in a dream and behaved badly — now that's something that should be contested. It does make me think of dream literal and dream metaphorical. When we talk about people's "dreams" in the waking life we're surely not talking about the same things as those things that happen to us while we sleep. Right there, then, stands a crossroads of what we do with words in various realms. The so-called dreams everyone's supposed to have — for their children, for their country, for their businesses, for their racing forms — someone should come up with a new name for those desires. Or dreams.

As far as sleep goes, *The Sleep of Reason Produces Monsters* is the name of an etching I've always thought terribly cruel. In it there's a man with his head fallen down on a table and all around him bats — maybe it's bats, maybe it's something else — attack his sleepy, exhausted head. Showing us what?

PF: It's bats and owls, and also a pretty big cat in the corner. (I looked it up.) What's really unnerving are the eyes. The bats don't have eyes, but the owls and the cats do, these lidless, bulging eyeballs. It reminds me of an image from my childhood — my parents hung it on the wall of their bedroom over the hamper. It's a photograph of a girl, maybe five years old, in a nightgown, blindfolded, sitting on a tree branch with an owl. At night. It's black except for the girl and the owl and the branch. And I think a crescent of moon in one corner. And the branch is very thin, so it's not really clear how it could hold the girl without bending or snapping altogether. And then of course the owl, being an owl, has those big owl-eyes, inscrutable and relentless. This image is imprinted way back in my early childhood memories, and the sense I guess it gives me is that after we close our eyes, something incomprehensible goes on watching . . .

DW: You're absolutely right about that. Something incomprehensible goes on watching. I don't seem to know how to sleep. I don't sleep all that much. Typically about five hours a night. So of course I worship sleep. I've stayed up late and gotten up early most of the time. I attribute the stay up late part to not wanting to miss anything. The up early part to getting up to feed the chickens. So then there is the question of the nap, and when and if that is possible. Do you nap?

PF: Once a year maybe. Probably because I sleep at least eight hours and often nine a night. I do like the nap, the feeling of not quite going all the way under — the world is still out there somehow during a nap; things are shuffling around, and I can hear it. This reminds me of something I read in a footnote of Oliver Sacks's piece "The Last Hippie": some researchers at NYU have posited that the only real distinction between waking and dreaming is the presence or absence of sensory input. Brain activity is otherwise essentially the same in both states, apparently. I don't know whether the implications of that are more alarming in terms of waking or in terms of dreaming.

DW: I don't know either. So of course influences of any sort — dreaming, awake, conscious, unconscious — tend to be beyond describing, elemental from the get-go and impossible to say too much about.

PF: That's what I love about it, that elemental quality. I get the feeling I'm wandering into some kind of hallowed ground. And it's uncanny-strange and uncanny-familiar at the same time. You really have to watch your step in that kind of territory. And language does seem to crumble when it approaches that elemental moment. Sometimes it almost holds together, though, I think. I feel like I'm always trying to get there. So what do you know about petrified wood?

DW: I know a little bit about it. When a child I found petrified wood absolutely fascinating to think about, and I took it literally. I couldn't wait to go out west where I knew the petrified forests were, to see them standing there terrified and stilled into their petrification by the fearfulness of our existence. I looked up to them. I thought they had the right idea. And you probably know the rest of that story.

PF: So the forests are afraid of us? That does make sense. And so what about the owls?

DW: No, I didn't think the forests were afraid of us; they were afraid of the same things we are.

PF: In the entry for *petrify*, my dictionary uses an expression I really like: "a stony replica by structural impregnation with dissolved minerals." It's great that there's this very slow, almost accidental process by which the thing becomes a statue of itself. Great and horrible, deathless and petrifying. How do you approach form when you write?

DW: I approach it on my knees, in awe, hoping it will be my friend, hoping I will see it when it flies by. Maybe catch it. Hope I notice. Keep it near enough to recognize a little something about it, to be for it or against it, depending on what it's doing.

Form — form is a good thing, shapes of things involving forms vaguely appearing somewhere in the distance, over the horizon, something taking shape. We've got a lot going for us when it comes to this stuff. Words. Good old syntax. Why we seem to admire patterns and how this leads to that. How we like to interrupt these things. Music. Weather. Have you ever interrupted the weather?

PF: Only in the most localized sort of way: umbrellas, etc. Although not often even that. As much as I like the shape of the umbrella, especially with the curved handle — it's almost like a flightless bird — I don't use them much. I might crouch under someone else's. But then I'm also thinking about a game I used to play when I was six or eight: I'd breathe on the falling snowflakes so as to melt them before they touched the ground. The key was to summon up the breath from the bottom of the lungs, because it has to be warm enough to melt the snowflake . . .

DW: I did recently have a problem proposed to me that made me think of form, especially established, regulation forms, the this the that of informed forms to address. Obstacle courses. If you start thinking about this you'll not get any sleep tonight and you won't dream. But I think you'll have some adventures, traveling around the world, involving horses, skates, skis, money, real estate, barrels, time, guns, animals, boards, fish, fires, insects, tides, protons, us, and everything else in the world. Now we maybe ought to ask you to come up with how form and repetition and cyclical things can not be . . . you name it?

PF: Formal? There is that scary moment when the elemental influences meet the artificial influences — artificial like language, form, artifice — and hopefully one doesn't completely eat the other one up. Hopefully it's not so easy to tell the one from the other. But what was the problem that was proposed to you?

DW: The problem involved how to describe the wonder of why we like to navigate an obstacle course. Why, whether we invent it or are assigned it, some of us sometimes find solving the problems of getting through an obstacle course worth doing. When you wrote your prose book, did you hesitate before you began it, or did you know you'd have to finish it up?

PF: I started with no idea whether I'd finish or not. And I wasn't worried about that at all. I conceived of the whole project as kind of a lark, for whatever reason, to avoid petrification maybe. One day I was just in the middle of a daydream, and a very long thread suddenly unravelled in my mind, and so I started following it. I knew where things were going, to a certain point anyway, but I took it very lightly. At least, that's the story I'm telling myself.

I'm curious about *Reverse Rapture*: how did that book come to be? How did it find its form?

DW: It began slowly, inside of a couple of poems just before *Reverse Rapture* settled into its form. To make a long story short, I wanted to write longer poems after having written shorter poems, so I assigned myself a couple of ways to do that, a poem called "A Thousand Words," a poem called "A Question of Stamina," and not long after that another poem with way too many parenthetical phrases showing up in it, so many that it seemed natural to do only parenthetical phrases for a while to see if ( ) could function just as clearly as regulation punctuation and syntax function to move through language and thinking, with logics maybe a little more nimble than usual.

So I got hooked on the nine line/nine stanza length and before too long something seemed to need to be followed. There was never a clear straightforward story in mind, though there soon was a necessary need to pay attention to what these characters had to say to one another. I was reporting what they were saying to one another as they traveled in dangerous circumstances. I found their various ways of reporting to one another compelling. They're reporting to one another out of necessity. Almost like touching someone in the dark to see where one is. Staying in touch with and by word so as to find one's way through something unknown.

Sometimes one of them would be afraid, and another would change the subject so as to give another one courage; sometimes one would have a lot to say, another time almost nothing; sometimes there were monologues, other times complicated dialogues. I think what kept me paying attention to them was how much they seemed to love one another, as the extremes of their being together determined a lot, but not all, of the ways they said things to one another. I wish I could say to you something exact about how the book got made but I can't. I do know it all happened in the dark. Because that turned out to be the only circumstance in which it was safe for them to travel.

Let's go back to dreaming and owls and twig branches and things we learned as children and eyes and petrified wood and the essentially parenthetical elemental nature of dreams. Oh, I don't know, maybe all forms and formal elements we have in language (and poetry and prose) parallel similar things in all else. You tell me now about artificiality, and what that's all about.

PF: I'm a little obsessed with the drama of this conflict between the natural and the artificial, and how we can try to synthesize the two. On one hand there's artificiality as banal, insidious bane of civilization, as in skyscrapers, cathode-ray tubes, nose jobs, and computers that won't let us back in our spaceships. And then there's nature as predatory and murderous, as in bats, owls, and big cats peering through the darkness. And then there are medications, biological weapons, genetic engineering, and ice caps, and where does language fit in, and where does poetry fit in? What to make of the architecture of grammar, or the landscape of vocabulary? What would a vow of silence feel like? Would it be more or less artificial?

Insects and small birds and chipmunks and squirrels and mice and such often seem like little machines to me, with their miniature skeletons and their tiny, crafted feet. Plus there are the artificial hearts and the iron lungs. And meanwhile, viruses for computers. So the whole question gets pretty foggy. There's this from Mallarmé's "An Interrupted Performance": "*Reality* is but an artifice, good only for stabilizing the average intellect amid the mirages of fact."

But to get back to things that happen in the dark, it seems perfect that *Reverse Rapture* should take place there — there's that way darkness has of blanketing everything, bracketing it and preserving it. Which is also exactly what ( ) does. And then there's that certain quality that conversations in the dark have, when your voice, and maybe someone else's, are the only real evidence you have that you're continuing in the act of existing. So the words start to take on a life of their own, and it's not always entirely clear who's saying what anymore — it doesn't even matter anymore who's saying what — or if the words are even being said, but instead are somehow just conjured out of the darkness. And pretty soon a phrase, any and every phrase, becomes tactile, almost visible — I guess a kind of radar. So the dark seems to me like this wonderful, elemental laboratory for language. Besides which, it's a place where all those mirages are cleared away. To make room for other mirages?

Let's go back. What did you learn as a child?

DW: That all these things were already synthesized. They came packaged that way. Though, thank god, their packaging was minimal, invisible and visible in the darkness you mention.

I'll keep on with the mirages. My favorite ones, as a child (are we going to call this "As a Child"?), were the heat mirages one sees on a highway when it's hot and before one it looks like coming up is a whole lot of water?

I think that last "?" was kind of a mirage.

Oh, oh, my god, I mean, Paul, is that what a question is, a mirage?

I learned that a river is a very good thing to live with.

I learned that farmers work all day long.

I learned that farmers' families work right along with them.

I learned that a farm stand is a portal and a window and a door.

I learned that a farmers' market is a good place to sleep and wake up after sleeping in it, French Market in New Orleans especially, as this was my market.

I learned that story about how rows of crops imitate lines of poems. From the back of our mule I learned how mules turn.

I learned I wanted to escape. Escape being a positive force. Go looking, go finding out.

I learned how wanting to escape relates directly back to your "conversations in the dark," and that is fine by me.

PF: There's a rare kind of mirage called fata morgana — I've never seen one in person, but still I like just the fact that it has its own name, after Morgan le Fay, a shapeshifting fairy. Werner Herzog made a documentary called *Fata Morgana* with lots of footage of mirages. I remember it starts with about five minutes of footage of airplanes passing through a wave of mirage-space as they land. It's nice to know that these things can be photographed.

DW: Yes, that is a good thing. Fata Morgana: who could resist that?

PF: At first I'm inclined to think that questions are less ephemeral than mirages, but maybe mirages aren't as ephemeral as I thought — they're these spaces in which whole big airplanes can exist. And we can take pictures. But then they can only exist at a certain distance.

DW: What's certain about this certain distance? I think we can be pretty certain at this point questions = mirages, mirages = questions. And why not?

PF: I want to know more about you wanting to escape: was there precisely something you wanted to escape from? Or to?

DW: No, nothing I wanted to escape from. I wanted to see the world, you know, in that dreaming kid's way. I was escaping day in and day out. Yes, no, nothing from, everything to. The ships on the river did come from somewhere else; I was hoping to see where someday.

PF: Did you ever hatch a plot for escaping?

DW: No, the boats were always going somewhere, north, south. I think I was mesmerized by the boats going so much, in their slow-motion watery ways; it wasn't part of the picture to hatch a plan.

PF: Do you feel like you escaped?

DW: Yes, I do feel that escaping daily is what perhaps we're all always doing. Death is coming, there's no doubt about it, so to zigzag and feint away and hide from that for a while just might be what escaping is all about. Yes, perhaps escaping is nothing more than wanting to put one foot down into the future, then the next foot, the next. One word after another. I didn't want to escape anything in particular. I wanted adventures. All of the ships on the river said, *Travel, go forth.* Turns out, my travels mostly do most well in imagining.

PF: I wonder if the impulse to escape is something perpetual, or cyclical, or not. Usually when we talk about escape and writing, it's a pejorative thing. Escapism is associated with irresponsibility and selfishness, but then again escape can be this vital force for change.

DW: I wouldn't jump from escape to escapism automatically. Say you were escaping from prison, that's not irresponsible or selfish, not in many circumstances. It's perpetual and cyclical all right.

It shouldn't be pejorative; we're talking about escaping (when you say "escapism" that's not what I meant) from an absurd situation we daily wake up to find ourselves in. I don't mean the day-to-day life I'm grateful to have.

We know almost nothing. I'd like to imagine we might sometime find a little comfort against that nothing. I'd like to imagine we can entertain one another against that nothing. Not to make too big of a deal about it. Okay, so escape isn't the precise advantage.

Rather than escape let's say I wanted to go elsewhere from the vantage I'd been given, though it's a vantage I love very much.

Escape does suggest *from* something. I meant to mean *to* something, as you suggested is possible. Maybe it would make more sense if I'd have said there's something out there I knew I needed to see. It's not exactly as if I climb mountains or explore the depths of the ocean. Imagination's the territory I love the most.

Hypnagogic

It began with the egg-and-dart,
sunrise, animal, diamondwork, palmette,

running ornament, tumbled brick, the fret.
Nothing for me to do but shut my eyes

and wait and they'd arrive. Cornices,
shafts and capital pediments, entablature,

gambrel gables, dentils and brackets.
I learned fast the part I had to take.

Not to make a move, not to edge my sight beyond.
They'd come around alone or not at all.

And they'd dissolve, one into the other
or they'd be gone. Not for me to invite

or rearrange or they'd shut down.
And when they upped the ante I obeyed:

in flayed hideous faces, in plain white skulls
without eyes, in griffins, in malevolent freaks,

in living dead chimeras. So I could not move,
fascinated, then afraid I'd have them with me

all my life to carry on. But they didn't stop
at that. They gave me the faces of strangers:

receptionist staring at the thermostat
as she takes my name, car wash money changer,

postal clerk ringing my receipt, i.d. checker,
customs officer, bank teller, airport security

guard, poll watcher, doorman, elevator operator,
bouncer. In remote silence I watched serial strangers.

In spite of my will to intervene I complied.
In the lull before sleep I waited for them,

lonely, adrift, and nearly lost, restless,
about as good as dead if they didn't appear.

They were training me to wait and not want
what I'd lose if I asked for it.

I had to pretend I didn't care
and this was against my nature.

Corrosion

(either way or not) (neither before nor after) (neither you nor I) (but not only us)
(but also them and their kin) (we couldn't
follow them) (we couldn't find a corridor)
(that hadn't been sealed off) (all of the
light switches were broken) (every window
was boarded up) (as if a hurricane were in
the forecast) (you could tell how the air
was coming from a long way off) (all the while

you were waiting) (you were filling up bottles
with water) (fashioning a collection of food
stock) (searching for batteries of many different sizes) (either it was going to hit hard
or it was not) (either you stayed put or you
left for elsewhere) (you gathered up some things)
(you didn't like leaving) (behind some things)
(there were other things behind everything) (you were
rethinking) (re-evaluating) (changing your mind

about everything) (it was a very low pressure
situation) (all of the barometers were falling)
(they fell the way night falls) (when you aren't
looking) (is when almost everything happens)
(when someone builds a throne of human skulls)
(is a very direct statement about someone's position) (in relation to what someone stands for)
(and is willing to make public) (& stand by)
(and to try to go as far as possible away from)

(to be evacuees) (always leaving) (never
having) (neither having a choice) (nor able
to choose) (we were like schools of fish
caught up in the waterspouts) (we weren't swim-

ming) (there was no lazy day in summer) (it
was one lousy picnic) (it was worse than that)
(we were out of our water) (we were in over
our heads) (we'd lost our gills) (our lungs
were over-loaded) (we were smothering) (we

wanted out of there) (we were approaching
a cutoff) (some of our relatives were from
there) (we'd hit the hinterlands) (we were
circling the outskirts) (we were like neck-
laces) (made of mercury) (we were almost out
of bounds) (at escape velocity) (almost mach
seven) (we were trespassing) (like sin) (we
were in the wrong airspace) (we could be
paying guests there) (we could be tenant

farmers) (we could be vassals) (we'd have to
turn the clocks back) (we'd have to go in
reverse) (pay homage) (pay tribute) (we'd
have to swear a lot) (swear to be very good
soldiers) (lay down our lives) (as if they
were pitchforks) (as if we were made out of
metal) (and treetrunks) (as if we'd been
made by a blacksmith) (as if we were good
for turning hayrows) (on good days) (when

there wasn't a cloud in the sky) (and you
could see forever) (there was good visibility)
(it was the least common denominator) (a high
pressure system had come through) (everyone
had grown a few inches taller) (their heads
were in the clouds) (it was a tall order)
(we were erring on the high side) (our thinking
was like a very tall building) (we had eleva-
tors in us) (terrible music was in us) (we

were many stories) (stacked up on top of one
another) (with stairwells in us) (that were
like echo chambers) (we were made out of concrete then) (we usually didn't have any windows)
(you could get lost in us) (and not know where
you are then) (or what you are doing here) (so
ask someone from upstairs) (someone who's seen
it all) (who knows everything) (who's been there)
(done that) (is like a wind gauge) (like a broken

thermometer) (it couldn't be put back together)
(and it had taken so long to make it) (it was
like the aftermath of a cyclone) (we were down
in the basement) (with the women and children)
(the men were out on the lawns drinking and
smoking) (idly scanning the horizon) (trying
to look as if nothing were happening) (not
betraying any emotion) (the picture of security)
(of conviction) (unerring) (strong) (silent)

MARK YAKICH | MARY LEADER

Pretzels Come to America

Legend has it that Houdini, the son of a rabbi, picked his first lock
Because he wanted a piece of boysenberry pie his mother was keeping

Dead-bolted in the pantry. A busted closet means trouble. Doesn't it
Seem that as soon as you get one thing fixed in the house something else

Falls apart? Say, I might as well punish myself for Mommy's cancer,
Because who else is there at the foot of the bed to discomfit. Bedrooms

Really are nice in all-white. Sheets, curtains, lamps, laser-white metal.
The most important place for a favorite painting is opposite the bed:

The last impression you see at night, the first when you rise. Upstairs
The house has an expiration date, just as Henry James did. Poor Henry

Was criticized for not liking dumb people. He avoided women especially
Because one lady had fallen in love with him and then committed
   suicide.

They say that before Henry died he thought he was Napoleon. And it
Turned out that he did know a lot about Napoleon, just not the right
   sorts

Of things that made dying easier. Houdini, James, Napoleon. Neither
Houdini nor James liked to be called by their first names. But Napoleon

Loved his first name so much he destroyed many lives in order to
Keep it popular. Three great men, three great holes. Like in the pretzel.

Medieval monks gave pretzels to children who had memorized their
   Bible
Verses and prayers. To reinforce a lesson: the three holes in the pretzel

Represent the Christian trinity. Today there are 28 different kinds of
Pretzels in the world and that number continues, in fits and starts, to grow.

An Untenable Nostalgia for Chernobyl

Unspeakable acts may be our epics and you
      May die in your sleep. Thus find
Your meaning between the lines
      Of mother's hands:

The best-paved streets of Chernobyl.
      All night long the points
Of view are punished. I, too, wanna be
      Ready for the little black dress

That's all the rage. I look into
      The bathroom mirror at that old baby,
The gaze after my own heart.
      What is it about our experience of

A great book? Like a disposable
      Yarmulke, it causes a question:
What to do when you're done with it?
      They say, if you go far enough away

You'll be on your way back
      Home. To a sacred still. I have to
Confess that in my flight
      Often I'm drinking alone.

But I'm sowing. And I hear my interred
	Relatives cheering. More
And more their memories make
	Mockery of the bookshelf. I stand over

The toilet poised and lustful. Happy as
	I am to enjoy the vanity
And vodka, the drunk don't make
	The rules. No. 1: Live long life.

No. 2: Quiver. I figure in a land blessed
	By compunction, what can't be
Lost again. I ape a dictator, a vial of
	Cyanide, a Geiger counter. I rewitness

The charcoal-burnt orange skin
	Imprisoning the fatty pork steaks. I shoot
Quatrains as if they fly from the trees.
	I say: Go now, Little Book,

	Make your way without my world.

MY: In the description of this anthology, the editors use a quote from Allen Grossman. I'll have to paraphrase, but it went something like "Poetry is the least solitary of the arts." And I was thinking, didn't you know Allen Grossman pretty well?

ML: Not well personally. But as a huge influence, absolutely. I met him at Warren Wilson. He was a guest there. Down there in the Blue Ridge mountains in a rustic campus. There he was in his rusty black suit, rusty black tie, white shirt — his Brandeis duds. And he gave a talk on the Philomel story that has stayed with me forever. The talk brought up weaving as a metaphor for poetry — not the Orpheus myth with the animals and the singing, but Philomel who was raped and who had her tongue cut out and, well, they all turn into birds. In any case, the idea that poetry can be mute. That you can have your tongue cut out and your hands cut off, and at that point you have to turn into a bird. But at the moment when you have just your tongue off but not yet your hands you can make poetry by weaving . . .

MY: And she wove the names of her attackers into a tapestry.

ML: Right. And that wasn't Allen's major point, but that trope has stuck with me, especially in one of my current manuscripts, "Readinesse." It's got all kinds of weaving tropes, with the distaff side and stitch and hemistich — like that poem I sent you a while ago, "Matrix"; that's part of it. "Readinesse" with an "e" on the end, George Herbert-style. The whole weaving metaphor is tricky, however, because especially women writers will use it as a code for saying that domestic subjects are worth writing about. So, they'll say such-and-such a quilt, but make no point of addressing the silence in which quilts are made, or the joint singing, or the gossip in which quilts are made. A woman cuts and makes the top piece by herself, and then gets together with others in a quilting bee — an interesting metaphor in itself — to put the layers together and stretch it on a frame, and many hands will go into that. On the other hand, I try to make poems look like rugs and fabrics and grids, but I don't like simply involving women's arts as a subject. No, that's just keeping it a ghetto.

MY: This reminds me of the phrase "The readiness is all" in Shakespeare. I think it's Hamlet to Horatio after Hamlet's taken the challenge to face Laertes in a duel.

ML: Well, that's what I think this book is about. "Readinesse" with an "e," and then the four subparts, are all based on Mondrian paintings. And they progress from what could be a George Herbert title to what absolutely couldn't be a George Herbert title — an insight actually had by Joshua Phillips — namely a section called "Exploded Box-Plan of the Salon for Ida Bienert," which is an interior space Mondrian designed on the page laid flat. So, what are you working on?

MY: Do you remember a poem I wrote titled "The Importance of Peeling Potatoes in Ukraine"? It was in the manuscript version of *Unrelated Individuals*, but then when I was revising I pulled it out; I decided that poem was the beginning of something else.

ML: And so this potato peeling — I want to say right here that that is radically different from the bourgeois poem we often hear, "Peeling Potatoes," where the speaker is doing a prosaic task, then has a sudden realization, a little insight out of the dailiness, and that's the closure of the poem. Usually something earthshaking, like "I have ovaries" or "My parents were my age once" or "My grandmother was Ukrainian" — peeling potatoes reminded the speaker of his grandmother, etc.

MY: This potato peeling...

ML: Yes, you've got it framed well. That is, the "importance of" gives it a meditative frame at the beginning, and then at the end of the phrase there is a narrative frame by locating the "peeling potatoes" in Ukraine. Right away, the title says this isn't about peeling potatoes, or rather, it is, but it's not about peeling potatoes in the usual way. Or rather, this poem is *more* about peeling potatoes than the other bourgeois one, where it was simply a fiction.

MY: You've already read the manuscript, haven't you!

Well, that title, "The Importance of Peeling Potatoes in Ukraine," started to become an emblem for everything else I was writing. Not only the old trope of *pomme de terre* (poem as potato, Francis Ponge, etc.) but also the idea that the poem, like the potato, is earthy and blank underneath. A potato is in no way special like, say, an orange.

[Parking the car in front of a jewelry store with a sign posted in the window: "Lapis Lazuli here!"]

Ah, a Yeats reference. And now it's time to eat.

[Walking over to Panera café.]

ML: Look — you can get your dentures here. *[Pointing to a sign that reads "One Day Dentures."]*

MY: Yes, one day I will have dentures.

ML: Oh no, it's "one day" dentures. So they're rentals. Just for, say, a wedding, the prom.

MY: Right, who needs the dentures the next day?

[Entering Panera café.]

ML: Smells like the Ukraine?

[Mark ordering a coffee and pineapple upside-down, lemon poppyseed muffin; Mary ordering an orange juice. There's a scuffle as to who's going to pay.]

[Sitting down, booth by a window, rather noisy.]

MY: Let's finish the Allen Grossman. It's generative after all: he, you, then me.

ML: After the MFA at Warren Wilson, I applied to Brandeis because Grossman was there, but it turned out that he wasn't there by the time

I got there. He had moved over to Johns Hopkins, but still maintained an office at Brandeis. So I put some poems in his mailbox and pleaded for him to meet with me, and we did meet a few times. I looked up to him. His seriousness about poetry. And then there were/are his eight tapes made from some "star" lecture series; some company put them out and I got them. Each lecture discusses one poem, starting with "London Bridge," then "Sir Patrick Spens," a later one on Dickinson.

MY: Dickinson, especially, we like her.

ML: He does an excellent job there on "I cannot live with You."

MY: "It would be Life — / and Life is over there / Behind the Shelf // The Sexton keeps the Key to."

ML: Right, and that poem, "640"— speaking of generative poetry, is an answer to "Come Live With Me and Be My Love."

MY: Sidenote on the poppyseed cake: it's dry, and it used to be moist. [Pause.] But it's still edible.

ML: Well, you're eating it.

MY: End sidenote.

ML: So, those things Grossman would say on the tapes, I would listen to repeatedly. Those tapes aren't extant anymore. Not on the backlist of that company. But I still have them; they're fragile.

MY: You've got to transfer to digital.

ML: Speaking of Grossman and poetic lineage, there's my friend Dan Morris at Purdue. He was an acolyte of Grossman's too. Dan teaches lit and has a small collection. He's wonderful. He cathected onto Grossman. Jamey Hecht was another. Not very many women. I think Grossman is kind of shy of women. When he first looked at my poems, he said, "These are very much the woman's poems." So when I got the three-volume Dickinson, he put his hand on top of the books and patted them saying, "Here's your man."

MY: Is women's poetry, then, his "Other"?

ML: Maybe. He values it in a way that keeps it strange.

MY: Who do you think is your Other?

ML: The poems that I value the most the radically unpublishable. Also the book itself, the space of the book. So that in "Readinesse" there is a poem, I put it last, that is an odd poem. But by that point in the book, at the very end, well . . . be prepared. Because what comes there, and occasionally before, are not what people would call poems.

MY: What would they call them?

ML: Designs. Visual designs. Typographical experiments. Gibberish.

MY: What does this last poem look like?

ML: It's long and it's got different forms. It's called "Queen Elizabeth the First's Period." It's a primer for someone who cannot and should not be writing — that would be me. So the idea of "Copying Copying it in," (a Stein line) allows me to take a book of needlework instructions, a *Reader's Digest* book, and the Elizabethan form of "blackwork," which was dense black embroidery on white linen. It was popular in Spain and then made its way over to England, when Catherine of Aragon transferred from the one brother to the other.

MY: Some credits didn't transfer.

ML: So, I spend some pages dealing with the credits from this *Reader's Digest* book — a crochet editor, a knitting editor, an embroidery editor, a needlepoint editor. And the companies — Coats & Clark and other sponsoring companies. I just copy all that in. I explain at the beginning of the poem, "Here's the poem, it's just a breakdown of how to find black-work of Great Britain in Europe," etc. A set up much like when you're a child and you say, "I live in this town, in this state, in this country, in this globe, in this universe" — it's a zooming in and out, step-by-step model. Then the poem says, "That was the poem, and now for the gloss," and the piece goes on for another 15 pages. And by this time in the poem, I've got so many names typed in, it's kind of a population study. A census. It says that the name is as important as the deed. After a while, anybody gets tired of doing that. Certainly anybody who's reading it is going to get tired of reading it. I myself would skip over it. The one and only time I read it aloud, that is what I did do. Skipped over it. And then in the next part of the poem, the memories of childhood start to come in.

MY: Into where? Into the gloss?

ML: Right, into the gloss. And there I can talk about the memories, but it's still not the poem — that is, I'm about to write the poem.

MY: Does the poem ever come?

ML: The poem finally does come, in a whispered, sent voice. A found, bi-furcated call-and-response, part Latin, part English.

MY: How did you decide on the call-and-response pattern?

ML: It was absolutely inspired. By the time I put in all the other parts — a big pastiche — certain ideas about menstruation started to come into play.

MY: Menstruation? Not of the minstrel variety, obviously.

ML: Thoughts about Elizabeth the Queen and about the Empire in gen-eral. And as I thought about my grandparents, I thought about my grand-father, whose goal in his old age was to see every country on earth. So they traveled everywhere, didn't make it to Africa except North Africa, and he had to get a foot cut off — gangrene. And each time they came back from a trip, he would take these colored pencils and laboriously fill in the country they'd been to on a large map. Purple circles around cities they'd been to, etc. He was conquering the world in that way. What could be more Elizabethan?

MY: Do you have that map of his?

ML: No, no. I don't have much. I do have my grandmother's charm bracelet. She would get a twenty-four carat gold charm in each place they went to — there's a poem using her bracelet in the book. And so I allow that poem and the book in general to put in pain — my mother's pain, my pain — the unhappiness of my parents — these elements come in as unbidden flashbacks, not as a poem but as memory. When the voice experiences the memories at their worst, the voice reverts to "knit, purl, knit, purl, knit purl" — it was the only thing that made sense, doing needlework when I was a child. And needlework wasn't something my mother did; my aunts taught me. My mother did nothing but write poems; she had nothing but disdain for traditional women's work. She hired somebody to clean the house, slapped supper on the table, spent all her time reading and writing poems and socializing. So needlework was rebellious for me. It would mean I had to get my dad's sisters, who were my mother's archenemies, to teach me to sew.

MY: Maybe that right there was the root of an Other — not the Other, but an Other.

ML: Yes. When you first said Other I thought of her. Because she's also in this book. There are all these devices for trying to reach her, ways of spinning a poem, of playing solitaire until she can be invoked. At one point she's figured as a woodcarver's ghost; that would be an Other for me. It's also an apology for me, for not being a good daughter. People say, You were a fine daughter. No, I was not. I let her suffer, and it was my job to keep her from suffering. She suffered all her life, and at the end she suffered physically, and I didn't do what she needed. But that's not in the poem. That's a personal note. The point is that this poem is experimental.

The point is to write in a form that explodes a three-dimensional life onto a flat surface — like an architectural plan, like the Mondrian. "Of Ida Bienert" is like "in the Ukraine," and I don't know or need to know who she was.

MY: Exactly. You never need to go to Ukraine to get the poem.

ML: Right, because the language itself is an act of the imagination.

MY: That's interesting, then, when you say that the book's the Other — then Ida Bienert becomes an Other too.

ML: Right. And I don't know whether I'm even saying her name properly.

MY: How do you spell Bienert?

ML: It's "b-i-e" or "b-e-i" — I always have to look it up. In the Mondrian book the names are in the index. I always figure Bienert and her husband were rich Jews, which is another kind of Other for me. Or any Jews for that matter.

MY: Interesting, because I have the same relationship with Jewishness. First, because of the unknown family background — I'm adopted as you know, half Lebanese. Maybe there's Jewish blood in me, and then, well, my wife is Jewish. A lot of my friends are.

ML: Allen Grossman is Jewish, Dan Morris is Jewish, Jamey Hecht is Jewish . . .

MY: It's like left-handed, isn't it — one always wants to be left-handed. Doesn't everyone want to be Jewish at one time or another? A left-handed Jew.

ML: Yes, wannabe Jews. Artists do, often. Because there's something — and I hate to say this, for it's a sheer and false stereotype — but, for me, it's hard not to associate Jews with suffering and enduring. And every artist has to be able to do both.

MY: A strange privilege.

ML: And you have to be born to it. I've tried converting. I've tried taking lessons, in Boston and then in Memphis. And I like the Orthodox tradition, because I sit among the women.

MY: That would be a serious conversion.

ML: Not only would that require serious conversion for me, but they don't want me. Although I have to say, there's a gender difference. The women welcome me. "Where are you from? Do you have any kids? We missed you last week," etc. But if I were a wannabe male Jew and wanted to sit among the men, with the prayer shawl, etc., I definitely would not be welcome there. I suppose we're getting away from — well, this isn't supposed to be about religion. I keep wondering when you're going to bring in Derek Walcott. You're going to replace me in this interview with Derek Walcott. [ML is referring to her earlier reported dream that MY fired her from this interview, explaining he'd gotten someone much better, namely Derek Walcott.]

MY: Oh no, not that. He's my Other. No no, you know who my Other is? Seamus Heaney. I mean, I like him fine — a poem such as "Dig," etc.— but he's a construction of Helen Vendler who herself is a construction. I wrote a poem called "Working Girl" about Vendler. It's ostensibly — well, just under the surface — okay just underneath ostensible and before sublimation — that's where I believe Helen Vendler created Seamus Heaney. It's a list poem, Googlism-style: "Helen is a world-class critic / Helen produces a lot of books / Helen is a pretty critic of the lyric / Helen is to be achieved / Helen is the author of Seamus Heaney," etc. I didn't use her last name, because I could get the Helen the Most Beautiful idea in there, too.

ML: Helen of Troy, nice.

MY: I had another lurking question. That last poem in "Readinesse" — you mention how you'd skipped over all those pages. I hate to consider the reader, exactly, but how do you see the reader there? Does the reader even matter?

ML: Interesting. I wouldn't say the reader is the Other. The reader is, I think, the gatekeeper. As in Kafka. That heavy irony. "You could have opened the door all along, but now it's too late, you can't, I'm going to close it. Goodbye." The ultimate paradox that all this time you've been kept out and yet you were the only one who could have gotten yourself in. And right when you're told that, you're kept out forever. Now I don't think of the reader as you, a Mark or a Josh (a friend of mine who referees my poems) or a specific person, but the reader as the gatekeeper who won't let my poems in — into the canon or whatever it is. Nor could I write those poems — the ones that might get me into the canon, the ones that might get me a Pulitzer. My friend Carl Dennis said after he got the Pulitzer, "Well, at least I won't have any trouble getting my next book published."

MY: Right, that's the goal: to be at a spot where you can write anything you like and not fear that it won't get printed.

ML: Exactly, and I write my poems as if I already have that license. But I don't have that license and I'm unlikely to get it.

MY: You're an untenured radical, in that respect.

ML: And I'm determined for my poems to be seen on their own terms. The temptation, for example with this poem, is to go back and take out and treat as separate pieces the parts that are emotionally charged. Several lyric poems are embedded within this text, but I'm determined not to do that. I'll give the reader preparation; I'll give other poems that proceed in mechanical, sewing-like ways, that proceed by stitch, stitch, stitch . . .

MY: So by the time you get to that last poem, you've educated the reader enough so that he or she should be able to read it.

ML: Yes, and there are references to earlier poems and precursors in the text. There's a poem called "Kommt Uns" [Come to Us] which says, Come to us with half-broken things, not finished things . . .

MY: . . . of what use are those to us . . .

ML: Yes, right — you know the poem? Did I get that poem from you?

MY: No no, I was just extrapolating.

ML: What I do in that poem is deal with someone I left out of the credits in the final poem. For example, Kreinik Manufacturing Company. So I say in the poem "Kreinik Mfg. Co. should not have been omitted," though you haven't gotten to the poem yet from which it was omitted. There are other poems that use Oulipo devices, shifting around nouns in a pattern. One is called "When the Wind Ever Shall Be Like a Black Thread."

MY: It's that weave you mentioned earlier.

ML: Yes, it's that weave, and any poem can be constructed that way, shifting around the nouns. See, the beauty of needlework is that basically anybody can learn it. Because there are patterns in the past, and because of the limits of the material — textiles being parts of plants and animals, not like language — and since you have the same tools, you must always be doing a variation on a theme. Which is true of poetry, too, in a way, though language seems like it could be all new. You don't have to be doing a variation on a theme in order to write a poem. And this brings back in Allen Grossman — he sees it all as one project. Social. Maybe that's what he means when he says, "Poetry is the least solitary . . . " He certainly doesn't mean something like slam poetry or worrying about the context for delivery.

MY: He means the activity of writing, the generative aspect. But what you're saying is that poetry is also *not* like quilt-making or needlework, because the materials *do* change.

ML: Because you're not bound. The only thing you're bound by is language which is such a multi-valenced material, so all-purpose, so cell-like . . .

MY: . . . that it mutates continually . . .

ML: . . . and there are predictable mutations and unpredictable mutations, but language as a medium, unlike any other medium, including painting. In painting, for instance, you must deal with a surface on which to make marks and something with which to make those marks.

MY: The bounds of dimensions.

ML: Yes, painting cannot exist in the air. Language can exist in the air, like music. So the beauty of poetry, of course, is that it proceeds in time like music, though it aspires to be still like painting.

MY: That "air" quality is the key. Because some people would say painting does have this other sense, because we see images all the time. There's a real life versus image battle going on. And yet, painting doesn't have the air. It doesn't have the wind-like quality — where did it come from and where is it going to go?

ML: I don't think anyone would say, "Your mind is a painting."

MY: They might say that in a poem. And sometimes when I've been painting a lot, six to eight hours in the basement, I come up to the surface and see the paint everywhere, in everything. I have tried painting the air before.

ML: Maybe you're right. Maybe language is no different. Maybe language isn't poetry until it has a physical form.

MY: You mean the product.

ML: A product.

MY: Then poetry doesn't need the air, does it?

ML: Yes, at that point, as a product, it doesn't need the air. But it assumes that somebody with air will come along.

MY: Say, Ginsberg, with his breath thing.

ML: Although the bag may not be inflated, oxygen will be flowing.

MY: This is your captain speaking. Don't be alarmed!

ML: Take care of yourself before assisting any others. Your seat cushion *may* be used as a flotation device . . .

MY: . . . though it doesn't have to be . . .

ML: . . . if you would rather drown . . .

MY: . . . that's perfectly okay with us. We realize dead bodies float well.

ML: Right, we understand.

MY: Thank God for verbal typos.

ML: And for typo typos.

MY: Right. In my classroom we've got this very loud air conditioner and people can't hear well, so there are all kinds of mishearings and misreadings. I jump on those, and after a while the students jump on those, and it becomes generative.

ML: And it's interesting about process and product. There again it's an idea that's in the zeitgeist but that I claim as an elite idea. Someone could look at these poems that I've been talking about and say, Well, that's just a lot of process. Or if you want to look outside of that box, you could say, Well, that's what the poem is about, how it got there, its making. And I will say that the last version of those lines is a better version than the first version. On a desert island I'd take that last version over any of the others, and yet I won't do that for the poem. I want the metonymy; I want all the parts there and not to have the last one be the metaphor for the process.

MY: Why is that — is it because it's too rarefied by that point?

ML: It's because it's too ungenerous.

MY: Ungenerous?

ML: Because it doesn't let the reader or the blank page know — let the air know — that it can do this too. It's to empower stupid people.

MY: So it's different than to have the facsimiles of Eliot's "The Waste Land" and consider the process — that's a different project?

ML: It is a different project, but that is including the process in a way that interests me. Superficially, the idea of a collage or pastiche, multi-scripted voices without the tags "he said/she said," without the reader's aids — and instead the dialing around on a radio and picking up voices.

MY: Those voices run through us anyway.

ML: Right, so "The Waste Land" is a poem I couldn't proceed without.

MY: I was thinking I can't read "The Waste Land" without looking at the facsimile version; without the facsimile it doesn't make as much sense to me.

ML: I feel a little bit that way about Dickinson's poems, her handwriting and the dashes, the capitals. You know, it's like Blake, too. You can write a typescript of *Songs of Innocence and of Experience*, but you're not getting Blake.

MY: You're not getting half of what he wanted. "The Tyger" — that one always interests me. The poem is a rather fearsome thing, but you look at the illustrations he has with it —

ML: — it's a little goo-goo tiger —

MY: — a pussycat tiger, and that's obviously part of his project. If you don't have that pussycat tiger — see it — you really miss out on the whole piece.

ML: And even the handwriting which will become part of the vines. But there's an irony here with respect to a democratic society. Shelley's poems were made on cheap paper, contained misprints — you know, the cheaper the better, because the more people that read the poems the better. And Blake, equally democratic in his politics, produced pieces that at least poor people couldn't afford. Blake was writing for an Other that was beyond — that was in the trees, with the angels, or for God; that was somehow beyond speaking to his fellow human beings. So hence the long lines and *The Four Zoas*.

MY: I was just going to mention *The Zoas*.

ML: Yes, *The Zoas*. It's beautiful because it's unfinished. It, too, is a process. You can't leave out a piece of it just because he never decided which ones to use. You have to reproduce the whole thing, like a facsimile. Close to the origins of the act of writing. You can picture the scene of production and picture what's going on in their mind as they're creating the text. So, back to the Oulipo in my poem. You can see the nouns, the Legos, being moved around. It's democratic in that artists are not on top of some hierarchy. And yet, at the same time, when I hear, "Oh process not product," I want to divorce myself from it, especially when it becomes the fodder of every feel-good workshop: "Oh just don't think about the product, just look at the process." But the problem is that there's no radical difference between the product and the process in that poet's hands.

MY: Neither the process nor the product ends up being very interesting.

ML: Nor will that work change what we think of as a poem. So, I might sound like an elitist when I espouse these ideas, but these ideas are in the interest of inclusion.

MY: It's a paradox, isn't it? Or fascist. And it's in *The Zoas*, where one of the characters declares, "You must create your own system or be imprisoned by another man's."

ML: Yes, exactly. That's the idea. Oulipo is a system, but I'm using it in my own way — process-evident, anyone-can-do-it, even a machine could do it, or part of it. And yet when the poems are done mechanically, as in when Oulipo did it at the time, they did it merely to disrupt.

MY: As acts of subversion.

ML: Right, to undermine, but I want to use their system as an act to establish. I'm interested in having the process also be as good a lyric poem as I can write. And for the work to be personal; for my work to have heart.

MY: This goes along with what you told me a long time ago about the "list poem." You want a list poem to *seem*, but not *be*, random.

ML: Must seem but not be random. Yes, the parallel is exact. Because the poem that I start with, before the noun-switching function takes over, must seem but not be random.

MY: Could you speak a bit more about the "personal" notion you mentioned earlier?

ML: To keep the personal in the experimental. For example, I like the project of Language poetry — the challenges to the underlying syntax, etc.— but too often there's not enough personal in it for me. I still want — I still want tears.

MY: Too often, frankly, their textures aren't that interesting to me. The syntactic textures have so many stumbling blocks that I have a hard time benefiting in a visceral way, a "personal" way.

ML: Which is interesting because we both have been so chary of autobiographical poems. Our situation is that we want the personal to be a large, extremely sophisticated, complex operation, not just "write what you know" or "write about your life." And yet what one knows about his or her unique circumstances belongs in poems, I believe.

MY: The reality is that one mainly sits at the end of the hall and writes in a closet. But one can't live in the closet.

ML: True, but if one's lived in the world for a while, one can be a writer. My situation is that I've lived a while in the tower and there's a fear that the work can become sterile.

MY: What do you do then?

ML: Good question. If the work has already been done to disrupt the culture, say, Language poetry, then what's the next thing? How to make sure the work is not going to be sterile? What I turn to is the things from my childhood that make me sad.

MY: "The profound sadnesses" is what I call them.

ML: Profound sadnesses, yes. And with those you're asking for trouble; you're asking to write a sentimental poem.

MY: For me, that's when I try to subvert myself.

ML: That's when you put in the Ukraine. That's when you move the potatoes.

MY: Right. That's when I put one filter — no, one rake — over the other. That's when things can get interesting.

ML: Especially if you design your own rake.

MY: So yes, "The Importance of Peeling Potatoes in Ukraine." The underlying current is to marry the serious and the personal with the social and the comedic. There's a poem, for example, in which Fidel Castro narrates a personal letter to a romance novel manuscript writer in New York City asking for advice. And another, "Weegee," where I assume the voice of the photojournalist, giving his side of the story for his voyeuristic photos of tenement fires, car crashes, murdered bodies. And then there's an incantation by Adorno — a persona poem — where the poet/theorist laments at having made his famous pronouncement about poetry after the Holocaust. And in "Quiz Show," I create a conversation between the painter Jackson Pollock and the Yugoslavian dictator Tito. I'm aiming in these pieces at a balance or a dialogue between earnestness and comedy. Gabe Gudding once wrote on his blog that tragedy teaches us to suffer, but comedy teaches us to endure. And I'd rather endure, even if it is through these characters and/or archetypes.

ML: Yes, you're good with the archetype poems. Being more familiar with the eastern European poets, or for whatever reason, you're better at that than I am. No dialogue between former teacher and former student would be complete without this progress.

MY: And this whole dialogue is good for me, Mary. It helps me reenter and/or re-spark the poems I'm working on now.

ML: For me, too: theory, poem, theory, poem. They exist in such a flickering relationship.

When the Wind Ever Shall Be Like a Black Thread

> "And then bargain with the wind
> To discharge what is behind."
> — George Herbert, "L'Envoy"

I clasp my long hair to listen to the ceiling.
Two sounds in concrete
Pace and knock, pace (what word from heaven?),
Knock.
My apartment sounds like an irritable mother,
The punctuation

Wrong in her presence,
Wrong because of it, snapping its tendons and cords.
The moving eye perversely plots to vacate.
A lasso of bees, pre-storm, swerves over water.
In the under-cabinet clip-light fluorescence
Mountains blanch, moraines flatten.

You, Sieve, enact slow departure.
Wail, Poor Kettle, duplicate crisis.
I, the daughter of the house, enunciate
What I want, all I want, like this:
Mazes that open toward breezed-out sleeves
That lead to exits grooved by machine;;;;;;;;;;;;;;;;;;;;

WHEN THE THREAD IS LIKE A BLACK WIND

I clasp the ceiling to listen to my long hair.
Two concretes in sound
Pace and knock, pace (what heaven from word?),

Knock.
My mother sounds like an irritable apartment,
The presence

Wrong in her punctuation,
Wrong because of it, snapping its cords and tendons.
The moving lasso perversely plots to vacate.
An eye of storms, pre-bee, swerves over cabinet.
In the under-water light-clip mountain
Fluorescences blanch, sieves flatten.

You, Moraine, enact slow kettle.
Wail, Poor Departure, duplicate daughter.
I, the crisis of the maze, enunciate
What I want, all I want, like this:
Houses that open toward sleeved-out breezes
That lead to machines grooved by exit;;;;;;;;;;;;;;;;;;;;;;

WHEN MY LONG HAIR IS LIKE A BLACK CEILING

I clasp the wind to listen to the thread.
Two words in heaven
Pace and knock, pace (what sound from concrete?),
Knock.
My punctuation sounds like an irritable presence,
The apartment

Wrong in her mother,
Wrong because of it, snapping its eyes and lassos.
The moving tendon perversely plots to vacate.
A cord of waters, pre-cabinet, swerves over bee.
In the under-storm fluorescence-mountain clip
Lights blanch, departures flatten.

You, Kettle, enact slow moraine.
Wail, Poor Sieve, duplicate house.

I, the maze of the crisis, enunciate
What I want, all I want, like this:
Daughters that open toward exited-out machines
That lead to breezes grooved by sleeve;;;;;;;;;;;;;;;;;;;;;;

WHEN THE CEILING IS LIKE MY LONG BLACK HAIR

I clasp a thread to listen to the wind.
Two heavens in word
Pace and knock, pace (what concrete from sound?),
Knock.
My presence sounds like an irritable punctuation,
The mother

Wrong in her apartment,
Wrong because of it, snapping its lassos and eyes.
The moving cord perversely plots to vacate.
A tendon of cabinets, pre-water, swerves over storm.
In the under-bee mountain-fluorescence light
Clips blanch, kettles flatten.

You, Departure, enact slow sieve.
Wail, Poor Moraine, duplicate maze.
I, the house of the daughter, enunciate
What I want, all I want, like this:
Crises that open toward machined-out exits
That lead to sleeves grooved by breeze;;;;;;;;;;;;;;;;;;;;;;

WHEN THE MACHINE IS LIKE A BLACK EXIT

I clasp my long sleeves to listen to the breeze.
Two mazes in house
Pace and knock, pace (what daughter from crisis?),
Knock.
My kettle sounds like an irritable departure,
The sieve

Wrong in her moraine,
Wrong because of it, snapping its mountains and fluorescences.
The moving light perversely plots to vacate.
A clip of cabinets, pre-water, swerves over storm.
In the under-bee lasso-eye cord
Tendons blanch, presences flatten.

You, Punctuation, enact slow mother.
Wail, Poor Apartment, duplicate heaven.
I, the word of the concrete, enunciate
What I want, all I want, like this:
Sounds that open toward ceiling'd-out hairs
That lead to threads grooved by wind;;;;;;;;;;;;;;;;;;;

WHEN THE EXIT IS LIKE A BLACK MACHINE

I clasp my long breezes to listen to the sleeve.
Two houses in maze
Pace and knock, pace (what crisis from daughter?),
Knock.
My departure sounds like an irritable kettle,
The moraine

Wrong in her sieve,
Wrong because of it, snapping its fluorescences and mountains.
The moving clip perversely plots to vacate.
An eye of waters, pre-cabinet, swerves over bee.
In the under-storm eye-lasso tendon
Cords blanch, punctuations flatten.

You, Presence, enact slow apartment.
Wail, Poor Mother, duplicate word.
I, the heaven of the sound, enunciate
What I want, all I want, like this:
Concrete that opens toward hair'd-out ceilings
That lead to winds grooved by thread.

MICHELLE ROBINSON | PAUL AUSTER

From This Miserable Mutineer a Stutter, for When We Are Reading Dostoevsky in Caves.

How can I describe to you the sadness of my precision?
I am Brendan, owner of dictionaries,

Whose intoxicating contents leveled me with one blow.

In Stockton, a fellow looked at me. We threw down right
there, behind a Mexican grocery store.
I pummeled him until the grease poured from my fingers.

Ah fuck it all sometimes!
I thought truth would speak from that thing that is
physical. I am wrong.
I want it on my grave:
                    I am wrong.

Whose product follows me, that ghost.
The scuffling sounds of dusty sneakers and sheets flapping. His constant
clumsiness!
["Don't leave me now. I can't get through this night without you."]

I pummeled him until the grease poured from my fingers. My —

(Has it been a hoax?

The man on Belton Street selling poetry. The man who laid hands on him.
The sandwich board for Johnny's Luncheonette.
And Damrosch, that quick-witted kitten, who will make me laugh anon!)

My fellows!

How can I persuade you of the imprecision of my sadness?
I have forgotten to take this body off

Whose letter ends, "I don't know what to write.
I don't know what you want to read. Not this."

Keith

His name is Nick. He is the guy at Vicki's housewarming party
who tells me how to make cocaine in my bathtub.
He looks like this guy on the cover of *The Snarkout Boys
and the Avocado of Death* (in the book he is Walter Galt
and his father is a sausage manufacturer). In this poem he is
the guy who leaves a note in my pocket.

There is a note in my pocket.

I feel like I'm shuffling through this, the fatness of it.
Let me explain:
      Here is when Nick leaves the note in my pocket.
      The note says Nick — the guy from Vicki's housewarming party.
         Call me.
The note means this:
Nick was the name Nick gave when the name Nick
gave was a variable assignment for Nick.

Here there is a break in the pattern;
After this I will refer to Nick as Keith only.

                    "Play out the play" (II.iv.490)

Last night I slept with a belt around my neck.

I say to Keith, "Nick, you must have spilled
Something on your shirt." Keith says, "This is not beer.
I just don't bathe." Keith smells like beer.
Keith talks like something beautiful.

We are eating red Jell-O. There is not a note
in my pocket.

The next day I'm walking down the street Vicki says
who did you sleep with last night I say this guy named
Shakespeare.

When Smithson Looked into
the Salt Lake What He Saw

When Smithson looked into the Salt Lake what he saw
was not the thing itself but the possibility
of the thing: what had in its approach the possible
consequence of stepping off the land, and into the water
and for which he would be made fun of by name:
clown, you irrelevant, shit-eater, Rob — not
Rauschenberg who erased deKooning's drawing, nor
Mitchum who could not see the picture, could only see
the frame, nor Stoppard, nor Shakespeare, no sucker
of stones was Smithson, no rocket scientist, whose roughly
carted rock trucked out to the rim of the lake a makeshift
anachronism: sediment, and grew steadily into land
because he did not *faire un trou* but a rotary, a gift and

what will be sweet to remember: swirling into the Salt Lake
he, who could have said "Take this!" one miserable rock,
who could have said "here is something

beautiful for you," who said, who could barely say
"Someone turned on a faucet inside me"

when he and the world became acquainted,
and thus succeeded in maintaining its mysterious
and wonderful affections, his hand dipping
into the water, occasionally, after the sediment
he was not certain was underneath in the same way he was not
certain the water would not rise about him, and it did: I did not
know for a long time generosity was rare,
or if the world is not eminently just and fair it is
sufficiently so, don't blame me, Smithson,
you were duly exiled: in the film: you run along
the Spiral Jetty, the helicopter cranes
above you, and reaching the end of the curving land
you rest briefly, dizzy and gratified, and start back, you,
who could do nothing: having skirted your way
along the scaffold could do nothing but run back
but I will explain:

MR: I was just reading some of *The Arcades Project* by Walter Benjamin, and at the very end of it, when he is comparing the work of Mallarmé to Baudelaire's poetry, he talks about Mallarme's poems resulting in a literature that doesn't have an object. He says that the poems revolve around absences, silences, emptinesses, and that they are highly esoteric. I felt that the same words could be used to describe some of your poetry. The *Collected Poems* and *Disappearances* are about the articulations of absences; so the question is, does your poetry occur in the world? Do you think about the relationship of your poetry to a physical world?

PA: Oh yes, definitely. In fact, I always thought of my poems as very down-to-earth and very concrete. What I was trying to do, when I wrote all these poems in my twenties (I haven't written a poem since 1979, so it's been a long time), was consciously limit myself to just a few elements, but all of them concrete, all of them from nature. There are obviously no references to the contemporary world whatsoever in what I wrote. We're dealing with landscapes, stones, earth, plants, sky, clouds, stars, night; just a few basic elements. And out of that, what you might call setting, I tried to create some kind of work that would speak to, on the one hand the aspiration for a better world, and on the other hand, the difficulties of communication. So I think in general, my work is about striving toward the other, and rarely achieving it. Am I making sense?

MR: Yes, definitely. You just mentioned that you stopped writing poetry in 1979 which is, incidentally, the year I was born.

PA: One leaves, the other arrives.

MR: Well, I wasn't writing poetry at that age.

PA: Potentially a poet.

MR: The fact that you don't write poetry now makes me want to ask if you stopped being a "poet" at the level of language or the level of ideas. What does it mean exactly to stop writing poetry?

PA: I guess I came to a wall. I didn't know how to go on. I was blocked. If you look at the movement of the poetry from the beginning to the end, there is, nevertheless, a gradual opening up. And I think the last poems have a much more narrative feel to them than the early ones did. The early poems, from *On Earth* for example, are very compact, very tight little fists of language, whereas by the end, some of those longer poems are very discursive, in a way. You see, underneath it all, I was always hoping to write novels, and concurrently with poetry I was writing fiction; I was just never really happy with it. I just didn't publish it; I didn't show it to anybody. And I hit that wall and didn't write anything for about a year. Then (I don't know if you've read about this; I've talked about this before) I went to a little rehearsal of a dance performance.

MR: Oh yes, I have read about that.

PA: And it was there that something happened to me, some kind of opening took place. I think I felt a kind of joyful understanding of the rift between words and the world. And it made it possible for me to write again. And when I picked up my pen to start writing, it wasn't poetry; it was suddenly prose. And that led to a short prose piece, which is in the *Collected Poems*, called "White Spaces." And that really was, I think, a breakthrough for me. It's much freer, much more open; it's much more filled with contradictions. The terrible irony is, the night I finished that piece, which was January 1979, that was the night my father died. And I worked on finishing it until about two o'clock in the morning. It was a Saturday night. I went to sleep and then the telephone rang the next morning at about seven. Nobody calls at seven o'clock on Sunday morning. It was my uncle, telling me that my father had died that night. Such a strange turn. I started writing *The Invention of Solitude* almost immediately — about a week later — and it flowed out of "White Spaces." That was prose and now I was writing prose again. And I've somehow never looked back. My whole life changed that moment. That book led to the novels that I've written since. It's a very strange story. I don't fully understand it myself. But I think the kind of poetry I was trying to write can only go so far. You can't keep doing it.

MR: One of the things that your absence from poetry always makes me recall is the fact that George Oppen and Carl Rakosi also had these long hiatuses from writing poetry.

PA: Absolutely. And they were two people that I knew very well and admired. And both stories are very, very strange. Who knows? Maybe some day I will start writing poetry again. At the moment, the only time I write poems is for family occasions . . . [laughs] Weddings, birthday parties, and I write very silly rhyming poems to make everybody laugh.

MR: Terrific.

PA: That's my sole poetic work at the moment.

MR: My poems usually make people laugh too.

PA: Good.

MR: I was reading some of your prose writing, your preface to *The Random House Book of 20th Century French Poetry* where you talk about the problems for Beckett translating *Endgame* from French into English. I often feel that in your poetry — in this way it reminds me of the poetry of the New Englander William Bronk as well — there's very frequently not the same heaviness or mundane specificity that gets associated with the English language. Bronk's work also seems to retain some kind of built-in abstractions. I was going to quote from one of his poems from *Silence and Metaphor* called "Missing." It starts off:

Whomever we might miss, it is not our friends, though there is no one else. Then isn't there anyone?

And I think in a way "White Spaces" does that too — it seems as if it's translated from another language. Do you think your writing is something that happens in English?

PA: Ah. Well, I don't know. I have a feeling just the opposite. Maybe "White Spaces" feels a little odd, but the poems themselves are really immersed in English, and I think they're almost untranslatable too — the poetry. People have tried here and there — I don't know to what degree they've succeeded — but I was always very drawn to the polarity in English between the Anglo-Saxon roots and then the French-Latinate additions, which made English this double language. I think it's perhaps the most flexible language, and certain writers I admire a great deal, like Emily Dickinson or John Milton, really played with those two kinds of English very brilliantly — the concrete Anglo-Saxon and the more abstract French — and I tried to do that consciously in the poems that I wrote.

MR: I was also wondering if you could talk a little more about the reception of your poetry, generally. You just mentioned that it hadn't been translated, although people have attempted to do so. But I know that your fiction is really popular abroad.

PA: It's been translated into a few languages — French, Spanish, German, and Japanese. And Finnish. Someone did a book in Finland. So maybe there've been seven or eight places where the poems have appeared, but other than the French I can't really judge. The French never seem to capture the earthiness of the English, the concreteness of the language. The reception of the poetry? Well, I was a very obscure poet. When I was writing and publishing it was always with little presses, very tiny editions. Nobody really saw the work. I published in tiny magazines for the most part. You know, once or twice I was in bigger places like *Poetry* or *Partisan Review* (which no longer exists, but it was an important magazine back in the '70s). Other than that, very, very, very small, marginal places. But I think that's the fate of most poets anyway.

MR: I was talking to my sister, and she said she read an article about you in a Finnish magazine, so I imagine you're very popular there.

PA: Ah-ha! That's very interesting. You see, it wasn't until I started publishing prose and novels that people got to know who I was, that there became some interest in reprinting the poems, and that's how *Disappearances* came about.

MR: Do you think about the poetry as something that's really integral to your body of work, then?

PA: I think of it as the foundation of everything I've done. And who knows? Maybe it's the best work I ever did. I don't know. But I do feel that all the concerns that I had then, I've continued. And my later work has been an outgrowth of that poetic work.

MR: The other issue I want to ask you about is your own translations. I've been writing a couple of papers on translating, mostly about Sir Philip Sidney's translations of the Psalms into English verse — he was working from the 1560 Geneva Bible in English and the French verse translations of the Psalms by Clément Marot and Théodore de Bèze (Les Pseaumes de David Mis En Rime Françoise). So I was wondering if you could talk about the hermeneutics of translation for you. What compels you to translate a particular French poet?

PA: Before I answer, speaking of the Psalms, a poet friend of mine from college did a beautiful translation of the Psalms about two years ago. You may have seen it; his name is Lawrence Weeder.

MR: I think I have seen it, yes.

PA: Good. Translating for me was a passionate act of discovery. And I started reading contemporary French poets when I was an undergraduate — eighteen, nineteen, twenty years old — and I got so excited by some of the work that I decided to translate it. That was it. I picked people that I cared about. And I think it was a very, very, very good thing to do. Translation is probably the best exercise a young writer can participate in to learn how to write. Because in some sense — of course you have to take a good text — but if it's something interesting, something of value, and then you give up your own ego, and enter into that text, it's certainly a way of penetrating it, better than reading and rereading, better than writing a paper about it. You're inside the tissue, the bones, the muscles of the work. You do your best to transform it into your own language, but in some sense the pressure's off. You know you don't have to be, so to speak, coming up with brilliant ideas every second. And so it gives you a chance to concentrate on the actual craft of putting together words. I think it was a very important part of my development as a writer, doing those translations when I was young.

MR: Are you still doing translations?

PA: No, I haven't translated in a long, long time. Again, it's that sense of wanting to do it — it just disappeared after a while. And I've just been so busy with my other work, I haven't had time. But it was interesting — this new book, the *Collected Poems* — of course it's the same publisher that did *Disappearances* (Overlook Press) and has been through a few printings. The book had gone out of print again at one point a few years ago. And the publisher, Peter Mayer, called me up and said, "Look, why don't we do something new this time? Why don't we do a bigger book?" He was the one who suggested putting some of my translations in the book as well, and I thought it was a good idea.

MR: Did you choose which translated poems would go in?

PA: Yeah, I chose the ones from many, many more than that, but it was just a selection.

MR: One other thing I wanted to ask about was last fall, I believe it was, I saw a performance at MIT with Don Byron, and you were there performing with him.

PA: Oh, you were there? Oh, how nice!

MR: We had gone to see Don Byron and didn't realize that you would be there as well, so it was really interesting. And at the time I didn't know what you were reading but now I think you were reading parts of "White Spaces."

PA: I think so. Don and I have performed together about three times so I can't remember what we did that time, but I think "White Spaces" was one of the pieces.

MR: So, I want to ask you how you understand the combination of music and poetry working. Is he accompanying you? Are you accompanying him? What's supposed to be taking place?

PA: Well, I think in some sense it's a failed activity from the start. It doesn't work. But at the same time, there are interesting moments. And I think it's those moments that make it worth trying. I would say the words come first. The music is accompanying the words. But every once in a while, there could be a moment when the two elements are working in some interesting harmony or just the opposite, against each other in some interesting way. And I'd like to keep an open mind about things and experiment. Don is a very good improviser. So, it seems . . . I don't know. What did you think?

MR: Well, once I realized that you were reading "White Spaces" and that you weren't improvising, it had a stranger quality to it. There was something about your poems being already written at that point, that they were existing in a kind of different realm than the music that was going on too.

PA: Right.

MR: But also, the act of performing made it seem like they were being re-written. So, in that sense maybe you were writing poetry then.

PA: Yeah, it's quite incredible.

MR: So is there anything else in particular you'd like to say about your poetry?

PA: No, I guess not. I always feel that the work has to speak for itself. And there's not a lot I can say about it. It's just *there* for you to make of it what you will.

MR: You mentioned the wall earlier. And there's the brick wall and the bricks in George Oppen's *Of Being Numerous*.

PA: Yes, true. True.

MR: Is there some kind of correspondence there?

PA: No, I don't really think so. But walls have always interested me. You know, there was a period while I was writing poetry in the mid '70s during which I wrote a few plays. One of them, which has the strange title — "Laurel and Hardy Go To Heaven" — is about two men, Laurel and Hardy, and they're in some undefined space, some meadow somewhere, and what they have to do is build a wall. And the whole play is them carrying these stones and building the wall, which slowly rises as the play progresses until, in the end, they're blocked off from the audience. And that was the play. It was a youthful work, not great, but it interested me. And I think that wall stayed inside of me and became the wall in *The Music of Chance*, a novel. I don't know if you've read it.

MR: I have read it.

PA: You have? So, there's another wall. It's been an image that's haunted me all my life.

MR: It's an interesting image too because it's also in Tom Stoppard's play about Hamlet. It begins with the building of a wall, kind of as a metaphor for language. But I'm thinking even earlier, in Poe's wall in "The Cask of Amontillado."

PA: Yes, yes. Well, walls are very pregnant images, I have to say. They can lock you in or they can keep people from coming in. It's double.

Narrative

Because what happens will never happen,
and because what has happened
endlessly happens again,

we are as we were, everything
has changed in us, if we speak
of the world
it is only to leave the world

unsaid. Early winter: the yellow apples still
unfallen
in a naked tree, the tracks
of invisible deer

in the first snow, and then the snow
that does not stop. We repent
of nothing. As if we could stand
in this light. As if we could stand in the silence
of this single moment

of Light.

from "White Spaces"

Something happens, and from the moment it begins to happen, nothing can ever be the same again.

Something happens. Or else, something does not happen. A body moves. Or else, it does not move. And if it moves, something begins to happen. And even if it does not move, something begins to happen.

It comes from my voice. But that does not mean these words will ever be what happens. It comes and goes. If I happen to be speaking at this moment, it is only because I hope to find a way of going along, of running parallel to everything else that is going along, and so begin to find a way of filling the silence without breaking it.

I ask whoever is listening to this voice to forget the words it is speaking. It is important that no one listen too carefully. I want these words to vanish, so to speak, into the silence they came from, and for nothing to remain but a memory of their presence, a token of the fact that they were once here and are here no longer and that during their brief life they seemed not so much to be saying any particular thing as to be the thing that was happening at the same time a certain body was moving in a certain space, that they moved along with everything else that moved.

Something begins, and already it is no longer the beginning, but something else, propelling us into the heart of the thing that is happening. If we were suddenly to stop and ask ourselves, "Where are we going?", or "Where are we now?", we would be lost, for at each moment we are no longer where we were, but have left ourselves behind, irrevocably, in a past that has no memory, a past endlessly obliterated by a motion that carries us into the present.

It will not do, then, to ask questions. For this is a landscape of random impulse, of knowledge for its own sake — which is to say, a knowledge that exists, that comes into being beyond any possibility of putting it into words. And if just this once we were to abandon ourselves to the supreme indifference of simply being wherever we happen to be, then perhaps we would not be deluding ourselves into thinking that we, too, had at last become a part of it all.

To think of motion not merely as a function of the body but as an extension of the mind. In the same way, to think of speech not as an extension of the mind but as a function of the body. Sounds emerge from the voice to enter the air and surround and bounce off and enter the body that occupies that air, and though they cannot be seen, these sounds are no less a gesture than a hand is when outstretched in the air towards another hand, and in this gesture can be read the entire alphabet of desire, the body's need to be taken beyond itself, even as it dwells in the sphere of its own motion.

On the surface, this motion seems to be random. But such randomness does not, in itself, preclude a meaning. Or if meaning is not quite the word for it, then say the drift, or a consistent sense of what is happening, even as it changes, moment by moment. To describe it in all its details is probably not impossible. But so many words would be needed, so many streams of syllables, sentences, and subordinate clauses, that the words would always lag behind what was happening, and long after all motion had stopped and each of its witnesses had dispersed, the voice describing that motion would still be speaking, alone, heard by no one, deep into the silence and darkness of these four walls. And yet something is happening, and in spite of myself I want to be present inside the space of this moment, of these moments, and to say something, even though it will be forgotten, that will form a part of this journey for the length of the time it endures.

BEN LERNER | AARON KUNIN

from *The Lichtenberg Figures*

We must retract our offerings, burnt as they are.
We must recall our lines of verse like faulty tires.
We must flay the curatoriat, invest our sackcloth,

and enter the Academy single file.

Poetry has yet to emerge.
The image is no substitute. The image is an anecdote
in the mouth of a stillborn. And not reflection,
with its bad infinitude, nor religion, with its eighth of mushrooms,
can bring orgasm to orgasm like poetry. As a policy,

we are generally sorry. But sorry doesn't cut it.
We must ask you to remove your shoes, your lenses, your teeth.
We must ask you to sob openly.

If it is any consolation, we admire the early work of John Ashbery.
If it is any consolation, you won't feel a thing.

from *The Lichtenberg Figures*

I'm going to kill the president.
I promise. I surrender. I'm sorry.
I'm gay. I'm pregnant. I'm dying.
I'm not your father. You're fired.
Fire. I forgot your birthday.
You will have to lose the leg.
She was asking for it.
It ran right under the car.

It looked like a gun. It's contagious.
She's with God now.
Help me. I don't have a problem.
I've swallowed a bottle of aspirin.
I'm a doctor. I'm leaving you.
I love you. Fuck you. I'll change.

from *The Lichtenberg Figures*

The sky is a big responsibility. And I am the lone intern. This explains
my drinking. This explains my luminous portage, my baboon heart
that breaks nightly like the news. Who

am I kidding? I am Diego Rodríguez Velázquez. I am a dry
and eviscerated analysis of the Russian Revolution.
I am line seven. And my memory, like a melon,
contains many dark seeds. Already, this poem has achieved

the status of lore amongst you little people of New England.
    Nevertheless,
I, Dr. Samuel Johnson, experience moments of such profound alienation
that I have surrendered my pistols to the care of my sister, Elizabeth
    Förster-Nietzsche.

Forgive me. For I have taken things too far. And now your carpet is
    ruined.
Forgive me. For I am not who you think I am. I am Charlie Chaplin

playing a waiter embarrassed by his occupation. And when the rich
    woman I love
enters this bistro, I must pretend that I'm only pretending to play a waiter
    for her amusement.

BL: Aaron, things aren't going very well for our empire, our species, or our planet. Who, besides politicians or the insane, would deny that our commitment to radical ecological destruction and the ever-increasing proliferation of murderous technologies threaten the survival not only of our culture, whatever that might be, but of culture generally? How does the very real possibility of holocaust influence your writing, your thinking about writing?

AK: Poetry is traditionally supposed to resist holocaust by preserving whatever is most valuable in human civilization, like in Shakespeare's sonnets, where the most valuable thing in the culture is the face of a particularly beautiful boy, and everyone who sees it wants to see more of it and gets angry at this boy because he isn't working harder to bequeath his beauty to the culture as some kind of legacy that can be enjoyed as a keepsake forever. The speaker in the sonnets argues that the beautiful boy should entrust his most valuable quality to some technology of preservation, such as sexual reproduction (so that his image will be preserved intact in the body of his son) or poetry (so that his image will be available to anyone who sees, hears, or recites these poems). The arguments fail; the boy apparently isn't convinced, because he isn't being offered a very good deal: in every scenario, his beauty is preserved in a form that won't allow him to enjoy it. He still has to die, but his beauty gets to live on.

So, even in the sonnets, which are the most familiar and influential articulation of the preservation fantasy in English literature, preservation turns out to be a rather unattractive plan against the fact of mortality and the possibility of holocaust. Either you aren't preserving the object of value, or you're preserving it in a form that won't allow you to experience it fully, or you're preserving it in a form that's actually toxic to whatever quality you value in the object which originally made you want to preserve it.

Shakespeare's preservation fantasy might also look unattractive because it is apparently compatible with a holocaust fantasy: in advocating the preservation of the beautiful image that he values, the speaker in these poems also incidentally calls for the destruction of everything else! "Let those whom nature hath not made for store, / Hard, featureless, and rude, barrenly perish." After the surpassing disasters of the last century, poets have at least learned to be suspicious of these proposals. I agree with Elias Canetti when he says that the content of the fantasy of living forever through culture is crazy, violent, and basically indistinguishable from the fantasy of destroying a town, an army, or a civilization. You want to see everyone else die so that you can prove to yourself that you are indestructible. Unfortunately, this deplorable fantasy is pretty hard-wired. If Canetti is right, people aren't going to change until they lose the instinct toward self-preservation — which basically means that they aren't going to change, right? He also says that we would have to stop giving commands, just take the imperative mood out of grammar (which sounds slightly more doable).

BL: Has anxiety about annihilation changed significantly since Shakespeare? Has the nature of the struggle for intergenerational cultural transmission been transformed by global warming and nuclear weapons?

AK: My usual response to that would be: that's a historical question, and I am not a historian, so I am not responsible for that. I'm not strongly committed to the project of representing a moment or period in time. I'm just not that interested in history or narrative or time for that matter. My biggest problem as a critic, because I specialize in seventeenth-century English poetry, has been to find ways of writing about old poems that do not entail writing history.

What could it mean to be on the side of history? There's a scene in the Gillo Pontecorvo film *The Battle of Algiers* where a captured rebel leader has a conference with the international press. One of the journalists asks, Did you really think that your tiny band of terrorists stood any chance against the entire modern French army? And the rebel says, Well, we thought that we had a much better chance of defeating the French army than the French army had of defeating history. That's a commitment to history in the future, "the history that will be," as Eduardo Galeano puts it. Particular historical events might not appear to be on the side of some individual rebel, but history is ultimately going to favor this rebellion.

History starts to look interesting to me when it's about modality rather than chronology. "What mood do you want to live in?" rather than "What tense?" History can be written in the mode of nostalgia (you study seventeenth-century history because you actually want to turn back the clock and live there) or in the mode of accuracy or positivism (you want to collect as much information as possible about what really happens) or in the mode of the probable (like Greek tragedy or Hollywood film). The probable is the most powerful mode for shaping belief, and it's the one most of us inhabit most of the time. If I'm a historian, if my work has any implications for history, I want it to be in the mode of the possible rather than the probable. One implication of the question you're asking is that the modality of apocalypse is shifting from the possible to the probable, or, to put it generically, from myth into history. Since moving to California, I notice that I've been spending a good part of each day indulging in apocalyptic fantasies. Everyone I talk to has them — I'm sure you've noticed it too. It's not like New York, where everyone seems to more or less agree on how the world will end; here, there are so many possible endings that each person can have one, or several. Why is this? It kind of makes sense to me that the world would end differently in each place, but why does California have more than its fair share of end-of-the-world scenarios?

BL: In *Terminator 2*, the current governor of California plays a machine sent back in time to preempt apocalypse. It was an ideologically rich fantasy — a supercomputer with an Austrian accent that could correct for holocaust. Now the Terminator is looking forward to becoming president. In a state where the fantastic and the real pass into one another seamlessly, I think apocalyptic speculation is bound to proliferate: that's not a real governor — that's Arnold Schwarzenegger playing the governor! That's not the real sky — it's some sort of special effect! California dreaming: the world could end without our knowing it, or could have already ended and been replaced with its image.

AK: I'm also wondering about the Midwest, where we both grew up. I find it difficult to imagine the end of the world in Minneapolis, for example. Since you've thought seriously about the particular kind of violence that happens in the Midwest, you might have an answer for this question: is there a midwestern apocalypse?

BL: Every sixty miles in the Midwest you can get off the highway and find yourself in the place you just left — that's the phenomenology of the chain, the franchise. In that sense time in the Midwest no longer exists, which is the condition of the postapocalyptic. Maybe that's why you find it difficult to imagine Central Standard Time ending?

Violence is often a strategy of orientation: pinch me so I know I'm not dreaming; punch me so I know that I'm real — wait, I'll just punch you. I wonder if apocalyptic fantasy, which is rampant in the Midwest, is just this desire on the grandest scale? My world must exist if it can be destroyed. The thirst for apocalypse in the Midwest is pronounced: the best-selling books are the *Left Behind* series of Christian fundamentalist texts, the AM radio stations are all talking about the cataclysmic clash of East and West. The Midwest is really able to come together over the issue of imminent destruction — apocalypse is a uniter, not a divider! Fundamentalism is a strategy for forging community through end-time fantasy.

California and the Midwest, of course, are two ways of talking about an identity crisis that is increasingly general. Our culture doesn't just worry about what it is, but if it is — we worry about keeping it real. On the one hand these are ancient concerns: skepticism, doubt, "the sense of an ending." On the other hand, the reality of Zeuxis's grapes can't be compared to our contemporary capacity for simulation. Simulating apocalypse, as in many of Governor Schwarzenegger's movies, is less a way of fantasizing about the end of the world than it is a fantasy about the end of simulation, even if the world has to go down with its stunt double. A culture that constitutes itself through images of its own destruction — that's very close to the kind of fascistic feedback loop described by Walter Benjamin.

AK: This reminds me of Alexander Kluge's idea that at any moment in our world someplace is always "Sarajevo, no matter what the place is called," where, if you do the wrong thing, you will cause a world war. In this place, the wrong action is not only possible but likely, because this is a place with multiple centers where no one can predict with any certainty what anyone else is going to do next.

BL: Alexander Kluge has interesting things to say about catastrophe — indeed, his *Learning Processes with a Deadly Outcome* takes place after the apocalypse. What is significant about Kluge's writing is the utter absence of style (which is, of course, a kind of style). He uses a flat, objective tone to describe the litany of disasters effected in the name of objectivity. What is eventually revealed is the complicity of such language in the violent processes it describes. While American writers who take on fascism, violence, etc., like William Vollmann, tend toward an excessive style presumably homologous to the excesses they document, Kluge does something much more vital: he makes visible the role that purportedly rational, sanitized rhetoric plays in fascistic organization. There is no passion in Kluge, because the greatest crimes of the last 150 years have not been crimes of passion, of unreason, but of systematic thinking and methodical execution. Kluge's prose is terrifyingly efficient. He has no voice. Or he has the voice of a machine.

Your first book, *Folding Ruler Star*, can be similarly scary. You reduce affect to biology; the body to its parts; *Paradise Lost* to a kind of structuralist *Fort/Da*. Your version of the *Carte du tendre* is anything but tender — it remaps the body into security zones that, instead of being thrilled by a lover's touch, are alarmed by their own description. It is a work of radical antihumanism, of negative anthropology, a work that reveals the degree to which the human is a construct, and reflects your suspicion of the humanist project of immortality. "The t.v. has a / human face," the book begins. If *Paradise Lost* were a computer program, *Folding Ruler Star* would be a vicious worm, deleting value claims from within the form. Not a serpent with an evil agenda, but a vermin immanent to the apple!

The formal strategies you apply to enact the antihumanism you thematize are similarly sinister. Auden celebrated the power of metrical form to free us from "the fetters of the self." Auden meant that metrical rules interrupt our habits — we want to say one word, but it doesn't scan, so we're forced to select another. The self, fettered or unfettered, is still the center of Auden's poetic paradigm. Your brand of formalism — your strict syllabic and stanzaic rules — frees us from the self but embraces the fetters ("inhuman / syllables"). I'll tell you when the reader realizes just how inhuman your syllables are: when she encounters the "found poem" on page 29 that functions as an expert segue into your sequence of "FIVE SECURITY ZONES." It consists of a warning message that appears on computer screens: "YOU APPEAR TO BE / USING A VERSION / OF TELNET SOFTWARE // WHICH IS NOT SECURE." What's startling is that this found text is perfectly consistent with the voice (or lack of voice) of all the other poems. The speaking subject of these poems is a machine. There may or may not be a human addressee.

AK: I admire the poem in *The Lichtenberg Figures* made entirely of clichés:

> I'm going to kill the president.
> I promise. I surrender. I'm sorry.
> I'm gay. I'm pregnant. I'm dying.
> I'm not your father. You're fired.
> Fire. I forgot your birthday . . .

The form of the poem recalls two quite different New York School models: O'Hara's "I do this, I do that" poems, and Barbara Guest's emphatic self-descriptions (e.g., in *Fair Realism*: "I float over this dwelling and when I choose / enter it"). But this is not a personal poem in either sense; the language is not the speech of a particular person. If it nonetheless has a powerful effect it's because, first of all, these clichés are speech acts — threats, promises, apologies, confessions, etc. Each phrase constitutes an action in itself, and in many cases the actions are violent. The violence is both descriptive and inflammatory, provoking instinctive physical response. Second, although you present the clichés raw, without any personal context or vocal signature in the phrase, there's nonetheless a strong narrative pull, because you've arranged them so that they appear to frame each other. It's possible to imagine them as the soundtrack for a sequence of actions (I threaten the president, I promise to carry out my threat, I surrender to the authorities, I apologize); there's also some suggestion that this is a riddle, in which readers can try to guess the common term that binds the statements. They produce an image of a person not prior but anterior to the phrases, just as, in another poem, you ask: "What am I the antecedent of?" The pronoun is the antecedent; the person is on the other side.

Even though the person in this poem is not someone but anyone, I want to say that it isn't an example of non-style. On the contrary, your book is an anthology of different styles. In classical rhetoric, style is conceived as a mask, a prophylactic device that detaches you from what you are saying and thus protects you from the dangerous effects of your own eloquence. In revising "figures of speech" into "Lichtenberg figures," you're imagining style as a tool that cuts both ways, imposing form on speaker and audience.

Do you realize that we've just congratulated each other for poems that are essentially found objects?

BL: Yes, we're complimenting each other on disappearing from our poems. It's like applauding a speaker for not showing up.

The found poem is an important form because it reminds us that all language is to some degree found — that writing is always manipulating the already written; reading is always rereading. If poetry is supposed to "make it new," poets have to practice creative recycling.

AK: "A cookie / is not the only substance that receives the shape / of the instrument with which it's cut." Coleridge's name for such a tool is "mechanical form": a limit on what can and can't be said in poetry, imposed from outside. By contrast, he prefers "organical form," where the poem discovers its own limits. A more productive statement of the same distinction, at least for me, occurs in Sol LeWitt's "Paragraphs on Conceptual Art." LeWitt talks about two strategies for art-making: in the normal, intuitive, organic way, at every stage of the project, you're constantly discovering new problems and having to respond to them. With every move, you have to start from scratch: what color should this be, what materials should I use, what scale am I working on? You have to make a whole new set of decisions every time you turn around. In the other, conceptual way, which is LeWitt's, you make all the decisions before you start working "and the execution is a perfunctory affair. The idea becomes a machine that makes the art." You can even get someone else to "fabricate" it for you. The distinction, whether intuitive/conceptual or organical/mechanical, is not between imposing form and not imposing form, because LeWitt understands, correctly, that you can't have art without some kind of control. It's just a question of where are you going to make the decisions, where are you going to make the cuts? Because I'm not very good at making decisions, I seem to need a lot of veils and baffles, a "secret architecture" with several procedural stages, before I can write a poem. Sort of like the character in the Wong Kar-Wai film *Fallen Angels* who says that he became an assassin because he isn't very decisive, and the great thing about being an assassin is that you never have to decide anything; someone else always tells you where to stand, who dies, how to escape, etc.

BL: Mechanical form isn't just procedural in *Folding Ruler Star*, it's thematic, in so far as the text is an argument against humanism. In *The Lichtenberg Figures*, mechanical form is similarly thematic in the sense that the arbitrary constraints of the cutting instrument, the sonnet, aspire to enact the violence the poems often describe. (My friend Eric McHenry has objected to my using the term "violence" in this sense, arguing that the concept of textual or linguistic or discursive violence debases the reality of physical violence. Not only do I believe that textual violence can have physical effects, but I think the phenomenon McHenry is describing — the emptying of a word through metaphorical transfers and repetition — is itself a kind of violence, one that poetry can explore.)

I'm very suspicious of any intuitive compositional strategy, of the concept of organic form. While the human is often associated with the spontaneous, and the mechanical with the predetermined, we know this association is largely mythical — humans are famously unable to avoid patterns; we rely on our machines for the generation of random numbers. "Free verse" is a silly concept for a variety of reasons. On the most obvious level, the decision to avoid metrical rules is a rule. An artist doesn't get to choose between spontaneous and procedural composition; she can only choose the degree to which she will make the composition of the compositional rules part of the artistic process. The freest verse is contained in books like Raymond Queneau's *Cent Mille Milliards de Poèmes*, not in the predictably lineated prose of our laureates.

Many contemporary poetic polemics are predicated upon an impoverished concept of form. Geoffrey Hill and Lyn Hejinian, for example, have more in common with each other than they do with weaker members of their respective coteries. *My Life* and *The Mercian Hymns* are brilliant exercises in autobiography in which the compositional procedures relate to the text thematically. Hill's versets — a form traditionally used to express fervent religious or patriotic sentiments — structurally stage the conflict between personal and historical memory the book explores. Hejinian's use of sentence count and repetition reveals how the structure of remembering can determine its objects, which is what the book, in part, is "about." "New Formalism" is nonsense — the position that a villanelle is somehow inherently more formal than Hejinian's techniques is reactionary. It's equally reactionary, however, when a young member of the self-declared vanguard dismisses Hill because he explores the potential of received techniques. From now on let's use "formalist" and "experimental" as superlatives, not as ideological affiliations that precede the poems in question. Geoffrey Hill is an experimental poet. Lyn Hejinian is one of our finest formalists.

AK: I don't want to give too much power to poetic form. Put it this way: poetic form is interesting only insofar as it produces a social relation or an image of one. This can happen rhetorically — e.g., a poet uses a formal device to have an effect on the minds and bodies of readers. Or poetic form can define a community of people who have read the same poems or write in similar forms, such as the Language poets. Form can also be understood as political allegory. For Pope, the closed couplet describes an enlightened society in which communication works: thought can be externalized, grasped, transferred. For Milton, the closed couplet represents an imposed order that should be resisted. Poetic form produces not one but many images of society.

BL: You are a formalist poet particularly interested in the poem as measure — "Affect lives in the face and is measured with a ruler. The measure is a five-syllable line arranged in three-line units." Would you talk a little bit about what this means?

AK: I'm very interested in the idea that a poem is an instrument of measure. What does it measure? The traditional answer is time. In classical prosody, you're measuring time in units called long and short syllables that have precise lengths. Because it measures time, this kind of poetic line also implicitly measures human life. It may also be thought to regulate, therefore to institute or control, time, to stop time, or to shield objects from the effects of time. (Shakespeare again: "And all in war with time for love of you, / As he takes from you, I engraft you new.") Lyn Hejinian's *My Life* is an unusual example of a prose poem in which the compositional unit, the sentence, measures time — not the time it takes to say the sentence, which is not precisely regulated, but a year.

"Time" is still a very good answer to the question of what poems measure. The typical, modern, vernacular answer is voice. In traditional English prosody, you're measuring voice in units called long and short syllables that bear a precise stress. It might not sound as though very much is at stake in the modern conception. Time sounds like a profound concept; accent doesn't, maybe because everyone has a distinct accent. No one speaks exactly the same English, no one puts stress in the same places or pronounces a stressed syllable in the same way, or not all the time. But that's what makes the reduction of voice — of a particular, accented voice — to a uniform, abstract pattern so ambitious. It's the dream of a universal language, and, beyond that, a common world. There's a poem by the German poet Christian Morgenstern in which only the title, which translates as "Fishes' Nightsong," is in Danish; the rest of the poem is written in accent marks. When you diagram voice as a pulse, human language looks the same as fish language.

In modern poetry, there's a tendency to distrust both the accuracy of any measuring system (early in the twentieth century, Henry Adams composed a "Prayer to the Dynamo" because he believed that it released an energy that could not be regulated) and the impulse to measure, which is considered deceitful at best and, at worst, violent. For Gertrude Stein, "paragraphs are emotional not because they express emotion but because they register or limit emotion." My shame poems are supposed to be emotional in that sense. Shame is dominant because part of its function is to limit or bind other affects. The five-syllable line is imagined as equivalent to a face, where affect is radically externalized on the outermost surface of a person.

BL: You have an ironic strategy for measuring affect — your ruler erases what it measures. Your version of the dream of an abstract language is a nightmare — the language of machines, the laughter of Odradek. How did it take me until now to think of Odradek!

> But it is not only a spool, for a small wooden crossbar sticks out of the middle of the star, and another small rod is joined to that at a right angle. By means of this latter rod on one side and one of the points of the star on the other, the whole thing can stand upright as if on two legs.

Odradek is a folding ruler star, a ruler that has taught itself to walk. In the effort to reduce language to the universal, the human disappears — fish can speak it, and so can fishhooks. Odradek knows the empty Esperanto of modern bureaucracy ("And where do you live?" "No fixed abode"). We've returned to the immortality project, which is the care of the family man: "Can he possibly die . . . The idea that he is likely to survive me I find almost painful." That's the anxiety *Folding Ruler Star* produces: these poems don't need me, thinks the reader, and, precisely for that reason, they will survive me. That's why Odradek is laughing at us: "no human / face smiles out of a / folding ruler star."

Enclosed Please Find

a lost green binder
with bridge inspection
criteria (un-

fold celestial guide)
my incoherent
message (truer words

were never spoken)
in the mush of the
brain (in a morass

of shame) I adapt
to you faithfully
(because I make no

care) and the plumbing
works incessantly
violently and

ironically
and (literally
riding on wings of

lightning) an engorged
cloud suddenly un-
covers head and sky

Enclosed Please Find

solitary male
walking softly (on
those curiously

sensitive little
appendages they
have) so he won't feel

as much (frequent and
terrifying pains
on the surface) of

the machine (they can't
blush cry or love but
it's precisely in

blushing crying and
loving that they are
most machine-like) like

an apple that did
not ripen (astral
physiognomy)

kindly no human
face smiles out of a
folding ruler star

The Sore Throat

I'm inventing a machine
for concealing my desire.
And I'm inventing another
machine for concealing the
machine. It's a two-machine
system, and it sounded like
laughter. And I'm inventing
a machine for concealing
the sound. You, to me: "Why are
you concealing the beauty
of your machine?" Every machine
has more beauty than the last,
for everything whose purpose
is to conceal seems to change,
in the end, into a sign
of what it's concealing. And
now the sound that once sounded
like laughter is so loud that
it seems more like sobbing or
laughter concealing sobbing.
All my inventing is a
complete disaster. It's not
concealing my desire, it's
talking about my desire
to conceal my desire, like
a voice on a message machine
that would say: "Hello. About
desire, I'd like to say a
word or two. It's not your eyes,
it's not the word you say, it's
not your complaining voice that
I desire. All I desire
is your applause." It's hard not
to hear what the message is

saying, also it's hard to
keep myself from inventing
another machine to keep
from hearing it. So invent
a machine for disinventing.
This will be the last machine
I ever invent, and its
purpose will just be to change
every machine into shit.
No more inventing (for me).

— What a shame. It once was a
wonder of a machine; now
it's more like a disaster.

— I think he left a message . . .

— You're wrong: he just left a mess.

Rae Armantrout's most recent book of poetry, *Next Life*, was chosen as one of the 100 Notable Books of 2007 by the *New York Times*. Other recent books include *Collected Prose, Up to Speed, The Pretext*, and *Veil: New and Selected Poems*. Her poems have been included in numerous anthologies, including *Postmodern American Poetry: A Norton Anthology*, and *American Women Poets in the 21st Century: Where Language Meets the Lyric Tradition*. Armantrout is professor of poetry and poetics at the University of California, San Diego.

Paul Auster is the author of the poetry collections *Ground Work, Disappearances*, and *Collected Poems*. He is also the author of multiple works of fiction including *City of Glass, Leviathan, Mr. Vertigo*, and *Timbuktu*. He has translated, from the French, Stéphane Mallarmé and Joseph Joubert. Auster has received numerous awards and his work has been translated into 27 languages.

Jennifer K. Dick, who hails from Iowa, is the author of *Fluorescence*, the art chapbook *Retina/Rétine*, and the ebook *Enclosures* from a longer work in process. Her manuscripts *Circuits* and *The Texture of What Surrounds* were finalists for the 2007 Poets Out Loud Prize. She lives in Paris and is a doctoral candidate in comparative literature at University of Paris III. She also teaches for L'Université de Lille III & Polytechnique.

Paul Fattaruso is the author of *Travel in the Mouth of the Wolf, Bicycle*, and the chapbook *The Submariner's Waltz*. He received his MFA from the University of Massachusetts and his PhD from the University of Denver.

Allen Grossman was born in 1932 in Minneapolis, Minnesota. His awards and honors include a Guggenheim Fellowship, the Witter Brynner Poetry Prize, and a MacArthur Fellowship. He was professor of English at Brandeis University and the Andrew W. Mellon Professor of the Humanities at the Johns Hopkins University. His books of poetry include *The Ether Dome and Other Poems, How to Do Things with Tears*, and *Descartes' Loneliness*.

Carla Harryman is known for her genre-disrupting poetry, prose, plays, and essays. Her most recent book, *Adorno's Noise*, is a collection of conceptual prose works. She is the coeditor of *Lust for Life: On the Writings of Kathy Acker* and a coauthor of *The Grand Piano*, an experimental memoir by ten poets. She currently lives and teaches in Detroit and will join the faculty of Eastern Michigan University in fall 2008.

Christian Hawkey is the author of *The Book of Funnels* (winner of the Kate Tufts Discovery Award), the chapbook *HourHour*, which includes drawings by the artist Ryan Mrozowski, and *Citizen Of*. In 2006 he received a Creative Capital Innovative Literature Award, and in 2008 he was a DAAD Artist-in-Berlin Fellow. He teaches at Pratt Institute in Brooklyn, New York.

Christine Hume is the author of *Musca Domestica, Alaskaphrenia*, and the chapbook (with CD by James Marks) *Lullaby: Speculations on the First Active Sense*. She is associate professor of English at Eastern Michigan University.

Aaron Kunin is a poet, critic, and novelist. He is the author of *Folding Ruler Star*, a collection of small poems about shame; a novel, *The Mandarin*; and a chapbook, *Secret Architecture*. He lives in California and teaches at Pomona College.

Mary Leader began writing poems in the midst of a career as a lawyer, primarily on the staff of the Oklahoma Supreme Court. Her books are *Red Signature*, a selection of the National Poetry Series, and *The Penultimate Suitor*, winner of the Iowa Poetry Prize. She holds a PhD in English and American Literature from Brandeis University and an MFA from Warren Wilson College. She now teaches at Warren Wilson and at Purdue University.

Ben Lerner is from Topeka, Kansas. His books are *The Lichtenberg Figures* and *Angle of Yaw*. He has been a Fulbright Scholar and a finalist for the National Book Award; he cofounded and coedits *No: A Journal of the Arts* and teaches at the University of Pittsburgh.

Mark Levine is the author of three books of poems, *Debt, Enola Gay*, and *The Wilds*, and a nonfiction book, *F5: Devastation, Survival, and the Most Violent Tornado Outbreak of the 20th Century*. He teaches at the University of Iowa Writers' Workshop.

Sabrina Orah Mark was raised in Brooklyn and received a BA from Barnard College and an MFA from the Iowa Writers' Workshop. Her poems appear in many journals, most recently in *Harvard Review, Boston Review*, and *Conduit*. She has received fellowships from the Fine Arts Work Center in Provincetown, the Glenn Schaeffer Foundation, and the National Endowment for the Arts. Her first book of poems, *The Babies*, won the 2004 Saturnalia Books Poetry Prize (judged by Jane Miller). She teaches at Agnes Scott College and the University of Georgia, where she is completing her PhD in English.

Laura Mullen is a professor at Louisiana State University. She is the author of five books: three collections of poetry and two hybrid texts. Her most recent book is the hybrid text murder mystery *Murmur*. Her honors include Ironwood's Stanford Prize, a National Endowment for the Arts Fellowship, and a Rona Jaffe Foundation Writers' Award, among other honors.

Sawako Nakayasu is the author of two books of poetry and two forthcoming books: *Hurry Home Honey* and *Texture Notes*. She has received grants from the National Endowment for the Arts and PEN for translating Japanese poetry. Her translations include *Four from Japan* and *To the Vast Blooming Sky* by Chika Sagawa. Her own poetry has been translated into Japanese, Swedish, Arabic, and Vietnamese.

Claudia Rankine is the author of four collections of poetry, including *Don't Let Me Be Lonely*, *Plot*, *The End of the Alphabet*, and *Nothing in Nature is Private*. She is also coeditor of *American Women Poets in the 21st Century: Where Lyric Meets Language* and *American Poets in the 21st Century: The New Poetics*. She teaches at Pomona College.

Srikanth Reddy's first book of poetry, *Facts for Visitors*, received the Asian American Literary Award for poetry in 2005. His poems have appeared in various journals, including *American Poetry Review*, the *Canary*, *Jubilat*, and *A Public Space*. Reddy is currently assistant professor of English at the University of Chicago.

Michelle Robinson's first book of poetry, *The Life of a Hunter*, was published by University of Iowa Press in 2005. She was born in Madison, Wisconsin, and grew up in northern Virginia. A graduate of Harvard University and the Harvard Divinity School, Robinson is currently a PhD student in American Studies at Boston University.

Tomaž Šalamun was born in Zagreb, Croatia, and raised in Koper, Slovenia. He has published thirty collections of poetry in his native Slovenian language and numerous collections in other European languages. His recent books in English are *The Book For My Brother*, *Row*, and *Woods and Chalices*. He lives in Ljubljana and occasionally teaches in the United States.

Karen Volkman's books of poetry are *Crash's Law*, a National Poetry Series selection; *Spar*, which received the Iowa Poetry Prize and the James Laughlin Award; and *Nomina*. Her poems have appeared in numerous anthologies, including *The Best American Poetry*, the Pushcart Prize anthology, and *The PIP Gertrude Stein Awards in Innovative Poetry*. She has received awards from the National Endowment for the Arts, the Poetry Society of America, and the Bogliasco Foundation, and she currently teaches in the MFA program at the University of Montana, Missoula.

Rosmarie Waldrop's trilogy (*The Reproduction of Profiles*, *Lawn of Excluded Middle*, and *Reluctant Gravities*) has been reprinted by New Directions under the title *Curves to the Apple*. Waldrop's other recent books of poetry are *Blindsight* and *Love, Like Pronouns*. She has translated most of Edmond Jabès's work, including *The Book of Questions* and *The Book of Resemblances* and her memoir/study, *Lavish Absence: Recalling and Rereading Edmond Jabès*, was published in 2003. She lives in Providence, Rhode Island.

Dara Wier's books include *Remnants of Hannah*, *Reverse Rapture*, *Hat on a Pond*, and *Voyages in English*. She lives and works in Amherst, Massachusetts, where she directs the University of Massachusetts MFA Program for Poets and Writers and codirects the Juniper Initiative for Literary Arts and Action.

Jon Woodward is the author of *Rain* and *Mister Goodbye Easter Island*. He currently lives and works in the Boston area.

Mark Yakich began writing poems while living in Brussels, Belgium, and working for the European Parliament. He later returned to the United States to pursue an MFA at Louisiana State University. He is the author of three poetry collections: *Unrelated Individuals Forming a Group Waiting to Cross* (National Poetry Series Winner), *The Making of Collateral Beauty* (Snowbound Chapbook Award), and *The Importance of Peeling Potatoes in Ukraine*. Mark is associate professor of English at Loyola University New Orleans.

ACKNOWLEDGMENTS AND PERMISSIONS

Rae Armantrout
"Sake" copyright © 2003 by the author. Originally appeared in *Up to Speed*, published by Wesleyan University Press in 2003. Reprinted by permission of the publisher. "The Subject" copyright © 2007 by the author. Originally appeared in *Next Life*, published by Wesleyan University Press in 2007. Reprinted by permission of the publisher. "Worth While" copyright © 2008 by the author. Reprinted by permission of the author.

Paul Auster
"Narrative," and the fragment from "White Spaces," copyright © 2007 by the author. Originally appeared in *Collected Poems*, published by the Overlook Press in 2007. Reprinted by permission of the publisher.

Jennifer K. Dick
"Anatomy," "In the Garden," "Claudia" copyright © 2004 by the author. Originally appeared in *Fluorescence*, published by University of Georgia Press in 2004. Reprinted by permission of the publisher.

Paul Fattaruso
"The Submariner's Waltz" copyright © 2007 by the author. Originally appeared in *The Submariner's Waltz*, published by Factory Hollow Press in 2007. Reprinted by permission of the author.

Allen Grossman
"Rain on a Still Pond," " 'Warble,' Says the Bird," "I Am That I AM" copyright © 2007 by the author. Originally appeared in *Descartes' Loneliness*, published by New Directions Publishing in 2007. Reprinted by permission of the author.

Carla Harryman
"Now. Word. Technology." copyright © 2005 by the author. Originally appeared in *Baby*, published by Adventures in Poetry in 2005. Reprinted by permission of the publisher. "Fish Speech" copyright © 1994 by the author. Originally appeared in *Memory Play*, published by O Books in 1994. Reprinted by permission of the publisher and the author. "Membership," "Matter" copyright © 1995. Originally appeared in *There Never Was a Rose Without a Thorn*, published by City Lights Publishers in 1995. Reprinted by permission of the publisher.

Christian Hawkey
"*Fräulein*, can you," "There is a Queen inside," "Unhoused Casements" copyright ©
2004 by the author. Originally appeared in *The Book of Funnels*, published by Verse
Press/Wave Books in 2004. Reprinted by permission of the publisher.

Christine Hume
"Comprehension Questions," "What Became of the Company You've Kept, According to One Who Left" copyright © 2004 by the author. Originally appeared in
Alaskaphrenia, published by New Issues Press in 2004. Reprinted by permission of
the publisher.

Aaron Kunin
"Enclosed Please Find," "Enclosed Please Find," copyright © 2005 by the author.
Originally appeared in *Folding Ruler Star*, published by Fence Books in 2005.
Reprinted by permission of the publisher. "The Sore Throat" copyright © 2008 by
Aaron Kunin. Appearing in a forthcoming collection to be published by Fence
Books. Reprinted by permission of the publisher.

Mary Leader
"When the Wind Ever Shall Be Like a Black Thread" copyright © 2008 by the
author. Reprinted by permission of the author.

Ben Lerner
"We must retract our," "I'm going to kill," "The sky is a big" copyright © 2004 by
the author. Originally appeared in *The Lichtenberg Figures*, published by Copper
Canyon Press in 2004. Reprinted by permission of the publisher.

Mark Levine
"Work Song" copyright © [1990]. Originally appeared in the *New Yorker* in 1990.
Reprinted by permission of the author. "Counting the Forests" copyright © 2000
by the author. Originally appeared in *Enola Gay*, published by University of California Press in 2000. Reprinted by permission of the publisher. "Triangle" copyright © 2006 by the author. Originally appeared in *The Wilds*, published by University of California Press in 2006. Reprinted by permission of the publisher.

Sabrina Orah Mark
"The Dumb Show," "The Song," "In the Origami Fields" copyright © 2004 by the
author. Originally appeared in *The Babies*, published by Saturnalia Books in 2004.
Reprinted by permission of the publisher.

Rosmarie Waldrop
"Music Is an Oversimplification of the Situation We're In" copyright © 2005 by the author. Originally appeared in the journal *Aufgabe* in 2005. Reprinted by permission of the author.

Dara Wier
"Hypnagogic" copyright © 1992 by the author. Originally appeared in *Blue for the Plough*, published by Carnegie Mellon University Press in 1992. Reprinted by permission of the publisher. "Corrosion" copyright © 2005 by the author. Originally appeared in *Reverse Rapture*, published by Wave Books in 2005. Reprinted by permission of the publisher.

Jon Woodward
"newer sore spots blossomed open," "looking over the bomb inventory," "it's not that he died" copyright © 2006 by the author. Originally appeared in *Rain*, published by Wave Books in 2006. Reprinted by permission of the publisher.

Mark Yakich
"Pretzels Come to America," "An Untenable Nostalgia for Chernobyl" copyright © 2008 by the author. Originally appeared in *The Importance of Peeling Potatoes in Ukraine*, published by Penguin Books in 2008. Reprinted by permission of the publisher.

The editors gratefully acknowledge the following journals in which some of the material of this anthology first appeared: *Chicago Review*, "Conversation between Christine Hume and Rosmarie Waldrop" and "Conversation between Christian Hawkey and Tomaž Šalamun"; *Jubilat*, "Conversation between Srikanth Reddy and Mark Levine"; *Denver Quarterly*, "Conversation between Ben Lerner and Aaron Kunin"; the *New Yorker*, "Work Song" by Mark Levine.

We are also deeply grateful to the contributing poets for their dedicated labors; to Eleni Sikelianos, Bin Ramke, Joseph Parsons, Allison Thomas, Rhonda Wetjen, Charlotte Wright, Holly Carver, Lisa Raffensperger, Frank Fennell, Joyce Wexler, and everybody at University of Iowa Press for their invaluable support and advice; and to the Department of English and the College of Arts and Sciences at Loyola University Chicago for their generosity.

Acker, Kathy, 155
Adams, Henry, 249
Adorno, Theodor W., 216
advertising, xvii
Against Language?, 86
Agamben, Giorgio, 12
Akhmatova, Anna, 8
Akiko, Yosano, 154
Albiach, Anne-Marie, 82
The Alphabet, 141
"Although the paths lead into the
    forest . . .," 121
*American Women Poets in the 21st
    Century*, xiii
"Anatomy," 2
"And when the nights . . .," 122
Antin, David, 140
apocalypse narratives, xv, 99, 240–44
appropriation, 8, 9
The Arcades Project, 226
Archimedes, 80
Aristotle, 127
Armantrout, Rae, xvi, xvii, 22–38, 141
Art Institute of Chicago, 11
Art News, 58
Aschheim, Eve, 6
Ashbery, John, xiv, xvi, 4, 8, 23, 24, 27,
    58, 59, 238
assonance, 22
Astrophil and Stella, 99
Auden, W. H., 8, 11, 244
Aufgabe, 80
Auster, Paul, 226–36
Austerlitz, 44
authenticity, 106

The Babies, 45, 46, 49
Baby, 141, 142, 145, 150, 156, 160, 168
Bacon, Francis, 108, 109
Ballad for Metka Krasovec, 63
Barney, Matthew, 12
Basho, 163, 167
The Battle of Algiers, 241
Baudelaire, Charles, 226
Beat poets, 84
Beckett, Samuel, 142, 228
Beckman, Joshua, 69
Belladonna publishers, 157
Benigni, Roberto, 45
Benjamin, Walter, 12, 44, 59, 226, 243
Benson, Steve, 163, 164–67
Berkeley, 165
Berkson, Bill, 161
Bernstein, Charles, 8, 49
Berryman, John, 31
Bible, 47, 49, 230
Bienert, Ida, 200, 206
Bishop, Elizabeth, 59
Black Mountain poetry, 148
Blackboards, 60, 61
Blake, William, xv, 26, 58, 78, 83, 144,
    145, 212–14
blogs, 28, 103, 216
Bloom, Harold, xiv
Blue for the Plough, 180
Böhme, Gernot, 87
Borges, Jorge Luis, 27
The Botany of Desire, 59
Brazilian poetry, 61
Breugel, Pieter, 7, 8, 11
Brock-Broido, Lucie, 45
Brodsky, Joseph, 8

Bronk, William, 228
Brooklyn, 64
Brown, Julie, 8
Brown, Norman O., 80, 81, 82, 83
Browne, Laynie, 8
Bruno, Giordano, 61
Buber, Martin, 64
Buchanan, Oni, 23
Buckley, William F., 103
Bunting, Basil, 58
Burroughs, William S., 59
Bush, George H. W., 9
Bush, George W., 64, 65
Butler, Judith, 146
Byron, Don, 231–32
Byron, George Gordon, 82

Cage, John, 80, 81, 82, 83, 86, 87, 88
Canetti, Elias, 241
canonicity, xix
Carroll, Lewis, 144
Castro, Fidel, 216
Catherine of Aragon, 203
Celan, Paul, 48, 50, 51, 59
Cendrars, Blaise, 58
Césaire, Aimé, 43, 44, 46, 48, 49
Chaplain, Charlie, 27, 28, 239
Chekhov, Anton, 25
Cixous, Hélène, 154, 155
Clare, John, 64
"Claudia," 3
Coleridge, Samuel Taylor, xix, 246
collaboration, xvii, 139, 140, 143, 148,
    149, 150, 163–68
collage, 8
Collected Poems (Auster), 226, 231
comedians, xvii, 27, 28
"Comprehension Questions," 72
confessional poets, 105
Coolidge, Clark, 58
Copernicus, 13

Cornell, Joseph, 11
"Corrosion" 191
"Corruption (II)," 98
"Counting the Forests," 115
Cranbrook Art Museum, 166–67
Crane, Hart, 59, 123
Creeley, Robert, 58, 81, 82, 142, 143
cummings, e. e., 26

Dada, 77
Dahlen, Beverly, 155
Danish language, 249
Dante, 6, 59, 171
de Bèze, Théodore, 230
Debt, 102, 105, 108, 109, 110, 111, 114–15
del Tradici, David, 63
Deleuze, Gilles, 108
Dennis, Carl, 208
Derrida, Jacques, 79
Descartes' Loneliness, 130–34
Dick, Jennifer K., xiv, xvi, xviii, 2–13
Dickinson, Emily, xv, 5, 59, 60, 87, 106,
    110, 144, 145, 202, 203, 212, 229
Differentials, 31
DiFranco, Ani, 7
Disappearances, 226, 230, 231
Dissonance, 79, 81
Donne, John, 110, 202
Donovan, Keith, 8
Don't Let Me Be Lonely, 43, 44, 45, 46,
    47, 51
Doris, Stacy, 8
Dorn, Ed, 58
Dostoevsky, Fyodor, 222
The Dream Songs, 31
dreams, xvii, 23, 29, 30, 31, 46, 121, 180–
    82, 185, 187, 207
Drucker, Joanna, 11
Ducornet, Rikki, 4
"The Dumb Show," 40
Duncan, Robert, 48

duPlessis, Rachel Blau, 155, 168
Dylan, Bob, 33, 104

Edson, Russell, 27, 31
Einstein, Albert, 80
Ekphrasis, 10
Eliot, T .S., xv, 6, 7, 58, 113, 212
Elizabeth I, 203
"Enclosed Please Find," 251, 252
The End of the Alphabet, 45, 47
Endgame, 228
England, 203–04; poetic tradition, 107, 110
English language: Anglo-Saxon roots, 229; French-Latinate additions, 229
Enola Gay, 99, 100, 102, 105, 108, 111, 115–16
ethico-political purpose of poetry, xv, 103–13, 154, 240–50
"Evening with Stars," 96

Factorial, 148, 158, 159, 161
Facts for Visitors, 96–98
Fair Realism, 245
fairy tales, 25
Fallen Angels, 247
fascism, 57, 244
fata morgana, 187
Fattaruso, Paul, xvi, 176–88
Feast, 60
feminism, 6, 152, 155
Fenollosa, Ernest, 78
film, 6, 9, 13, 27, 30, 45, 87, 141, 187, 241, 242–43, 247
Finland, 229
Finnish, 229
"Fish Speech," 170
Fluorescence, 2–3, 7, 8
Folding Ruler Star, 244–45, 247, 250–52

For Love, 142
Forces of Imagination, 80, 81
formal constraints, 23, 184, 213, 226, 244, 248
Förster-Nietzsche, Elizabeth, 239
Fort/Da, 244
found poetry, 33, 34, 246
Four from Japan, 149, 158, 168
The Four Zoas, xv, 213–14
Foust, Graham, 28–29
"*Fräulein*, can you," 54
French: language, xvii, 152, 157, 159, 229, 230; poetry, 58, 228; theorists, 155
Freud, Sigmund, 46, 244
From the Other Side of the Century, 141, 168
"From This Miserable Mutineer a Stutter . . .," 222
Frost, Robert, 8, 140
futurity, xv

Galeano, Eduardo, 241
Gardener of Stars, 155, 160, 168
German language, 76, 77, 159, 162, 229, 249
Ginsberg, Allen, xv, 58, 211
Godard, Jean-Luc, 6, 141
Gómez-Peña, Guillermo, 139
Graham, Jorie, 4, 27, 31
The Grand Piano, 142, 147, 168
Greek: language, 59; mythology, 26; poetry, 29, 33, 123, 124, 125, 127, 129; tragedy, 242
Grinnell, E. Tracy, 157
Grossman, Allen, xiii, xv, xvii, 123–34, 199, 201–03, 206, 209
Gudding, Gabriel, 216
Guest, Barbara, xvi, 80–87, 245
Guiterman, Arthur, 144
Gumilyov, Nikolay, 10

Hall, Donald, 80
Hamlet, 200, 233
Handke, Peter, 7
Harryman, Carla, 8, 139–73
Hatter, Madelyn, 5
Hauser, Kaspar, 7
Hawk, Tony, 101
Hawkey, Christian, xiv, 54–66
Hawthorne, Nathaniel, 6
Heaney, Seamus, 207
Hecht, Jamey, 202, 206
Heidegger, Martin, 61
Hejinian, Lyn, xviii, 23, 24, 25, 149, 151, 162, 168, 248, 249
Helen of Troy, 207
Heliotropes, 157
Helmholtz, Hermann von, 80
Herbert, George, 59, 61, 199, 200, 217
Herzog, Werner, 187
Hill, Geoffrey, 248
Hill, Peter, 167
Hillman, Brenda, 4, 11
Hölderlin, Friedrich, 59, 61, 63, 64
Hole (music group), 6
Hollo, Anselm, 58
Hollywood, 126, 241
Holocaust, 49, 127, 129, 216, 242
homesickness, 14
Hopkins, Gerard Manley, 110
Horace, 123
"Hotel Lullaby," 97
Houdini, Harry, 196
Housman, A. E., 8, 83
How to Win Friends and Influence People, 4
Howe, Susan, 8
Hume, Christine, xvii, xviii, 72–88
Hurry Home Honey, 150, 168
hybridity, 157, 158, 159
hymns, xvi, 26, 28, 248
"Hypnagogic," 189

"I Am That I AM," 133
"I opened the brushed steel box," 176
"I'm going to kill . . .," 238
Imperial Palace Garden (Tokyo), 61
The Importance of Peeling Potatoes in Ukraine, 196–98, 200, 201, 216
"In the Garden," 3
"In the Origami Fields," 42
In the Room of Never Grieve, 5
incipient doxy, 74
indeterminacy, 91
Information Show (MOMA), 58
The Invention of Solitude, 227
Iraq war, 113, 154
irritable departure, 219
Ito, Hiromi, 154
"it's not that he died," 21

Jabès, Edmond, 88
Jackson, Laura Riding, 9
James, Henry, 6, 196
Japan, 44, 60, 61, 62, 145, 153, 154, 160, 161, 164, 229; poetry, 145, 149, 154, 155, 157, 158, 161, 167
Johnson, George, 8
Johnson, Samuel, 239
jokes, xvii, 5, 28
Judaism, 48, 206–07

Kabbalists, 48
Kafka, Franz, 6, 27, 208
Kane, Daniel, 24
Kane, Thomas, 68
Kant, Immanuel, 145
Kar-Wai, Wong, 247
Keaton, Buster, 27
Keats, John, 13, 59, 102, 110
"Keith," 223
A Key to the Language of America, 86
Khlebnikov, Velimir, 58
Kluge, Alexander, 243–44

Knott, Bill, 10
Koch, Kenneth, 58
Kristeva, Julia, 154, 155
Kunin, Aaron, xv, xviii, 240–54

Language poetry, 140, 143, 214, 248
Latin, 6, 204, 229
Lautrémont, Comte de, 58, 59
Lawn of Excluded Middle, 79
le Fay, Morgan, 187
Leader, Mary, xv, 199–220
*Learning Processes with a Deadly Out-
come*, 244
Lease, Joseph, 4
Lerner, Ben, xiv, xv, xviii, 238–50
Levertov, Denise, 27
Levine, Mark, xv, 99–117
Levine, Philip, 109
Lewin, Kurt, 78
LeWitt, Sol, 246–47
The Lichtenberg Figures, 238–39, 245–
46, 247
Life Is Beautiful, 45
Light and Humorous Verse, 144
Litmus Press, 157
"looking over the bomb inventory," 20
Love, Like Pronouns, 86
Lucas, John, 47
lyric poetry, xv, xvi, 8, 110, 123–30, 214

Mac Low, Jackson, 81, 82
Made to Seem, 29
Mallarmé, Stéphane, 185, 226
Mandelstam, Osip, 8, 59, 62, 65
Mark, Sabrina Orah, xiii, xvi, xviii, xix,
40–50
Marot, Clément, 230
Marxism, 147
Maso, Carole, 4, 8
The Master Letters, 45
"Matter," 173

Mayer, Peter, 231
McHenry, Eric, 247
McShine, Kynaston, 58
Means without End, 12
medusa's whips, 67
"Membership," 171
Memory Play, 141, 142, 160
The Mercian Hymns, 248
Michaux, Henri, 58
Midwest, xv, xviii, 242–43
Miller, D. A., 4
Milosz, Czeslaw, 10
Milton, John, 229, 248
Minashita, Kiriu, 148, 149
modernism, 107
Moloch, 166
Mondrian, Piet, 200, 206
moon, 74, 181
Morgenstern, Christian, 249
Morris, Dan, 202, 206
Moscow Mansions, 82
Mouré, Erin, 4
Mullen, Laura, xiv, xv, xvii, 4–17, 26, 31
Murmur, 8
music, xvi, 6, 10, 13, 23, 57, 80, 140, 143,
144, 154, 166, 183, 210, 231–32
"Music Is an Oversimplification of the
Situation We're In," 89
The Music of Chance, 233
My Life, 248–49

Nabokov, Vladimir, 47–48
Nadja, 44
Nakayasu, Sawako, 136–69
Napoleon, 196
narrative, 24, 234
"Narrative," 234
A Narrow Road to the Deep North, 163
The Natural Philosophy of Time, 80
negative capability, 13, 102
Nerval, Gérard de, 58, 63

New Formalism, 248
New York School of Poets, 84, 148, 245
New York Times, 158
"newer sore spots blossomed open," 20
Nijinsky, Vaslav, 59, 61
"9.19.2004," 136
"19.IX.1982," 67
Nomina, 120
nothing fictional but the accuracy or arrangement (she, 164–65, 169
Nothing in Nature Is Private, 45
Notley, Alice, xvii
"Now. Word. Technology.," 170
nuclear holocaust, xiv, xvii

Odradek, 250
Of Being Numerous, 233
"of course. of course.," 52
O'Hara, Frank, 6, 7, 12, 48, 58, 62, 245
OHO group, 58
Olson, Charles, 7, 58, 78
On Earth, 227
Open Box, 154, 156
opera, 144
Oppen, George, 7, 228, 233
"Or one meaning of here is . . .," 51
"Or Paul Celan said that . . .," 51
Orpheus, 199
Oulipo, 213–14
Oxota, 23, 24, 25
Oz, Amos, 50

Palmer, Michael, 7
Paradise Lost, 244
Partisan Review, 229
Pasternak, Boris, 8
Paterson, 10
Paz, Octavio, 10
Perelman, Bob, 58
performance, 139, 143, 166, 227, 231–32; gender as, 146

Perloff, Marjorie, xviii, 31
Peter Pan poetry model, 104
Phillips, Joshua, 200
Phillips, Tom, 83
Philomel, 199
physical memory, 137
Pinsky, Robert, 6
Piper, Adrian, 139
Pittsburgh, 64, 65
Plath, Sylvia, 4
Plot, 45, 49, 52
Poe, Edgar Allan, 233
Poetics Journal, 169
Poetry (journal), 229
Poinsot, Louis, 80
political poetry, 103
The Politics of Poetic Form, 8
Pollan, Michael, 59
Pollock, Jackson, 216
Ponge, Francis, 201
Pontecorvo, Gillo, 241
pop culture, 6
Popa, Vasko, 112
Pope, Alexander, 248
postmodern fiction, 148
Pound, Ezra, xix, 6, 10, 58, 78, 83
preprogrammed words, 21
"Pretzels Come to America," 196
prose poetry, 46, 79, 84, 98, 249

Queneau, Raymond, 248

Rain, 20–21, 23, 24, 25, 27, 28
"Rain on a Still Pond," 31
rainmaking, 3
Rakosi, Carl, 228
The Random House Book of 20th Century French Poetry, 228
Rankine, Claudia, xiii, xvi, xvii, 43–52
Rauschenberg, Robert, 8
Reddy, Srikanth, xv, 96–113

Reluctant Gravities, 83, 86
Renaissance, xiii
repetition, 23, 183
Reverse Rapture, 184, 186
revision, 10, 24
rhyme, 22, 160, 161
rhythm, 79, 80, 82, 83, 112, 160
Riley, Denise, 160
Rimbaud, Arthur, 8
Robinson, Edwin Arlington, 202
Robinson, Michelle, 222–33
Rotar, Braco, 57
Rothenberg, Jerome, 141
Roubaud, Jacques, xviii
Rousseau, Henri, 60
Roussel, Raymond, 58
Royet-Journoud, Claude, 82
Russian poetry, 8
Ryman, Robert, 11

Sacks, Oliver, 182
Sagawa, Chika, 154
Saint Augustine, xvii
Saint Christopher, 177–79
"Sake," 35
Šalamun, Tomaž, xiv, xviii, 57–69
Samuels, Lisa, 11
San Francisco Renaissance, 84
Sandburg, Carl, 155
Sappho, xvi, 123, 124, 125
Sarajevo, 243
Sarraute, Nathalie, 142
Sartre, Jean-Paul, 155
Schwarzenegger, Arnold, 242–43
Sebald, W. G., 44
Sekiguchi, Ryoko, 157–58, 159, 162
self as repertoire, 36
The Seventy Propositions, 9
Shakespeare, William, xv, xviii, 26, 110, 125, 127, 144, 145, 200, 224, 240, 241, 249

shame, 249–54
Shelley, Percy Bysshe, xix, 213
Sidney, Philip, 99, 230
Silence, 83
Silence and Metaphor, 228
Silliman, Ron, 28, 141
Simic, Charles, 46, 65
Sisyphus, 10
"6.21.2003," 138
"The sky is a big...," 239
slam poetry, 5
The Sleep of Reason Produces Monsters, 181
Smithson, Robert, 225
Snow, Carol, 4, 8, 9
So We Have Been Given Time Or, 147, 160
Socrates, 140
Some Thing Black, xviii
"Something happens, and from the moment," 235
"The Song," 41
Songs of Innocence and Experience, 144, 212
sonnet, 26, 120, 240
"Sonnet ('I asked every flower')," 120
Sophocles, 127
"The Sore Throat," 253
The Sound of Music, 9
Spahr, Juliana, xiii
Spanish language, 229
Spar, 121–22
Speak, Memory, 47–48
Spicer, Jack, 62
"Spring Street," 69
Stalin, Joseph, 65
Stein, Gertrude, xvi, xix, 4, 7, 8, 11, 12, 13, 60, 140, 143, 203, 249
Stevens, Wallace, 10, 58, 59
Stoppard, Tom, 233
Streets Enough to Welcome Snow, 82

"The Subject," 36
Subject, 7, 10, 11, 12, 14–17
subjectivity, xv
The Submariner's Waltz, 176–79
Sukenick, Ronald, 147
The Surface, 7
surrealism, 29, 31, 109
Swensen, Cole, 8, 11, 157
switching cadences, 117
Sylvester, David, 108
S/Z, 10

Tales of Horror, 10
Tarkos, Christophe, 7
Tate, James, 27, 31, 63, 65
television, xvii, 44, 47, 124, 244
Templeton, Fiona, 139
Tender Buttons, 11, 13
Terminator 2, 242
Texture Notes, 136–38
theater, 140, 143
"There is a Queen inside," 55
There Never Was a Rose without a Thorn, 168
Thomas, Dylan, 8
Tito, Josip Broz, 216
Three Poems, 23, 24, 58
"3.21.2004," 137
Toscano, Rodrigo, 11, 149
Tower of Babel, 47
Trachtenberg, Amy, 148
Trakl, Georg, 59, 61, 64
translation, xviii, 149, 157, 159, 160, 161, 228, 230–31
Travel in the Mouth of the Wolf, 184
"Triangle," 116
Trieste, 57
troubadours, xiii
True, 27
Tsim Tsum, 48
Tsvetaeva, Marina, 8
"The Tyger," 213

Ukraine, 200, 206, 215
"Unhoused casements," 56
Unrelated Individuals Forming a Group Waiting to Cross, 200
"An Untenable Nostalgia for Chernobyl," 197
Up to Speed, 32

Vallejo, César, 59, 60
Vega, Suzanne, 7
Velázquez, Diego Rodríguez, 239
Vendler, Helen, 207
Veronezh, 65
Vice, 160, 169
Vicuña, Cecilia, 6
video games, 30, 32
villanelle, 22, 248
visual art, xvi, 10, 11, 12, 60, 83, 108, 109, 140, 166, 210, 213, 216, 246
Volkman, Karen, xv, xvii, 120–30
Vollmann, William T., 244

"Wake," 14
Walcott, Derek, 207
Waldman, Anne, 5
Waldrop, Rosmarie, xv, xvii, xviii, 8, 51, 76–94
"'Warble,' Says the Bird," 132
The Waste Land, 113, 212
"We must retract our . . . ," 238
Weeder, Lawrence, 230
Welish, Marjorie, 88
"What Became of the Company You've Kept," 74
"When Smithson Looked into the Salt Lake What He Saw," 224
"When the Wind Ever Shall Be Like a Black Thread," 217
Whitehead, Alfred North, 77
Whitman, Walt, 57, 105, 123
Whitrow, G. J., 80
The Wide Road, 149, 151, 162, 167

Wier, Dara, xvi, 180–93
The Wilds, 100, 102, 111, 112, 116–17
Williams, William Carlos, 10, 28, 58,
   77, 78, 107
Wilson, Emily, 99, 113
Winter Conversations, 123
Wittgenstein, Ludwig, 87
Woodward, Jon, xiv, xvi, xvii, 20–34
Woolf, Virginia, 49, 52
*The Words: After Carl Sandburg's
   Rootabaga Stories and Jean-Paul
   Sartre,* 155, 160, 168
The Words of Selves, 160
Wordsworth, William, 99
"Work Song," 114

workshops, xv, 101, 213
World War II, 76
"Worth While," 37
Wyatt, Thomas, 110

Yaddo, 58, 63
Yakich, Mark, xv, 196–216
Yau, John, xvi
Yeats, W. B., 201

Zajc, Dane, 57, 58
zen garden, 9
Zukofsky, Louis, 58
Zupancic, Oton, 57